Dear Shinji Moon

May we all commit to doing
whatever it is we are pursuing!

Yoon Sun Yang
August, 31, 2017

From Domestic Women
to Sensitive Young Men

Harvard East Asian Monographs 405

From Domestic Women
to Sensitive Young Men

Translating the Individual in Early Colonial Korea

Yoon Sun Yang

Published by the Harvard University Asia Center
Distributed by Harvard University Press
Cambridge (Massachusetts) and London 2017

The Harvard University Asia Center publishes a monograph series and, in coordination with the Fairbank Center for Chinese Studies, the Korea Institute, the Reischauer Institute of Japanese Studies, and other facilities and institutes, administers research projects designed to further scholarly understanding of China, Japan, Vietnam, Korea, and other Asian countries. The Center also sponsors projects addressing multidisciplinary and regional issues in Asia.

Publication of this book was supported by the Sunshik Min Endowment for the Advancement of Korean Literature at the Korea Institute, Harvard University.

Library of Congress Cataloging-in-Publication Data

Names: Yang, Yoon Sun, author.
Title: From domestic women to sensitive young men : translating the individual in early colonial Korea / Yoon Sun Yang.
Other titles: Harvard East Asian monographs ; 405.
Description: Cambridge, Massachusetts : Published by the Harvard University Asia Center, 2017.
    | Series: Harvard East Asian monographs ; 405
Identifiers: LCCN 2016055283 | ISBN 9780674976979 (hardcover : alk. paper)
Subjects: LCSH: Korean literature—20th century—History and criticism. | Korean literature—
    Western influences. | Individuality in literature. | Identity (Psychology) in literature.
Classification: LCC PL954 .Y36 2017 | DDC 895.7/09003—dc23
LC record available at https://lccn.loc.gov/2016055283

Index by Amron Gravett

♾ Printed on acid-free paper

Last figure below indicates year of this printing
26   25   24   23   22   21   20   19   18   17

For Juna

Contents

Contents

Acknowledgments

While completing this book, I was guided by a number of friends, colleagues, mentors, and teachers, near and far. I was lucky enough to begin my long journey with brilliant teachers at the University of Chicago. I would like to thank, in particular, my dissertation committee—Kyeong-Hee Choi, Norma Field, and Elaine Hadley—for their tireless support and encouragement.

This book could not have been finished without an exceptionally engaging and open-minded group of specialists in world literatures and vigorous comparatists in the Department of World Languages and Literatures at Boston University. J. Keith Vincent read each and every chapter of my manuscript and gave me encouraging and thorough feedback while carrying out the gargantuan task of restructuring the whole department as newly appointed chair. Words can never be enough to express how grateful I am for his unbelievably generous support. I could not wish for a better mentor than Sarah Frederick. Her unwavering support and timely advice helped me survive many uncertain moments in the process of writing and publishing this book. It turned out to be surprisingly opportune that Catherine Yeh, one of my most enthusiastic interlocutors, shared with me part of an earlier manuscript of her *The Chinese Political Novel* when I was about to start reframing my book project. Her work helped me better understand the relationship between early colonial Korean domestic novels and East Asian political novels. Peter Schwartz read an earlier iteration of this project and pushed me to polish my thinking concerning some key concepts. Sunil Sharma generously shared his wisdom with me on numerous occasions when I felt lost. Abigail Gillman, Margaret Litvin, and Yuri Corrigan helped me understand the global dimension of the figures of sensitive young men. I want to express my appreciation of William Waters, Wiebke Denecke, Anna Zielinska-Elliott, Roberta Micallef, Gisela Hoecherl-Alden, and Jungsoo Kim for their unstinting moral support and collegiality. In addition, I am grateful to the dedicated members of the Boston University Faculty Gender and Sexuality Studies Group for introducing me to the critical power of queer studies. Chapter 4 could not have been written without reading groups, workshops, and lectures organized by them. My gratitude is extended to Sanjay Krishnan for sharing his insights on postcolonial studies. Thanks to the participants of the Boston University Center for the Humanities Fellow Seminar in Spring 2015—including James A. Winn, Abigail Gillman, Erin Murphy, Erin Salius, and Jack Matthews—for giving me thoughtful feedback on a part of the manuscript of this book.

I am also immensely indebted to friends and colleagues outside Boston University. This book was nurtured by countless discussions over the years with Sunyoung Park, occasionally in person but mostly over the phone. I am thankful to Ruth Barraclough for her unfailing encouragement and friendship. Kelly Y. Jeong, Jin-Kyung Lee, Hyangsoon Yi, Sam Perry, Faye Kleeman, Shinyoung Kwon, Hyun-Suk Park, Suzy Kim, Ellie Choi, Stephen H. West, John Zou, Xiaoqiao Ling, Sookja Cho, Michael Tueller, John Creamer, and Young Oh read parts of the manuscript at varying stages and offered invaluable advice on how to improve it. Kang Hyŏnjo and Bae Gaehwa generously helped me obtain some rare materials. Yu Kwangsu (Yonsei University) patiently answered my numerous questions regarding "The Tale of Changhwa and Hongnyŏn." Youngju Ryu, Dafna Zur, Yumi Moon, Aimee Nayoung Kwon, Hyun-Suk Park, Jinsoo An, Youngmin Kwon, Moonim Baek, Sun Joo Kim, Si Nae Park, and Carter Eckert invited me to present parts of the manuscript at their home institutions. Theodore Hughes, Huangwen Lai, and Ayako Kano kindly invited me to present my work at their panels at annual meetings of the Association for Asian Studies. I am grateful to Valerie Levan, Hongjian Wang, and Liang Luo for their invitations to the seminars they organized for conferences of the American Comparative Literature Association. Hyaeweol Choi was extremely generous in helping me when I was embarking on my academic career. I am deeply indebted to my copy editor, Daniel McNaughton, for his amazingly efficient work. The quality of this book was significantly enhanced by thoughtful comments and constructive criticism by two anonymous readers for the Harvard University Asia Center. Janet Poole later identified herself as one of them, and I am humbled by her enthusiastic support of this book.

The early stage of research for this book was made possible by a Century Fellowship, a Hanna Holborn Gray Fellowship, and a Center for East Asian Studies Travel Grant from the University of Chicago, as well as a Korea Foundation Fellowship for Graduate Studies. A Daesan Foundation Grant for Translation, Research, and Publication of Korean Literary Works and a Boston University Center for the Humanities Junior Faculty Fellowship allowed me to take time off from teaching duties to write my book. The last stage of writing was made possible by my Junior Scholar Leave, which was generously offered by the College of Arts and Sciences at Boston University. I would like to thank the faculty of the Korea Institute at Harvard University for welcoming me to their vibrant academic community of Korean studies and permitting me to access the extraordinary collection of the Harvard-Yenching Library.

Chapter 1 originally appeared in *positions: asia critique* 22, no. 1: 103–30 (copyright ©2014) with a slightly different title: "Enlightened Daughter, Benighted Mother: Yi Injik's 'Tears of Blood' and Early Twentieth Century Korean Domestic Fiction." It is republished in this book by permission of Duke University Press (www.dukeupress.edu). Chapter 2 originally came out in *Comparative Literature Studies* 51, no. 4: 644–73 (copyright© 2014) as "From Female Ghosts to Ghostly Womanhood: Mt. Ch'iak (1908–1911) and Birth of Modern Korean Fiction." This article is used by permission of The Pennsylvania State University Press.

Teena Purohit's friendship sustained me through the process of writing. Young Bum Koh and Sandra H. Lee opened their home to me as my emotional sanctuary, whenever possible. I would like to thank my mother, Sungja Kwon, for teaching me the value of hard work, and my father, Yonggyu Yang, for his unyielding moral support. My younger sister, Yoonsu Yang, deserves special thanks. As a talented librarian, she patiently helped me get my hands on a number of early colonial Korean materials. My daughter, Juna, was quite literally born and has grown up with this book project, enriching it in so many unexpected ways. It is to her that I dedicate this book.

Belmont, Massachusetts
November 2016

INTRODUCTION

Yi Kwangsu's 1917 novel *The Heartless* (*Mujŏng*) recounts the process through which a young Korean man comes to learn how to "think like an individual."[1] The protagonist of the novel, Ri Hyŏngsik, appears to be fully adapted to modern culture from the beginning—he has a college degree in English literature from a Japanese university, knowledge about Western classics, entrée into Japanese literary society, a prestigious teaching job at a high school in the capital city, and the implicit prospect of marrying a nubile daughter of an affluent elder of a Protestant church. For him to come to terms with his inner self, however, he must go through a series of eye-opening moments, a process that the narrator compares to "the growth of crops in a field":

> The inner person (*soksaram*) within Hyŏng-sik had opened its eyes. He could now see the inner meaning of all existence with his inner eyes. . . . Hyŏng-sik's inner self had long been ripe for bursting from its shell. A grain seedling will swell as much as it can within its shell, inside the soil, and then sprout overnight after a light drizzle. Hyŏng-sik's inner self had grown, nourished by religion, literature, and Hyŏng-sik's actual social experiences, which were more abundant than those of most people. This inner self had then suddenly burst through its shell when it met with the

---

1. Yi, *Yi Kwang-Su*. Throughout this book I slightly modify this translation by Ann Sung-hi Lee, based on Kim Ch'ŏl's comprehensive annotated edition, *Parojabŭn Mujŏng* (*Restored Mujŏng*). Armstrong, *How Novels Think*, 10.

two young women named Sŏn-hyŏng and Yŏngch'ae, and spring rain and breezes.[2]

This passage describes the discovery of *soksaram*, or "the inner person," as an internal and clandestine phenomenon. The narrator almost sounds tautological when stressing that "only one whose inner self has awakened can know their inner self and know what it is like for their inner self to be awakened."[3] It is a matter of realizing that one has "a self," "an intelligence, will, location, mission, and appearance of his own" that are "not necessarily the same as those of other people," and of learning how to see, think, and feel nothing but from one's own perspective.[4] As a man's inborn quality, *soksaram* will remain dormant inside until it is sufficiently nourished through "religion," "literature," and "social experiences."[5]

Unlike Confucian awakening, Hyŏngsik's discovery of *soksaram* does not teach him how to act benevolently toward others as the ancient sages did. Nor does it lead him to grasp the nothingness of worldly desires as Buddhist awakening would have. If anything, Ri Hyŏngsik's new selfhood makes him restless, impetuous, and, in a way, lost. As soon as he discovers *soksaram*, around the midpoint of the novel, he sets himself free from his emotional debt by cutting short his search for Pak Yŏngch'ae, the missing and possibly dead daughter of his former benefactor, the late Pak Ŭngjin, to whom he, as an orphan, owed his survival and primary education. He does so with no hint of remorse—in fact, he experiences a feeling of boundless happiness. Upon returning from his aborted mission to rescue Yŏngch'ae, he resigns from his teaching position, allegedly because he is offended by his students' and colleagues' erroneous accusation that he has frequented the pleasure quarters, but more fundamentally out of his pent-up frustration with their inability to share his ambition and vision. After this heedless act, however, he is seized with regret over his "heartless" decision to give up his search for Yŏngch'ae (who he now believes is dead). Overpowered by unbearable guilt, he is taken with the idea of finding her corpse and giving it a proper burial, only to forget

2. Yi, *Yi Kwang-Su*, 139.
3. Ibid.
4. Ibid., 221.
5. Ibid., 139.

all about her once again when the church elder proposes that Hyŏngsik marry his daughter while promising to support his study at a college in the United States. Later in the story he questions again whether he has been true to himself.

Ri Hyŏngsik's quest for self-discovery is what makes *The Heartless* "the first modern Korean novel"—so goes the canonical account of modern Korean literature.[6] Jongyon Hwang observes that the "search for the modern man constitutes the major impulse for Yi Kwangsu's story of the self-formation of a youth"; "in Korea the novel was a project that worked toward the transformation of people by seeking an interior life."[7] This claim is, of course, derived from the study of European, especially English, literature, where the individual is considered the quintessential novelistic character. As an emblem of modernity, the individual defies traditional moral strictures in the quest for an inner self, turning inward to make sense of an unpredictable, fast-changing world and to find values in life from a subjective perspective. In his classic study, *The Rise of the Novel*, Ian Watt identifies as prototypical individuals an economically independent castaway in *Robinson Crusoe*, a sexually promiscuous criminal woman in *The Fortunes and Misfortunes of the Famous Moll Flanders*, and a maid resisting her master's sexual advances in *Pamela, or Virtue Rewarded*.[8] More recently, Nancy Armstrong has proposed that "wherever novels are written or read," the ideological core of the genre—"the presupposition that novels think like individuals about the difficulties of fulfilling oneself as an individual under specific cultural historical conditions"—remains unchanged.[9] This line of inquiry is explored by those scholars of Korean literature who point to *The Heartless* as the first "modern" Korean novel for its similarities to modern European novels, especially the main character's search for individual selfhood.

---

6. In more-recent iterations of this literary history—such as Michael Shin's reading of *The Heartless*—a similar story is told in poststructuralist terms. Shin, "Interior Landscapes," 248–88; Shin finds his theoretical basis in Japanese critic Karatani Kojin's concept of "the discovery of interiority" to emphasize Hyŏngsik's awakening to his inner self as a definitive epistemological break with the past. See Karatani, *Origins of Modern Japanese Literature*, 45–75.

7. Jongyon Hwang, "The Heartless," 781; "Story of the Novel," 222.

8. See Watt, *Rise of the Novel*.

9. Armstrong, *How Novels Think*, 9–10.

In the present study I offer a different story about the beginning of modern Korean fiction. I propose that the individual did not burst onto the Korean literary scene through one innovative work but emerged gradually through a trajectory of translation, as described by Lydia Liu's concept of "translingual practice."[10] According to Liu, translating European languages into Chinese at the turn of the twentieth century was not so much a matter of choosing a Chinese equivalent for a European word within the existing Chinese lexicon as a process of establishing a new equation between two languages. From this point of view, what matters is not how accurately European concepts were translated into Korean, but through what processes two languages worked together to create a new discursive and cultural space in-between. The notion of the individual was unknown to Koreans until it was translated into various terms in the late nineteenth century. There was no one definitive rendering of this term then.

The "unorthodox" Korean translations of "the individual" appear as significant sources for cross-cultural inquiries once we view, following Liu, translation as a meaning-making process rather than as the transmission of a fixed meaning from one language to another. These translations are "where the guest language is forced to confront the host language," and "where the irreducible differences between the host language and the guest language are fought out, authorities invoked or challenged, and ambiguities dissolved or created."[11] Instead of trying to determine which Korean translation reproduces the "original" European meaning of the individual most faithfully, we have to ask which extralinguistic, as well as intralinguistic, factors came into play in the making of early colonial translations of this term and in what forms the "guest" culture was circulated within the "host" culture.

This book focuses mostly on works of fiction published and a literary style established during the so-called transitional period, between approximately 1906 and 1918, which I refer to as "the early colonial period." In Kyung Moon Hwang's words, this was when "the Japanese takeover of Korea" was in progress.[12] Korea was not officially annexed by Japan

10. Liu, *Translingual Practice*.
11. Ibid., 32.
12. Kyung Moon Hwang, *History of Korea*, 151–53.

until 1910, but the process of Japan's colonization of Korea broke the surface as early as "1904 with the onset of the Russo-Japanese War."[13] It was not until the end of the first decade after annexation that the colonial apparatus was fully implanted in Korea. During the early colonial period—that is, for more than a decade before the initial serialization of *The Heartless*—a number of works of prose fiction came out through the burgeoning print media. Working from the assumption that the modernity of Korean literature should be evaluated by the standard of modern European literature, the canonical account of Korean literary history tends to view these works as partial or transitional forms of modern fiction. By following this teleological and Eurocentric paradigm, one runs the risk of reading the entire archive of Korean literature as a series of failed or successful attempts to imitate European examples. Certainly the power of Western influence was evident in Korean literary texts during this period. Korean writers did develop new types of characters inspired by the European notion of the individual—but not as mere imitators. They were addressing issues unique to their social and cultural context, issues that mattered to them and their readers. To explain the cross-cultural encounter between Western literature and Korean literature in the early colonial period outside the Eurocentric paradigm, then, I suggest that the key question should not be "Which Korean literary figures most resemble the European prototypes of the individual?" but rather "How do

13.   Ibid., 153. During the brief period between the Protectorate Treaty and Japan's annexation of Korea, Korea was engulfed by intense nationalist campaigns, anticolonialist struggles, and reform movements that aimed to spread "civilized" mores and "enlightened" views to the people in Korea. As recent scholarship on modern Korean history has tended to emphasize, however, these movements did not always coalesce into a united effort to regain the country's lost sovereignty but often broke into radically contrasting voices. Yumi Moon argues, for example, that the Ilchinhoe (Advancement Society), a "populist" political group, collaborated with the Japanese government's attempt to colonize Korea because their priority was not "Korea's exclusive sovereignty" but "its domestic reforms" and "substantial welfare" for the people. Moon, *Populist Collaborators*, 284; see also Chandra, "Outline Study of Ilchinhoe." For Andre Schmid, even nationalist newspaper editorials appeared to have ambivalent attitudes toward Japan because the kind of nationalism that they sponsored had already been entrenched by a discourse on civilization and Pan-Asianism that paradoxically buttressed Japan's imperialist claim as the leading civilizing power in East Asia. Schmid, *Korea between Empires*, 101–38.

Korean literary characters function as translations of new notions of subjectivity?"

This new question allows us to challenge the conventional belief that individuality was primarily embodied by male elites in Korean literature. I suggest that the earliest iterations of the Korean individual are in fact female figures in a group of works loosely classified as *sinsosŏl* (the new novel). *Sinsosŏl* were serialized by male reformist writers in newspapers and magazines, and reached their widest circulation between 1906 and 1915. The majority of them are domestic novels, and they tend to assign the leading role of advocating reform and criticizing traditional norms to female figures. In these novels, female figures often transgress traditional gender and social hierarchies. Some of them become suitable modern wives for reform-minded men by pursuing a degree in a modern school, advocating scientific and rational thinking in place of superstition, rejecting child marriage and concubinage, condemning domestic abuses, and calling for egalitarian marriage. Others more confrontationally challenge traditional male authority by fulfilling their sexual desires outside marriage, relentlessly pursuing an insatiable desire for money, and even creating an alternative form of family.

The stories of domestic women's defiance of traditional gender norms reverberate with the popular political slogan of "civilization and enlightenment" (*munmyŏng kaehwa*) and the nationalist premise that the level of women's education should be a barometer of a nation's progress. In response to the pressure of reform and modern nation building, Korean reformist activists and writers envisioned women as members of the nation, wherein people were no longer classified by their hereditary status distinctions but were treated, at least in principle, as equal citizens. As I show in detail in the first four chapters of this book, the nationalist roots of these female characters do not necessarily make them less individualistic, because claiming one's selfhood and enabling the nation's prosperity are often taken as one and the same thing in the context of early colonial Korea. These female characters embrace their domestic identities as wives, daughters, mothers, and daughters-in-law in the process of finding their modern selfhood. No matter how strange it may sound to contemporary readers, they suppose the recognition of individuals' rights, desires, and selfhood to be in line with the reformist effort to strengthen the nation. To a certain extent, these stories of the transformation of old-fashioned women into standard-bearers for individual rights and free-doms border on wishful tales about the nation's future. On the other hand, these female figures' failures to hold on to their domestic identities become allegorical signs of the loss of national sovereignty. These seem-ing contradictions point up the reality that domesticity, individuality, and collective identity coexist within the female figures of the early colo-nial domestic novel as inseparable elements. Rather than taking the form of secluded interiority (as is often the case with the sensitive male characters that Korean novels and short stories often center on in the late 1910s), the selfhood of female characters in early colonial domestic nov-els tends to be externalized through their acts of advocating for individual human rights, their insurgent attempts to dismantle the traditional pa-triarchy, or their open pursuit of their sexual or monetary desires.

Whereas previous scholarship casts the shift from "domestic women" to "sensitive young men" in the late 1910s as an unambiguous process of modernization, in which women represent the past (that is, remnants from premodern literature) and men the future (that is, the de facto modern subject taking its initial shape in Korea), I stress that both must be un-derstood as much more complex and aleatory practices of translating the individual into Korean. It is only from this perspective that we can begin to move beyond the Eurocentric and male-centered bias that has shaped our understanding of modern Korean literature. By disposing of the questionable assumptions that one literary figure is *a priori* more "ad-vanced" and closer to the "original" form of the individual than others, and that the standard type of a self-governing subject must first and fore-most be represented by a male rather than a female, we will be able to open up a new avenue for the understanding of the narrative form of early colonial Korean literature on its own terms. The driving questions of this study include: How did the literary translation of the individual change over time during this period? What might have caused one type of iteration of the individual to be more prevalent than others in a given time? What historical and cultural components came into play in differ-ent iterations of the individual? What pre-twentieth-century narrative elements remain, either residually or with extensive modification, in the new figure of the individual? What innovative literary devices did writ-ers borrow from other literary traditions, and how did they refashion them to translate the individual? Furthermore, rather than reading the mid-1910s shift from domestic women to sensitive men simply as "progress," we should ask what domestic women and sensitive men share as well as what sets them apart, not only what sensitive men brought to the Korean literary landscape afresh, but also what was lost in the transition from domestic women to sensitive men.

Translating the Individual in Early Colonial Korea

By revisiting the global spread of European individualism in terms of translingual practice in Korea, I am taking up a question rarely posed in scholarly inquiries about the relationship between individualism and the novel: What constitutes "the individual" in literary modernity outside European cultural domains? As a first step, it should be noted that the genealogy of individualism is not uncontested within Western thought. If it is more or less agreed that the contemporary theoretical underpinnings of individualism were laid down by seventeenth and eighteenth-century philosophers such as Thomas Hobbes, John Locke, Adam Smith, and Jean-Jacques Rousseau, the historical roots of individualism are often traced back to earlier times, sometimes to early Christian thought, as represented by St. Augustine's *Confessions* (397–400) or even in Greek antiquity.[14] Furthermore, the definition of the individual has shifted between the notions of privatization and of socialization. Joan Wallach Scott points out that the individual means not only "a unique being," "different from all others of its species" but also "the abstract prototype of the human."[15] Similarly questioning the monadic interpretation of individuality, Etienne Balibar uncovers that the dimension of socialization coexists with the better-known concept of privatization in Locke's concept of possessive individualism.[16]

The intrinsic ambiguity of the notion of the individual was peculiarly amplified in early colonial Korea. There was no equivalent for this term in the Korean lexicon when it was introduced to Korean

14.   Taylor, *Sources of the Self.*
15.   Scott, *Only Paradoxes to Offer,* 5.
16.   Balibar, "'Possessive Individualism,'" 299–317.

culture in the late nineteenth century. Numerous records indicate that the notion was incomprehensible to Korean writers and readers, just as it was to Meiji intellectuals who had been trying to reconfigure the foundation of Japanese society according to a Western model for a few decades by that point. Yanabu Akira details the trials and errors of Meiji translators and intellectuals in translating a series of words key to the ideology of Japanese reform, words denoting the Western European and American concepts of society, individuality, modernity, beauty, liberty, and rights. According to Yanabu, the Japanese translators ultimately chose the unfamiliarity of compound words made of Japanese *kanji* (Chinese characters) over reutilizing wholly or in part native Japanese vocabulary, believing that the Chinese compounds would better convey the novelty of Western terms. The same line of thought informed the Japanese translation of the word "individual." The Japanese educator, journalist, and translator Fukuzawa Yukichi settled on the Chinese compound *kojin* as the translation of "individual," after experimenting with more-familiar Japanese words such as *hitotsu* (ひとつ, or 一つ), *ichi kojin* (一個人), *hito ono ono* (人各々), *hitori no tami* (一人の民), and *hitobito* (人々).[17] Even though the ideographic loanword from Japanese was eventually taken as the standard translation of the English term in Chinese and Korean, to be read as *geren* and *kaein*, respectively, there were other translations in use in China and Korea. The Chinese *geren* was used interchangeably with *ziwo* (自我), *wo* (我), *ji* (己), *xiaoji* (小己), *gewei* (個位), and *geti* (個體), for example.[18] In early colonial Korea, "the individual" was also translated as *inmin* (人民), *punja* (分子), and *paeksŏng* (百姓).[19] Yi Kwangsu's *soksaram* was one of the Korean translations of the term, though it was not widely accepted.

17. Yanabu, *Hon'yakugo seiritsu jijō*, 23–42. See also Howland, *Translating the West*.

18. Liu, *Translingual Practice*, 82.

19. Focusing on the signifier *kaein*, literary scholar Pak Sukcha's study of individuality in Korean literature omits the early colonial domestic novel from her discussion. Pak Sukcha, *Han'guk munhak kwa kaeinsŏng*. Jin-kyung Lee aptly points out that "the construction of a colonial-modern 'individual' was a cumulative, ongoing process of transformation." Paying little attention to the complexity surrounding translation of this notion, however, she defines the individual simply as an autonomous being. Lee, "Autonomous Aesthetics," 1.

One of the earliest Korean sources in which the "individual" appears is *Tongnip sinmun* (The Independent, 1896–99). As a Korean-English bilingual newspaper that often published dual-language versions of articles, it offers a rare opportunity to observe the uneasy process of translating the European notion into Korean, as well as the ways in which historical and contingent factors seeped into early colonial Korean translations of the term. An editorial of March 9, 1897, for example, lays bare the ways in which the Korean translation was mediated by inherently transnational political subtexts. The word "individual" appears as a key word of the editorial. The opening passage of the English edition reads: "The first indication of progress in a nation is the knowledge of asserting individual rights. The Korean people have been, for centuries, living under the heavy yoke of oppression from their own officials, so that they have practically forgotten the words 'personal rights,' much less knowing the meaning of them."[20] From the beginning, the passage endorses individual rights less for the sake of discrete individuals than as a marker of national progress. In the Korean vernacular version of the editorial, the phrase "individual rights" appears as "their own rights as *paeksŏng*" (*chagi tŭl ŭi paeksŏng toen kwŏlli*). To present-day readers, *paeksŏng* would be an unlikely choice for a Korean translation of "individual." This ancient Chinese compound word, widely used in China, Korea, and Japan, literally means "one hundred families" and, more commonly, "people in distinction to the royal family or state officials." As if aware of the lack of equivalence between "individual" and *paeksŏng*, the Korean version adds a detailed explanation about the new usage of the age-old expression: "What I call *paeksŏng* are not the people without government rank. Those who live in a nation are the nation's *paeksŏng*. God gives each of the *paeksŏng* some (*ŏlmak'ŭm*) rights. These rights cannot be taken by anyone else. It is the duty of the *paeksŏng* to act properly as such in order to raise the status of the king and also that of the nation as a whole."[21]

The Korean-language version of the editorial, "Ronsŏl," shows a strong intent to indigenize the term by describing "individual rights" not as a foreign idea derived from modern European and American political thinking but as naturally given universal rights that Koreans had known

20. "Editorial Notes," *The Independent*, March 9, 1897.
21. "Ronsŏl," *Tongnip sinmun*, March 9, 1897.

once but had forgotten "under the heavy yoke of oppression from their own government officials."[22] The introduction of individual rights demanded a radically different way of imagining the community as well as its people, a community not delineated by the hierarchical four-tier status system of Chosŏn Korea but by each person's unmediated relationship with God. Reading further in this editorial, what may seem at first an innocent introduction of a "modern" concept was in fact occasioned by a recent dispute with political overtones between a Japanese settler and a Korean student at the all-male *Paichai* (*Paejae*) School. The latter had been insulted by the former, and, in response, his fellow students at *Paichai* submitted a joint complaint to the Japanese consul and, through the consul's intervention, received an official apology from the offender. On the premise that there should be interreliance among Koreans, the Korean version of the editorial emphasizes that the *Paichai* students vindicated not only the rights of the victim but also those of the entire people of Korea: "If the people of Korea defend each other's rights, foreigners will no longer insult nor look down on Koreans."[23]

The editorial's emphasis on the importance of joint actions against overbearing foreigners points to the national community as the indispensable ground for individuals to exercise their rights. While defining individuals not only as bearers of inalienable rights but also as integral parts of the national community, the editorial in *Tongnip sinmun* pushes to the fore the question of what political infrastructure would enable individuality.[24] With hindsight, it is easy to identify a penchant for allying with the Japanese behind the call for individual rights. The editorial sets the incident against the backdrop of the Kanghwa Treaty (1876) and the Sino-Japanese War (1894–96), while claiming that "after Korea opened its doors," Koreans let themselves be treated badly by foreigners, especially

22. "Editorial Notes," *The Independent*, March 9, 1897.
23. "Ronsŏl," *Tongnip sinmun*, March 9, 1897.
24. For a comprehensive review of the translations of *kaein* in *Tongnip sinmun*, see Pak Chuwŏn, "Kŭndaejŏk kaein sahoe kaenyŏm," 207–38. Pak observes that *Tongnip sinmun* (1896–99) and primers of politics of the mid-1900s (mostly eclectic translations from Japanese and German sources) frame their discussions about the rights of the *kaein* along the lines of the demand for strong laws and a strong nation, not for the reining in of state power.

the Chinese, "owing to their incorrigible tendency to put up with abuse."[25] Oddly enough, even though the incident in question involved a Japanese settler and a Korean student, the editorial labels the Chinese as the key villains while cautiously pointing out that it is only the "lower-class Japanese" (*hadŭng ilbon saramdŭl*) who have been denying Koreans their rights. Furthermore, the editorial ends by highlighting the Japanese consul's apology to the student as a hopeful sign of the civilized future for the relationship between Japan and Korea.[26] Thus, the editorial promotes the questionable image of Japan as Korea's ally in its modern reform efforts.

One might reasonably suggest that the "nonindividualistic" translation of the individual is in part an effect of the choice of the semantically plural *paeksŏng* in this early translation. Yet the allegedly more modern and widely accepted translation of *kaein* invited no less confusion. An abridged translation of Samuel Smiles's *Self-Help* in the editions of *Taehan maeil sinbo* (Korean Daily News, 1904–10) from October 25 and October 27, 1907, is a case in point.[27] The term appears in the opening passage, a liberalist epigraph taken from John Stuart Mill's *On Liberty*: "The worth of a State is the worth of the individuals [*kaein*] composing it." Yet *kaein* seems removed from Mill's definition of the individual, as the translation makes the unlikely equation between the Confucian concept of *susin* (the cultivation of the person or self-disciplining) and this mid-Victorian liberalist notion of individual progress by adding a passage from one of the Confucian classics, *The Great Learning*: "From the Son of Heaven down to the mass of the people, all must consider the cultivation of the person [*susin*] the root of everything besides."[28] Another Confucian interpretation of the individual is evident in Chang Tŏksu's essay "Society and Individuals" (Sahoe wa kaein), which was published under his pen name, Sŏl San, in 1917 in *Hak chi kwang* (*Lux Scientiae*, 1914–30),

25. *Tongnip sinmun*, March 9, 1897.

26. Relevant here is Alexis Dudden's observation that, starting from the time of the Sino-Japanese War, Japan posed as a supporter of Korea's "independence" and the ending of the centuries-old suzerain relationship between China and Korea, only to pave the way for the "legalizing" of its colonization of Korea with the language of international law. See Dudden, *Japan's Colonization of Korea*.

27. "Kungmin kŭp kaein" (Citizens and Individuals), *Taehan maeil sinbo*, October 25 and October 27, 1907.

28. Confucius, *Confucian Analects, Great Learning*, 358.

the monthly organ of the Fraternal Society of Korean Students in Japan (Chosŏn yuhaksaeng haguhoe), an organization made up of those pursuing college or high school degrees in Tokyo.[29] At first Chang claims that acknowledging the self-interests of individuals is the foundation of a modern economy. But later he likens the relationship between *kaein* and society to that of children and their parents, concluding that children should dedicate themselves to the renewal of society (*sahoe kaeryang*) because they owe their existence to it, just as they are indebted to their parents for their lives.

The Korean translation of the English word "individualism," *kaienjuŭi*, often had a pejorative connotation. In "Don't Live by Individualism" (Kaeinjuŭi ro saeng ŭl ku ch'i maljiŏda), an editorial that *Taehan maeil sinbo* had run a year before the annexation, *kaeinjuŭi* is blamed for creating the current crisis of national sovereignty and casting a shadow over the future prosperity of Korea.[30] Another pejorative usage of the term appears in the article "Nationalism and Individuals" (*Kukkajuŭi wa kaein*) published in 1915, about five years after the annexation, in the only nationally distributed Korean-language newspaper of the 1910s, *Maeil sinbo* (The Daily), an organ of the Japanese government-general.[31] Citing the observation of a Japanese army commander residing in Korea, Iguchi Shōgo, the article claims that Chinese immigrant workers are valued less than their Korean and Japanese counterparts despite their excellent productivity and high energies because of their *kaeinjuŭi* and *igijuŭi* (self-centeredness) as opposed to Korean and Japanese workers' prioritization of the state (namely, Japan) over their personal and familial interests.

Thus, early colonial Korean translations of the notion of the individual vacillated across a wide semantic spectrum, contingently referring to an agent of universal human rights, a specific group within a national community, a rational man pursuing wealth for his own interest, a unique being with an inimitable distinction (as in the case of Yi Kwangsu's *soksaram*), a selfish person blindly caught up in her or his own self-interest,

29. Sŏl San, "Kaein kwa sahoe." About the Fraternal Society of Korean Students in Japan, see Wells, "Background to the March First Movement," 5–21.

30. *Taehan maeil sinbo*, November 21, 1909.

31. *Maeil sinbo*, June 4, 1915. Another Korean vernacular newspaper of the 1910s was *Kyŏngnam ilbo* (The Kyŏngnam Daily), a local newspaper based in the South Kyŏngsang province, which was published until 1915.

the vanguard of social reform, and even Chinese immigrant workers sup-posedly living without a sense of national belonging. Many of the Korean translations may seem simply inaccurate, if one assumes that, in the process of translation, the language receiving the term should act as an empty vessel for the language providing the term. Needless to say, this assumption merely reproduces the alleged cultural hierarchy between East and West by positing that all non-Western cultures made a teleo-logical transition from their indigenous traditions to Western-influenced modernity. To intervene in this Eurocentric and teleological line of think-ing, one must shift the focus to how the seemingly inaccurate transla-tions of the notion of the individual contribute to a meaning-making procedure in non-European literary tradition. As a step toward the trans-national understanding of individuality, I propose to examine how the figures of domestic women—female characters whose primary identities are defined by their roles in the family—participated in translating the notion of the individual in early colonial Korea.

Domestic Women as Early Colonial Korean Iterations of the Individual

In examining the figures of domestic women as early iterations of the individual, I suggest that the domestic novel (*kajŏng sosŏl*) played a crucial role in the formation of modern subjectivity in Korea and offered a lim-ited degree of political agency to women. My reading of Korean *kajŏng sosŏl* questions the recurrent assumption that, targeted toward unedu-cated female readers, it either addresses women's trivial concerns or un-imaginatively reflects nationalism or nationalist gender politics. Instead, I engage with feminist debates on the gendered politics of modern domestic fiction that originated in Victorian British and American liter-ary and cultural studies in the late 1970s. In her classic study, *The Femi-nization of American Culture* (1977), Ann Douglas opened the debate with a critique of nineteenth-century American women writers of the domestic novel for the way their words tended to code emotions as femi-nine in compliance with the gendered division between the domestic and the public.[32] In response to Douglas, Jane Tompkins emphasized the subversive aspect of domestic fiction, offering a revisionist interpretation of Harriet Beecher Stowe's *Uncle Tom's Cabin* as a radical discourse of female empowerment and as "a monumental effort to reorganize culture from the woman's points of view."[33] However, one may argue that she nonetheless subscribes to Douglas's premise that domestic and sentimental culture was female subculture, in distinction to an allegedly masculine mainstream culture.

Subsequent studies have moved away from the theoretical premise shared by Tompkins and Douglas by locating domestic fiction at the heart of modern middle-class culture, not on its margins. Nancy Armstrong, in *Desire and Domestic Fiction: A Political History of the Novel* (1987), states that "narratives which seemed to be concerned solely with matters of courtship and marriage" pivot around the struggle of the middle class for moral superiority in relation to the aristocracy by striving to represent female sexuality in psychological terms. Instead of describing the female characters of Victorian British domestic novels as powerless under the reign of male dominance or as potentially subversive agents of liberation, Armstrong argues that these novels played an instrumental role in bringing "the middle-class into power" not only by holding "the authority to say what was female" but also by universalizing a set of moral norms that "exalted the domestic woman over and above her aristocratic counterpart."[34] Gillian Brown, in her study of nineteenth-century American culture, emphasizes how the literary and cultural artifacts of domesticity feminized the very notion of selfhood, even as, paradoxically, they made "individualism mostly available to (white) men."[35] More recently, Amy Kaplan urges us to take another political dimension into account in our inquiries about domestic fiction—the cultural politics of U.S. imperialism. In her account, American domestic novels "produced a racialized national subjectivity in contested international spaces" during the time of overseas expansion and of shifting national borders. The result was to leave

32. Douglas, *Feminization of American Culture*, 3–13.
33. Tompkins, *Sentimental Designs*, 124.
34. Armstrong, *Desire and Domestic Fiction*, 5.
35. Brown, *Domestic Individualism*, 4–10.

traces of the attempt to domesticate the foreign other within "the interiority of the female subject."[36]

The first four chapters of *From Domestic Women to Sensitive Young Men* elaborate on the different ways in which Korean domestic novels translated the individual as a variety of female figures within discourses such as the early colonial campaigns for women's education, egalitarian marriage, remarriage by widows, and the abolition of child marriage. These concerns may seem familiar to scholars of Victorian women's culture, and this is no accident. The link between early colonial Korean *kajŏng sosŏl* and the Victorian domestic novel is not merely theoretical but also historical. As I detail in chapter 1, the term *kajŏng* was a turn-of-the-century Korean neologism derived from a Japanese translation (*katei*) of the English word "home," as it was used in Victorian Britain.[37] The early colonial Korean domestic novel came into being in a complex process of translating Victorian domestic norms such as love marriage, the nuclear family, and the separation of public and private spheres, often via their initial translations into Japanese.[38]

Under what conditions, then, did the domestic novel thrive in early colonial Korea? Just as importantly, why did it lose its cultural power almost as quickly as it gained that power? I have already suggested that nationalist politics, reformist movements, and the influx of the Victorian discourse of domesticities all played their parts.[39] And yet we must ad-

36. Kaplan, *Anarchy of Empire*, 43.

37. Muta, "Meijiki sōgō zasshi," 12–25.

38. On North American missionaries' role in introducing modern domesticities in Korea, see Hyaeweol Choi, *Gender and Mission Encounter*.

39. As Partha Chatterjee's study of the nineteenth-century Bengali discourse of domesticity shows us, the discourse of modern domesticity did not always flourish along with the rise of nationalism. Chatterjee observes that the "women's question," which had been at the center of controversies about social reform in Bengal in the early and mid-nineteenth century, disappeared from "the agenda of public debate" toward the end of the century, as Indian nationalist discourse succeeded in designating the "feminine" space of the home as the source of national identity and conferring upon women the duty of preserving the traditional Indian spirit through the daily practice of properly feminine virtues. Unlike in Bengal, the women's question in Korea never vanished from public debates during the colonial period, because it was utilized by various political actors with widely differing agendas—from elite-centered bourgeois feminism to cultural nationalism and from socialist feminism to fascist wartime propaganda—all without ever prompting a nationwide movement for women's rights. Chatterjee,

mit that these broad historical factors alone do not explain why domestic novels were published on a mass scale by the burgeoning print market after the Russo-Japanese War (1904–5) and the Protectorate Treaty (1905), only to lose their cultural dominance by the mid-1910s. Never again would the Korean domestic novel regain its dominant position in the literary scene. I now attempt to explain this peculiar phenomenon by taking a closer look at the early colonial literary landscape.

The Domestication of Reform in Early Colonial Korean Fiction

The early colonial Korean domestic novel is typically considered a major subgenre of *sinsosŏl*, a representative genre of turn-of-the-century Korean fiction. The term *sinsosŏl*, however, resists stable definition, as it has been often arbitrarily used by writers, publishers, and critics. In this section I explore the various early colonial usages of the term not to suggest a new definition but to shed light on the cross-cultural, institutional, and political aspects of the evolution of Korean prose fiction as well as to call attention to a distinctive tendency in the Korean literary scene in this period, which I call "the domestication of reform in early colonial Korean fiction."

Korean prose fiction was departing from traditional *sosŏl* in several ways in the early colonial period, and *sinsosŏl* epitomizes this change. According to the literary scholar Kim Yŏngmin, the term came into being through the fortuitous attachment of a then-voguish Chinese prefix, *sin* (new), to one of the common traditional terms for fictional narratives, *sosŏl*. Kim goes on to argue that *sinsosŏl* made the transition from a common noun to a literary genre in the 1930s when, to support their evolutionist view of the Korean novel's development, the Marxist literary historians Kim T'aejun and Im Hwa used it to classify a group of early colonial domestic novels written by reform-minded writers such as Yi Injik, Yi

Nation and Its Fragments, 114; Sinha, "Gender in the Critique," 452–72; Dutta, "Identifying Mother India," 4–10; Hyaeweol Choi, *New Women in Colonial Korea*; Kyeong-Hee Choi, "Another Layer of Pro-Japanese Literature," 61–87; Park, *Proletarian Wave*, 197–231; Barraclough, *Factory Girl Literature*, 13–55.

Haejo, An Kuksŏn, Kim Kyoje, and Ch'oe Ch'ansik.[40] When the early colonial domestic novel came onto the literary scene, however, neither writers nor publishers consistently distinguished *sinsosŏl* from *sosŏl*. It was often the case that a literary work was marketed as *sinsosŏl* by one publisher but later reprinted by another and marketed as *sosŏl*.[41]

Translations of a broad range of foreign literature were also called *sinsosŏl*. For example, the prolific translator Hyŏn Kongnyŏm refers to Yano Ryūkei's political novel, *Illustrious Tales of Statesmanship* (*Keikoku bidan*, 1883), as *sinsosŏl* in the preface to his 1908 Korean translation of the book, *Kyŏngguk midam*, even though present-day scholars of Korean literature tend to draw a clear line between *sinsosŏl* and the political novel (*chŏngch'i sosŏl*). *A Tale of a Patriotic Lady* (*Aeguk puinjŏn*, 1907), a Korean translation of a biography of Joan of Arc, was published with the term *sinsosŏl* on the front cover and advertised as such.[42] *Long Dream of Regret* (*Chang han mong*, 1912), Cho Ilchae's popular translation of Ozaki Kōyō's Japanese domestic novel *The Gold Demon* (*Konjiki yasha*, January 1, 1897–May 11, 1902) was also advertised as *sinsosŏl* when it was serialized in *Maeil sinbo* in 1912.[43]

40.   Kim Yŏngmin, *Han'guk kŭndae sosŏlsa*, 123–35.

41.   *Maeil sinbo* advertised the initial serialization of *The Heartless* as *sinsosŏl* in 1917. A little more than a year later, Yi Kwangsu used the term to indicate the type of fiction that he had been trying to move away from: "Let's set aside the question of whether it is worthwhile to discuss the literary value of *sinsosŏl*, which always receives our *contempt and sneers*. Nevertheless, we should not remain oblivious that it helped [in] proliferating the vernacular and increasing [the public's] desire for reading a little." Yi Kwangsu, "Puhwal ŭi sŏ kwang," 28 (emphasis added).

42.   Advertisement, *Taehan maeil sinbo*, October 8–December 12, 1907.

43.   The initial confusion has been carried forward in various anthologies of *sinsosŏl* published from the late 1960s on, as well as in academic writings about this genre. The compilation of *sinsosŏl* published by Ŭlyu munhwasa (1968), for instance, includes a number of adapted translations of Japanese domestic novels. Hinting at the compilers' awareness of the blurry boundaries of *sinsosŏl*, the first set of *Kaehwagi munhak ch'ongsŏ* (Series of Literature from the Enlightenment Period), the two-set facsimile anthology of turn-of-the-century Korean fiction published by Asea munhwasa (1978), puts *sinsosŏl* and translations and adapted translations of foreign novels (*pŏnyŏk* and *pŏnan sosŏl*) into the same category without clearly delineating the differences between them. This classification, too, is far from consistent. Whereas the Korean renditions of the American pulp-fiction writer Frederick van Rensselaer Dey's *New Nick Carter Weekly* (1907) and Maria Edgeworth's *The Lottery* (1799) are classified in the first set as *sinsosŏl* and *pŏnan* (*yŏk*) *sosŏl*, those of John Bunyan's *The Pilgrim's Progress* (1678), Daniel Defoe's *Robinson*

The emergence of *sinsosŏl* may be less about a genre strictly understood and more about the rapid expansion of the print industry and the literary marketplace. Compared to the most common methods of premodern textual reproduction, such as woodblock printing and hand-copied manuscripts, the spread of the latest printing technologies at that time greatly reduced production time and cost and enabled the number of printed periodicals and books to increase rapidly. Unlike the traditional network through which *sosŏl* had been circulated—family and friends, private book rental shops (*sech'aek chŏm*), and book peddlers (*ch'aekk'oe*)—the mushrooming nationwide sales system of newspapers and publishing houses helped new forms of fiction reach broad audiences within a much shorter period of time.[44] After the Russo-Japanese War and the Protectorate Treaty, major newspapers, such as *Taehan maeil sinbo*, *Mansebo* (Three Thousand Generations, 1906–7), *Hwangsŏng sinmun* (Capital Gazette, 1899–1910), *Cheguk sinmun* (Imperial Daily, 1898–1910), and *Kyŏnghyang sinmun* (The City and Country Weekly, 1906–10), added separate sections for serialized prose fiction, probably to increase circulation.[45] It was a common practice among these newspapers to advertise their new serialization of *sosŏl* or *sinsosŏl* days before the first installment.[46] Publishers regularly

---

Crusoe (1719), and Jules Verne's *Deux ans de vacances* (1888) are included in the second set of the anthology as "historical and biographical novels." (See Kang Hyŏnjo, "Kim Kyoje pŏnyŏk pŏnan sosŏl," 197–225). The most comprehensive compilation of facsimile reprints of *sinsosŏl* by Kyemyŏng munhwasa (1987) includes a number of six-penny fictions (*yukchŏn sosŏl*), many of which were traditional folk tales republished using the latest printing technology in the 1910s and 1930s. A more recent collection of *sinsosŏl* published by the Seoul National University Press (2003) lists several translations of foreign literature, in addition to the novels written by canonical "*sinsosŏl* writers" such as Yi Injik, Yi Haejo, Kim Kyoje, and Ch'oe Ch'ansik.

44. Chŏng Chinsŏk, "Kŭndae minjok chuŭi hyŏngsŏng," 7–38. Published in the vernacular version and the mixed style in addition to the English weekly edition, *Taehan maeil sinbo* had the largest number of subscribers during this time. It was circulated nationwide through eighteen distribution outlets in May 23, 1907. The number had reached fifty-two by January 7, 1909. However, this newspaper was not evenly distributed across regions: about half of the branches were located in P'yŏngan province, a region historically marginalized by the Chosŏn court.

45. Kim Yŏngmin, *Han'guk ŭi kŭndae*, 42–57.

46. A Japanese-Korean bilingual newspaper founded by the Japanese politician Adachi Kenzō (1864–1948) with the financial support of the Japanese Ministry of Foreign Affairs (*Gaimushō*), *Hansŏng sinbo* (Seoul Newspaper, 1895–1904) started running

marketed their latest titles in various periodicals and other print media. From a contemporary perspective, copyright seems more fluid than would be expected, with an editor or publisher frequently named *chŏjakcha* (author) instead of the actual author. Nevertheless the book form of *sosŏl* or *sinsosŏl* would include a copyright page, which would list a publication date, the publisher's name(s) (often both that of a publishing house and that of its head), an author, at times a *kyoyŏlcha* (copy editor), addresses of local sales agents, and a list price. The notice of copyright was commonly printed in a larger font in a separate box (*p'ankwŏn soyu* [copyright reserved] or *pokche pulhŏ* [reprinting prohibited]).

Whatever else the term *sinsosŏl* signified, it clearly registered the growing aspirations for the reform of traditional stories, which were, in the eyes of turn-of-the-twentieth-century reformists, as much as in those of the Confucian literati, nothing but a shameful indulgence mainly targeted toward women and commoners. The renovation of fiction was emphatically called for as a part of the larger project of "civilization and enlightenment," reflecting the rising sense of political crisis among Korean elites in the wake of the Protectorate Treaty in 1905. The July 8, 1908 editorial of *Taehan maeil sinbo*, "Note to Today's Writers of Vernacular Fiction" (Kungmun sosŏl ŭl chŏsul hanŭnja ŭi chuŭihalil), is a case in point:

> As I always say, the world's greatest achievements are not carried out by great heroes and masterminds like Ŭlchi Mundŏk or Yŏn'gae Somun but by women, children, and servants; great social trends are not started by great philosophy or knowledge such as religion, politics, and law but by vernacular *sosŏl*. . . . Therefore how can we think lightly of *sosŏl*? Pessimistic and morally depraved *sosŏl* will affect people (*kumgmin*) as such; morally uplifting *sosŏl* will affect the people as such. As a Western scholar (*sŏyu*) said, "Fiction is the soul of the people." The novel that has been passed down in Korea . . . only corrupts popular sentiments and customs. I would say that it is urgent to replace it with *sinsosŏl*.[47]

---

a *sosŏl* section and regularly publishing prose fiction, mostly in vernacular Korean or the mixed style, for the first time in 1897. See Kim Chaeyŏng, "Kŭndae kyemonggi sosŏl," 18–28.

47. "Kungmun sosŏl ŭl chŏsul," *Taehan maeil sinbo*, July 8, 1908.

Often attributed to the nationalist historian Sin Ch'aeho, this editorial draws a parallel between the renovation of *sosŏl* and that of the people—especially the traditional subclasses of "women, children, and servants"—while endowing both with unprecedented capacities. *Sosŏl* has the potential to elevate the moral character of the people; ordinary people and women have the potential to act as leaders on the world stage. In this passage *sinsosŏl* signifies an elevated form of traditional *sosŏl* that would help women, children, and nonelites improve their moral character.

One must not overlook, however, the transnational dimension of the call for the renewal of fiction. Clearly Korean writers and readers were no strangers to stories and narratives originating outside Korea, given that Korean *sosŏl* had evolved through close exchanges with and translations of Chinese fictional narratives. The term *sosŏl* is the Korean reading of the Chinese *xiaoshuo*. The ancient term, made up of the two Chinese characters for "small" and "talk," initially denoted various types of "trivial" writings supposedly less serious than Confucian classics and official histories. According to Judith Zeitlin, the category of *xiaoshuo* began to include "consciously made-up stories designed to entertain and edify" in the tenth century and became an "umbrella literary genre, covering works long and short, in both classical and vernacular idioms" in the late seventeenth century.[48] *Sosŏl* owed much of its pre-twentieth-century development to the importation, translation, and adaptation of Chinese *xiaoshuo*. It is commonly believed by scholars of premodern Korean literature that Korean *sosŏl* emerged sometime between the late Silla and early Koryŏ periods (between the tenth and eleventh centuries), when the lost collection of short stories and tales *Eccentric Tales* (*Suijŏn*) was compiled by Pak Illyang. Twelve pieces in the original version of *Suijŏn* were transmitted through seven different sources between the thirteenth and the seventeenth centuries.[49] Save for them, five remaining pieces of *chuanqi* (stories of the marvelous) in Kim Sisŭp's fifteenth-century collection, *New Stories from the Golden Turtle Mountain* (*Kŭmo sinhwa*), are probably the oldest extant examples of *sosŏl*. The invention of the Korean vernacular script Han'gŭl in the mid-fifteenth century played a significant role in

48. Zeitlin, "Xiaoshuo," 249–61.
49. Im Hyŏng-t'aek, *Han'guk munhaksa ŭi sigak*, 9–25; Yi Tonggŭn, *Suijŏn ilmun*, 7–31.

expanding the *sosŏl* readership from elite men to women and common-ers. Not only did many Chinese *xiaoshuo* become available in Korean vernacular translations, but Korean *sosŏl* in the vernacular began to ap-pear from the sixteenth century on. More often than not, those first writ-ten in the vernacular script were translated into classical Chinese.[50] In this uniquely polyglossic milieu, *sosŏl* grew into more diverse and sophisticated forms and, accordingly, gained broader audiences from the seventeenth century onward. Yet early colonial Korea saw the scope and complexity of transnational interaction increase substantially, due to its contact with Japan and the West as well as to its renewed cultural exchange with China.

For example, the aforementioned July 8, 1908 editorial in *Taehan maeil sinbo* essentially restates the main points of two essays by the late Qing public intellectual and reformist writer Liang Qichao, with slight modifications: "On the Relation between Fiction and Mass Government" (Lun xiaoshuo yu qunzhi zhi guanxi, 1902), which appeared in the inau-gural issue of his literary magazine, *Xin xiaoshuo* (New Novel, the same Chinese characters as *sinsosŏl*), and "Preface to the Translation and Publi-cation of Political Novels" (Yiyin zhengzhi xiaoshuo xu, 1898), which was added to his translation of *Chance Encounters with Beautiful Women* (*Kajin no kigū*, 1885–97), the first Chinese translation of a Japanese po-litical novel.[51] Liang Qichao's writings were widely read by Korean elites who had easy access to the original, thanks to their knowledge of literary Chinese (*hanmun*). They were also translated into the Korean vernacular, for less-educated readers, and were frequently incorporated into Korean editorials and essays, as was the case with "Note to Today's Writers of Vernacular Fiction," often without proper citation.

As Catherine Yeh shows, Liang Qichao's understanding of what fic-tion could achieve owed much to the global migration of the political novel, a genre pioneered by the English politician and novelist Benjamin Disraeli (1804–81) with the high-profile publication of his so-called Young

---

50. Chŏng Ch'urhŏn, "P'yogi muncha chŏnhwan," 163–98.

51. "To renovate the people of a nation, the traditional literature of that nation must first be renovated. Thus, to renovate morality, we must first renovate fiction; to renovate manners, we must first reform fiction. . . . Even to reform people's hearts and remold their character, we must first renovate fiction. Why? It is because fiction exer-cises a power of incalculable magnitude over mankind." Wang, *Fin-de-siècle Splendor*, 24; U Rimgŏl, *Han'guk kaehwagi munhak kwa Yang Kech'o*, 149–53.

England trilogy: *Coningsby* (1844), *Sybil* (1845), and *Tancred* (1847).[52] Unlike in Japan and China, the political novel did not grow into a discernible genre in Korea but nevertheless left an indelible mark on the early colonial literary scene. To examine the political novel's distinctive impact on the evolution of early colonial Korean fiction, we need to take a brief look at the border-crossing paths of this genre before it reached Korea.

According to Morris Edmund Speare's classic definition, the political novel is "a work of prose fiction which leans rather to 'ideas' than to emotions . . . and where the main purpose of the writer is party propaganda, public reform, or exposition of the lives of the personages who maintain government, or of the forces which constitute government."[53] Disraeli's unapologetic use of the novel form to propagate his political views sets his novels apart from the dominant mode of nineteenth-century European realism. The political novel not only boasted a remarkable sales record in England during the nineteenth century, but also found a number of passionate readers and emulators in East Asia. Yeh emphasizes that it is precisely the political novel's built-in linkage to political reforms—which she identifies as one of "the core political and literary features of the genre"—that made this genre appealing to writers and readers in China, Japan, and Korea from the late nineteenth through the early twentieth centuries.[54] The presumed seriousness of the subject of the political counteracted the age-old bias against fiction as a trivial genre of writing. Like Disraeli, many authors of the political novel in East Asia were participating in contemporary political reform efforts in one way or another. For these activists, the primary importance of fiction lay in its potential power to influence public opinion, not in its aesthetic value.

If the first political novelists in East Asia were the Japanese activists of the Freedom and Popular Rights movement—a series of grassroots political endeavors in the 1870s and 1880s to curtail the government's authoritarian power by establishing a constitution and parliament—one should keep in mind that the Japanese political novel (*seiji shōsetsu*) arose from translation and adaptation as much as it was, in Yanagida Izumi's words, "generated for the political struggles for the freedom and popular

52. Yeh, *Chinese Political Novel*, 15–25.
53. Speare, *Political Novel*, ix.
54. Yeh, *Chinese Political Novel*, 109.

rights, reflecting the movement, and used as a weapon for the movement."[55] Despite the tepid interest of later scholars and readers in this genre, the Japanese political novel enjoyed immense popularity in the 1880s, often selling millions of copies.[56] Seki Naohiko's first Japanese translation of Disraeli's *Coningsby* was not merely enthusiastically received by the reading public upon its initial publication in 1884 but also enabled a number of activists to attempt writing their versions of the political novel.[57] Peter Kornicki identifies one of Disraeli's major contributions to the development of the Japanese political novel as the introduction of a new perception of fiction, suggesting that, even before his *Coningsby* became available in Japanese, Disraeli's career as a politician-cum-novelist was already shaking the Japanese reading public's accepted view that fiction was a genre of writing unsuitable for respected men of politics.[58]

The Japanese political novel in turn offered a model for Chinese versions between 1901 and 1910. Translations into Chinese by reformist writers like Liang Qichao enjoyed enormous popularity among urban elite readers while inspiring late Qing writers to compose their own versions (*zhengzhi xiaoshuo*).[59] Akin to its Japanese and English counterparts, the Chinese political novel was mainly written by political actors and activists who explored the future of China's constitutional reforms. The Japanese political novel was connected to public debates about the shift to a constitutional monarchy and parliamentary system to such a degree that

55. Yanagida, *Seiji shōsetsu kenkyū*, 33.

56. Some examples are Yano Ryūkei's *Keikoku bidan* (1883), a fictional retelling of the struggle of Thebes and other ancient Greek cities to put an end to Sparta's autocratic rule; Suehiro Tetchō's *The Plum Blossoms in the Snow* (*Setchūbai*, 1886); and Shiba Shirō's incomplete novel *Kajin no kigū* (1885–1897). See Sakaki, "Kajin no kigū," 83–108.

57. Kornicki, "Disraeli and Meiji Novel," 35–36.

58. Ibid., 47–48.

59. Some examples are Liang Qichao's unfinished novel *The Future Record of New China* (*Xin zhongguo weilai ji*, 1902), Xuanyuan Zhengyi's *A Prophecy on the Calamity of Being Carved Up* (*Guafen canhuo yuyan ji*, 1904), Chen Tianhua's *The Roar of the Lion* (*Shizi hou*, 1906), and Siqi Zhai's *Citizen Novel: The Rights of Women* (*Guomin xiaoshuo: Nüzi quan*, 1907). The Japanese political novel left its own formalistic imprints on Chinese works like Liang Qichao's *Xin zhongguo weilai ji*. On Liang's adaptation of Suehiro Tetchō's political novel *The Future Record from Meiji Year 23* (*Nijusannen miraiki*, 1890) in his *The Future Record of New China*, see Yeh, *Chinese Political Novel*, 87–93, and Willcock, "Meiji Japan," 1–28.

the genre lost its raison d'être when those issues were no longer relevant. Similarly, Catherine Yeh suggests that the heyday of the Chinese political novel coincides with the period of the Xinzheng Reforms (Reforms of Governance), an extensive series of measures instituted by the Qing court in response to the antiforeign upheaval following the Boxer Rebellion (1899–1901), which resulted in an unfair treaty between foreign powers and the Qing dynasty.

Considering the close relationship between the political novel and the efforts to modernize political institutions in Japan and China, one might be tempted to ascribe the arrested development of the Korean political novel to Korea's colonial condition. Indeed colonial censorship played a detrimental role in the growth of the political novel in early colonial Korea. Though officially enacted through the Newspaper Law (1907) and the Press Law (1909), colonial censorship was already being implemented right after the outbreak of the Russo-Japanese War, when Japanese headquarters started imposing prepublication screenings upon Korean newspapers under the pretext of military security and public safety. It was as colonial censorship was taking its initial shape that a limited number of Japanese political novels—including Yano Ryūkei's *Illustrious Tales of Statesmanship*, Suehiro Tetchō's *The Plum Blossoms in the Snow*, and Katō Masanosuke's *Enchanting Tales about Restoration* (*Kaiten kidan*, 1885)—became available in Korean.[60]

It is not clear that the Korean translations of Japanese political novels were seen as a genre distinct from the more numerous, latest translations of historical or semihistorical narratives that revolved around successful or unsuccessful struggles for national sovereignty and political reforms,

60. An incomplete, hybrid-style translation of Yano Ryūkei's *Illustrious Tales of Statesmanship* was serialized in *Hansŏng sinbo* in 1904. Korean translators probably preferred Chinese translations of Japanese political novels over the original Japanese texts because Chinese was more accessible to many of them, since they had grown up reciting the Chinese classics. As Hotei Toshihiko suggests, it is also possible that a Chinese rendition was chosen intentionally because it revised the original Japanese text in a way that could accommodate the Korean reading public's political aspirations. Hotei, "Futatsu no Chosen yaku." On Hyŏn Kongnyŏm's Korean translation of *Enchanting Tales about Restoration, Hoech'ŏn kidam,* see Tian Ming (Chŏn Myŏng), "Aeguk kyemonggi chungyŏkpon chŏngch'i sosŏl"; regarding Ku Yŏnhak's Korean translation of Suehiro Tetchō's *The Plum Blossoms in the Snow,* see No Yŏnsuk, "Ilbon Chŏngch'i sosŏl ŭi suyong."

such as *A Record of the Founding of Switzerland* (*Sŏsa kŏngukchi*, 1907), *History of the Loss of Vietnam* (*Wŏlnam mangguksa*, 1906, 1907), *Modern History of Egypt* (*Aegŭp kŭnsesa*, 1905), *A History of the Philippine War* (*Piyulbin chŏnsa*, 1907), and *Three Heroes of the Foundation of Italy* (*Itaeri kŏnguk samgŏlchŏn*, 1907, 1908). These were mostly translations of Chinese or Japanese texts, some of which were in turn adaptations or translations of the original texts in other languages—Spanish, German, French, or English.[61] A number of the Korean translations of these historical narratives were rendered by leading nationalist writers—including Sin Ch'aeho, Pak Ŭnsik, Chang Chiyŏn, and An Kuksŏn—who were outspoken about their political stances. Sin Ch'aeho penned Korean iterations of globally circulated historical narratives apropos of national sovereignty—such as *The Tale of Ŭlchimundŏk* (*Ŭlchimundŏk chŏn*, 1908), *The Tale of Yi Sunsin* (*Yi Sunsin chŏn*, 1908), *The Tale of Ch'oe Tot'ong* (*Ch'oe Tot'ong chŏn*, 1909)—while revisiting moments of crisis in Korean history associated with invasions by the Chinese, the Japanese, and the Mongols.

Another genre of fiction that comes close to the political novel among early colonial Korean narratives is "the debate novel" (*t'oronch'e sosŏl*), which revolves around fictional or semihistorical figures and discussions of various reform-related issues; examples include An Kuksŏn's *Minutes of a Forum among Animals* (*Kŭmsu hoeŭi rok*, 1908), Yi Haejo's *Freedom Bell* (*Chayujong*, 1910), Yu Wŏnp'yo's *Meeting Zhuge Liang in a Dream* (*Monggyŏn Chegallyang*, 1908), and Kim P'ilsu's *Warning Bell* (*Kyŏngsejong*, 1910).[62] Significantly, within a few years after their publication, political

61.   *Wŏlnam mangguksa* (*History of the Loss of Vietnam*) is a Korean translation of Liang Qichao's *Yuenam wangguo shi* (1905), Liang's interview with a Vietnamese expatriate, Phan Boi Chau, about France's brutal colonial rule of Vietnam. *Sŏsa kŏngukchi* (A Record of the Founding of Switzerland, 1907) translates Zheng Zhe's Chinese rendition of the story of the legendary Swiss hero Wilhelm Tell, *Ruishi jianguo zhi* (The Founding of the Swiss Republic, 1902). *Aegŭp kŭnsesa* (Modern History of Egypt, 1905) was originally written by Shiba Shirō as *Egibuto kinseishi* (1889), although the Korean translator Chang Chiyŏn probably used one of the Chinese translations, likely that of Zheng Zhe. See No Yŏnsuk, "20 seji ch'o hanjungil chŏngch'i sŏsa," 35–64; Yeh, *Chinese Political Novel*, 87–88.

62.   The literary critic Im Hwa called An Kuksŏn's *Minutes of a Forum among Animals* the "greatest Korean political novel" in his *Introduction to New Korean Literature* (*Kaesŏl Sinmunhaksa*, 1939–41) many years before Serikawa Tetsuyo and, more recently, Sŏ Chaegil showed that it was indeed an abridged translation of Satō Kuratarō's *Ani-*

novels, historical narratives about colonialism and nation building, and debate novels, whether translations or original texts, were rendered extinct by the state authorities through the banning and confiscation of the texts, the conviction and incarceration of writers and translators, and, perhaps most effectively, the closing down of the nationalist newspapers in which these works were serialized and/or advertised.[63]

Nor was the publication of Japanese and Chinese political novels free from state intervention. For example, Meiji censors expurgated two passages from a widely popular Japanese political novel, Shiba Shirō's *Chance Encounters with Beautiful Women* (*Kajin no kigū*, 1885–97), where a male character with the author's own pen name, Tōkai Sanshi (Wanderer of the Eastern Sea), discusses his experiences and concerns about imperialist oppression around the world with three compatriots from China, Spain, and Ireland, respectively.[64] The Chinese political novel emerged when the late Qing Chinese court was trying to put a gag on reformists via the Press Code enacted in 1901. Yet censorship did not put an abrupt end to the political novel in either Japan or China the way it did in Korea. According to Atsuko Ueda, the decline of the political novel in Japan was precipitated not only by state censorship but also by the epistemological shift sparked by the spread of the depoliticized discourse of "the autonomy of knowledge," the institutionalization of *shōsetsu* (a Japanese translation of "the novel") within the academic discipline of national literature, and the inward turn in literature.[65] Despite the court's severe censorship, Chinese reformist writers managed to publish political novels under the protection of Shanghai's International Settlement and even "engaged in court-sponsored reform processes" using the literary form as a medium.[66]

---

mals' Meeting: Attack on Mankind (*Jinrui kōgeki: kinjū kaigi*, 1904). Im, Hwa, *Im Hwa sin munhaksa*, 145. Serikawa, "Hanil kaehwagi uhwa sosŏl," 164–79; Sŏ Chaegil, "*Kŭmsu hoeŭirok* ŭi chŏbon," 67–93.

63. A few political novels written after the annexation—such as Sin Ch'aeho's *The Dream Sky* (*Kkumhanŭl*, 1916) and *Great Battles between Two Dragons* (*Yong kwa yong ŭi taegyŏkchŏn*, n.d.), and Pak Ŭnsik's *Meeting the Founder of the Jin Dynasty in Dream* (*Mong paekŭm t'aejo*, 1911)—were authored by exiles and remained unpublished for decades after the end of the territorial colonization.

64. Sakaki, "Kajin no kigū," 86–87.

65. Ueda, *Concealment of Politics*, 11–15.

66. See Yeh, *Chinese Political Novel*, 230.

The domestic novel, on the other hand, continued to flourish in Korea even after the Japanese government-general drove the political novel from the publication market. Because publishers kept on using the term *sinsosŏl* to market their fiction collections, now dominated by the domestic novel, this term became detached from the political novel and more closely attached to the domestic novel. The contrasting fates of the domestic novel and the political novel after the annexation may invite the predictable assessment of the domestic novel as politically benign and trivial. But things are not that simple. It would be more accurate to say that, whether classified as domestic novels, debate novels, political novels, or *sinsosŏl* by later literary historians, many literary works published between 1906 and 1910 share reformist aspirations, whether they had nationalist, pro-Japanese/colonialist, or anticolonialist viewpoints as their impetus. As is the case with the political novel and the debate novel, the narrators and characters of the domestic novel act as mouthpieces of reformist writers. It should also be noted that, just like Japanese and Chinese authors of the political novel, many writers of early colonial Korean domestic novels—such as Yi Injik, Yi Haejo, Pak Yŏngun, Yuk Chŏngsu, and An Kuksŏn—were also active in reform movements. Yi Injik's career had much in common with those of the Japanese political novelists: he graduated from the Tokyo School of Politics (Tōkyō seiji kakkō), worked as chief editor for several newspapers, served in the Japanese army as a Korean interpreter during the Russo-Japanese War, and assisted Yi Wanyong, the pro-Japanese prime minister, during the process of the annexation. Another prolific writer, Pak Yŏngun, was constantly under police surveillance for his anticolonialist activities during the colonial period and went to jail a few times during the 1920s and 1930s.[67] Commonly classified as a *sinsosŏl* writer, Yi Haejo also translated a politically sensitive biography of a key figure of the American Revolution, George Washington, and authored a debate novel, *Freedom Bell*. Both were banned, in 1910 and 1913, respectively.[68]

Although it is true that the early colonial domestic novel tended to present reform as a family or private matter rather than as a public concern, and was therefore less vulnerable to censorship than the political

67. Chang Nohyŏn, "Sinsosŏl chakka Pak Yŏngun," 129–55.
68. Ch'oe Wŏnsik, " 'Hwasŏngdon' chŏn yŏn'gu."

novel, it is not the case that the domestic novel was always unaffected by colonial surveillance. Despite Yi Injik's pro-Japanese collaboration, the 1907 edition of his domestic novel *Tears of Blood* (*Hyŏl ŭi nu*, 1906) was banned in June 1911 by the Government-General Police Bureau (Chōsenfu sōtoku keimu sōkanbu).[69] The redacted edition published by Tongyang sŏwŏn in 1912 not only excised the author's nationalistic comments, but also featured a new title, *Peony Hill* (*Moktanbong*), to make it sound less gruesome and politically explosive than the original. Yuk Chŏngsu's two-volume novel *Pine Wind Zither* (*Songroegŭm*), which was marketed as *sinsosŏl*, was not approved for publication in 1912.[70] The Government-General Police Bureau's records show that Pak Yŏngun's lost works such as *The Hall of Aeryŏn* (*Aeryŏn tang*) and *The House of Kangsŏn* (*Kangsŏn ru*) were banned, although their titles follow those of the domestic novel.[71]

The list of "censored" novels suggests that the domestic novel as a genre survived the harsh colonial censorship laws not necessarily because it was generically indifferent to politics or exclusively concerned with sup-posedly trivial family matters. If most domestic novels in early colonial Korea were engaging in one way or another with the question of how to renovate traditional kinship structures through egalitarian marriage and women's education, one should remember that the renewal of domestic-ity was in fact an important topic for public debates in Korean newspa-pers and magazines between 1895 and 1910 and remained so even after almost all the Korean-run newspapers were closed down by the newly es-tablished government-general in 1910. As Andre Schmid points out, the reformist discourse of "civilization and enlightenment" often obscured the differences between Korean nationalists and Japanese colonialists, as it was endorsed by both.[72]

The domestic novel came to be preferred by Korean reformist writers who were learning how to get their works published despite the severe

69. Chōsenfu sōtoku keimu sōkanbu, *Keimu geppō* 3, no. 13: 213.
70. Chōsenfu sōtoku keimu sōkanbu, *Keimu geppō* 4, no. 23: 416.
71. *The Hall of Aeryŏn* has a descriptive lable, "*sinsosŏl* about the red-light district" (hwaryu sinsosŏl), and *The House of Kangsŏn*, "sosŏl of ethics" (yulli sosŏl). Chōsenfu sōtoku keimu sōkanbu, *Keimu geppō* 16, 278; Chōsenfu sōtoku keimu sōkanbu, *Keimu ihō* 32, 590.
72. Schmid, *Korea between Empires*, 14–15.

colonial censorship, because it allowed them to engage in the reform discussion without necessarily addressing thorny topics such as national sovereignty and colonization, which were likely to draw the attention of colonial authorities. Thus, the novelistic discourse of reform was increasingly "domesticated" throughout the early colonial period, but more visibly after the annexation in August 1910. To understand this tendency in early colonial Korean fiction, we should be careful not to assume that there are clear, universal distinctions between public, domestic, and individual that early colonial Korean domestic novels unambiguously reproduce. On the contrary, each domestic novel imaginatively redraws its own version of the world in which the home displaces the space of the nation, and where an individual character's destiny foreshadows that of her family as well as that of her nation. At the heart of the fictional space of the early colonial Korean domestic novel are the figures of domestic women.

From Domestic Women to Sensitive Young Men

By the mid-1910s, it was clear that the Korean domestic novel had lost its place of dominance in Korean literature. As a conspicuous sign of this trend, *Maeil sinbo* no longer published Korean domestic novels after the serialization of Yi Haejo's *Passersby in the Rain* (*Ujung haengin*) was completed in May 1913, and focused more on various translations of foreign works of literature, ranging from Japanese domestic novels (such as Kikuchi Yūho's *My Sin* [*Ono ga tsumi*] and Ozaki Kōyō's *The Golden Demon* [*Konjiki yasha*]) to French and English novels (Alexandre Dumas's *Le Comte de Monte-Cristo*, Fortuné du Boisgobey's *L'oeil de chat*, Mary Elizabeth Braddon's *Diavola; or The Woman's Battle*, and Victor Hugo's *Les misérables*) to early modern Chinese classics (Cao Xueqin's *Dream of the Red Chamber* [*Honglou meng*] and Kong Shangren's *The Peach Blossom Fan* [*Taohua shan*]).[73]

73. The Korean translations of French and English novels were rendered from Kuroiwa Ruikō's Japanese translations. For a more detailed account of translations and adaptations, see Pak Chinyŏng, *Pŏnyŏk kwa pŏnan*. Also see Hyo Kyung Woo, "Korean Englishes, Uneven Asias," 52–88.

During this time the term *sinsosŏl* was more frequently associated with an inferior quality of writing than with aspirations for reform and novelty. It was no longer taken as being unequivocally superior to traditional fiction, nor expected to supplant the latter in the near future. On the contrary, traditional fictional narratives were experiencing a revival in the publishing market as, from 1912 on, a number of them became available in mass-market editions called "six-penny fiction" (*yukchŏn sosŏl*) or sometimes "old movable type editions" (*ku hwalchabon*). In the first half of 1912, *Maeil sinbo* serialized Yi Haejo's four modern adaptations of *p'ansori* novels (a traditional genre derived from Korean one-man folk opera, *p'ansori*): *The Song of Ch'unhyang* (*Ch'unhyangga*), *The Song of Simch'ong* (*Simchŏngga*), *The Song of the Underwater Palace* (*Sugungga*), and *The Song of Hŭngbo* (*Hŭngboga*). At the same time, traditional literature came to be seen in a more positive and perhaps fairer light, compared to a decade earlier. It is hard to imagine, for example, that between 1906 and 1910 Korean reformist writers would have advocated that the writers of *sinsosŏl* needed to seek inspiration from traditional Chinese and Korean novels, as did the scholar of Chinese classics Yun Hŭigu (1867–1926) in his 1916 essay "*Sinsosŏl*."[74]

The trivialization of *sinsosŏl* was often combined with the hopeful expectation for a newer style of novel. While criticizing *sinsosŏl* for offering no helpful insight regarding real life but merely ascribing "destructive" (*p'agoejŏk*) and "decadent" (*t'oep'yejŏk*) meanings to it, Paek Taejin voices his longing for the advent of new literary writers with rigorous principles and in tune with the Zeitgeist (*sidaean*).[75] Similarly, the writer and translator Yang Kŏnsik describes *sinsosŏl* critically as "a series of tedious and low-quality works written without a vision or wit," while expressing his unreserved excitement about Yi Kwangsu's upcoming serialization of *The Heartless* in his essay "Welcoming Ch'unwŏn's Novel [*sosŏl*]."[76]

The emphasis on aesthetic quality and elitism distinguishes the discourse on fiction of the late 1910s from that of the late 1900s. Between 1906 and 1910 the conception of *sosŏl* was predicated upon the sense that

74. Yun Hŭigu's essay was published under his pen name, U Tang. U Tang, "*Sinsosŏl*," April 5 and 8, 1916.

75. Paek, "Sinnyŏn pyŏktu e," 13–16.

76. Kukyŏ (Yang Kŏnsik's pen name), "Yŏ nŭn Ch'unwŏn ŭi sosŏl," *Maeil sinbo*, December 29, 1916. Ch'unwŏn was Yi Kwangsu's pen name.

nation building and reform would be accelerated by renovating fiction. Writers, commentators, and publishers all agreed that good *sosŏl* should lift the spirit of the nation and thus must be produced by and accessible to people from all corners of the nation regardless of their social status, gender, or level of education. Certainly the hope for a universal readership of *sosŏl* was wishful thinking: the literacy rate was still extremely low, especially among women; only a small group of reform-minded elites actually wrote and published *sosŏl* during this time; and some writers implicitly limited their readership to the elite population simply by writing in classical Chinese or a hybrid style. Nevertheless, the question of who among the people of Korea would be in a better position to write and read *sosŏl* rarely came up. In the late 1910s, on the other hand, the task of the renewal of fiction was most frequently imposed upon "educated young men." In the aforementioned essay by Yun Hŭigu, for instance, the author singles out "young people of letters" (*ch'ŏngnyŏn haksik*) as the leading lights in the renovating of *sosŏl*. Yi Kwangsu's unrealized plan to serialize *The Heartless* in an elite-targeted mixed script was intended to appeal to "the circle of educated young people" (*kyoyuk innŭn ch'ŏngnyŏn kye*), in contrast to what he considered to have been common practice in "the previous *sosŏl*."[77] However, he came to see the mixed style as unsuitable for newspaper serialization, so he eventually chose the unmixed vernacular for his novel while still holding onto his hope that *The Heartless* would help "some young people with education" (*ilbu yu kyoyukhan ch'ŏngnyŏn*) to pave the way to a new land (*sint'oji rŭl kaech'ŏk*).[78]

What Yun Hŭigu and Yi Kwangsu meant by "young people of letters" and "educated young people" were not the traditional Confucian literati but rather the growing number of people familiar with modern disciplinary knowledge through secondary or post-secondary education in Japan or Korea. As early as 1906, the semi-scholarly periodical *Boys of the Peninsula* (*Sonyŏn hanbando*, 1906–7) included concise introductions to modern academic disciplines such as mathematics, sociology, finance, psychology, economy, geography, engineering, biography, physics, mineralogy, zoology,

77. Advertisement, *Maeil sinbo*, December 26–29, 1917.
78. "On the Change in the Style of the Novel" (Sosŏl munch'e pyŏngyŏng e taehaya), *Maein Sibo*, January 1, 1917.

botany, physiology, hygiene, and commerce.[79] The significance of subject-based modern knowledge became more pronounced in the mid-1910s, as those specializing in one or more fields of study emerged as leading actors of modernization. Yi Kwangsu's well-known essay "What Is Literature?" (Munhak iran hao, 1916) is an attempt to disseminate the "disciplinary" notion of literature to the Korean public, even though he stresses that the Korean translation of literature (*munhak*, which consists of an ancient East Asian term for belles lettres, *mun*, and a suffix attached to academic disciplines, *hak* [studying, learning]) should aim to express *chŏng* (feelings), as opposed to the objectivity other academic disciplines (*hak*) should express.[80] Within the new system of knowledge that Yi Kwangsu introduces in this essay, *sosŏl* are not just stories meeting the need for entertainment, but a subgenre of literature that has its own purpose, rules, and history.

The emergence of what I refer to as the sensitive young man—another iteration of the individual in Korean literature—should be understood as a response to the growing demand for an aesthetically more sophisticated form of fiction in the late 1910s. Korean prose fiction published during this time and thereafter frequently portrays young male figures who suffer from physical or mental illness, unrequited love, lovers' deaths or betrayals, the loss of a job, or perennial poverty. It often focuses on their main characters' negative feelings—including anxiety, fear, loneliness, disappointment, remorse, sorrow, and grief. The majority of sensitive men's narratives appeared in two elite-targeted magazines published by those who were attending or had attended schools in Japan. One of these was *Hak chi kwang*, and the other was *Ch'ŏngch'un* (Youth, 1914–18), a cultural magazine published by Sinmun'gwan (The New Culture House), a well-known publishing company established by Ch'oe Namsŏn (1890–1950), who had embarked on a publishing career after dropping out of Waseda University in 1908.[81] Other venues for sensitive men's narratives included two Korean-language cultural magazines founded by the Japanese publisher Takeuchi Rokunosuke: *Sinmun'gye* (New Culture, 1914–17) and *Pando siron* (The Currents of the Peninsula,

79. *Sonyŏn Hanbando*, vols. 1–6 (November 1906–April 1907).
80. Yi Kwangsu, "Munhak iran hao."
81. Besides *Ch'ŏngch'un*, Sinmun'gwan put out four different periodicals between 1908 and 1918: *Sonyŏn* (Boys, 1908–11), *Pulgŭn chŏgori* (Red Shirts, 1912), *Aidŭl poi* (Reading to Kids, 1913–14), and *Saebyŏl* (Morning Stars, 1913–15).

1917–19).[82] Yang Kŏnsik published his short story "Sad Contradictions" (which I examine in chapter 5) in the latter, even though reformist Buddhist journals such as *Pulgyo chinhŭnghoe wŏlbo* (Society for the Promotion of Buddhism Monthly) and *Chosŏn pulgyo kye* (The Korean Buddhist Circle) were more often the publishers of his work.

The major magazines that published sensitive men's narratives were neither coterie journals nor did they specialize in literature. Sensitive men's narratives came out together with sundry essays covering a vast range of topics including science, music, religion, philosophy, national history, the history of language, current affairs, economic development, geography, travel, and so forth. It was often the case that one writer contributed several pieces to one issue while serving on the journal's editorial board. One can identify the elitist tendency of sensitive men's narratives in the stylistic choices made by their authors. Whereas early colonial domestic novels were mostly written in the vernacular and did not incorporate Chinese letters (*hanja*), writers of sensitive men's narratives preferred the hybrid style, implicitly limiting their readership to a relatively small number of elites or elites-to-be. The guidelines for the submission of short stories to *Ch'ŏngch'un's* regular literary prize contests required "the latest style [*simunch'e* 時文體], which slightly mixed with Chinese characters."[83] Through the literary contests, a number of sensitive young men's narratives were published, such as Chu Yohan's "Village Home" (Maŭljip, 1918), and Kim Yŏnghyu's "A Matter of the Heart" (Yujŏng mujŏng, 1917), to name but a few.

Almost all writers of sensitive men's narratives had advanced proficiency in Japanese, although not all of them had attended high school or college in Japan. Writers like Yang Kŏnsik (1889–1944), Yi Sangch'un (n.d.–1920), and Paek Taejin, for example, acquired their skill in Japanese within the government-run modern school system, which was established by royal ordinance in 1896 and closed down by the Japanese government-general in 1911. These writers' fluency in Japanese allowed them to stay in tune with the ever-changing intellectual and cultural scenes in Japan. While sensitive men's narratives were flourishing in Korea,

---

82.   Paek Taejin published a number of short stories in these journals while working as a reporter for them.

83.   *Ch'ŏngch'un* 11 (November 1917) (n.p.).

Japan was experiencing unexpected economic prosperity. World War I (1914–18) held European competitors at bay, allowing Japanese traders to seize control of the Asian markets and increase their exports exponentially. Mainstream cultural life in Japan was marked by optimism and "dreams of a modern life whose bywords were 'rationality,' 'science,' and 'culture,' and whose favorite adjectives were 'bright' and 'new.'"[84] This period of Japanese history was marked not only by the ascendance of party government and an interest in liberalism but also by rising class disparities and inflations. In response to growing economic and social disparities, a series of mass movements were organized to demand the expansion of civil rights, universal male suffrage, economic justice, political reform, and so forth. Japanese intellectuals, politicians, and the press were debating new democratic visions. This early twentieth-century Japanese iteration of liberal democracy is often referred to as "Taishō democracy," after the emperor who reigned between 1912 and 1926. Andrew Gordon suggests an alternative name, "imperial democracy," pointing out that the ideals of the "democracy" of the time rarely clashed with Japan's imperial expansionism and nationalism.[85]

The traces of liberal discourses are easily detected in sensitive men's narratives. One way or another, many of these writings delve into the questions of equality, freedom, liberty, and social progress. The writers of these narratives also published essays in the same periodicals that championed industrial modernization, economic progress, liberalism, the advancement of science and technology, and rationalism. The advocacy of liberal beliefs by Korean writers at this time may seem quixotic, however, given that they lacked freedom of speech, one of the basic tenets of liberalism. Korean writers could not share their thoughts and ideas publicly without being subject to the scrutiny of the rigid colonial surveillance system—censorship laws and security law (Poan pŏp)—whose severity has been summed up as "military rule" (*mudan t'ongch'i*).[86] Censorship in Korea was much more stringent than in Japan, demanding prepublication

84. Gordon, *Modern History of Japan*, 155. See also Jung-Sun Han, *Yoshino Sakuzō*, 14–40.

85. Gordon, *Labor and Imperial Democracy*, 7–10.

86. Though much less influential than liberalism, anarchism and socialism gained some adherents among Korean students in Japan in the late 1910s. See Han Kihyŏng, "Ch'ogi Yŏm Sangsŏp ŭi anakijŭm"; Park, *Proletarian Wave*, 46–48.

screening and a three-step examination of the manuscript, typeset copy, and specimen copy.[87] Under the Press Law, *Youth* was banned for two years (April 1915–April 1917).[88] The editor's postscript in the May 1917 issue notes that two works submitted for a literary contest had been expurgated. The sale of several issues of *Hak chi kwang* was prohibited between 1915 and 1916.[89]

Under the weight of the state apparatus as well as that of the ideological power of social Darwinism, young Korean writers' campaigns for social progress rarely confronted colonialism directly until the outbreak of the March First Movement in 1919. On the contrary, they more often held their fellow Koreans responsible for the failure to rise to the challenge of global competition. This line of thinking is well represented by Hyŏn Sangyun's "The Power Principle and Korean Youth" (Kangnyŏk chuŭi wa Chosŏn ch'ŏngnyŏn, 1915). While attributing the decline of Korea to its lack of power, he claims that Korean young men must cultivate "military spirits" (*muyongjŏk chŏngsin*), "promote the dissemination of natural science" (*chayŏn kwahak pogŭp*), and bring about an "industrial revolution" (*sanŏp hyŏkmyŏng*) in order to regain power. In this essay, Japan is not presented as a colonizer but rather as a role model for Korean youth wishing to strengthen their nation.[90]

However, in an essay in Japanese titled "Demand of Education for Koreans" (Chōsenjin kyōiku ni taisuru yōkyu, 1916), Yi Kwangsu does criticize the Japanese colonial government, not only for blatantly discriminating against Koreans in legal disputes and business licensing and favoring Japanese settlers in Korea, but also for providing a lower-quality curriculum and instruction in the Korean public school system than in Japan. Published in a Japanese liberalist journal, *Kōzui igo* (After the Deluge), this essay takes the form of a warning to Japanese policy makers: the current discriminatory policy will institutionally reproduce the subordinate status of Koreans and ultimately cause Koreans to become angry with the colonial regime.[91] His irate undertone notwithstanding,

---

87. Chŏng Kŭnsik, "Singminji chŏk kŏmyŏl," 5–46.

88. *Ch'ŏngch'un* 10 (September 1917), 112.

89. *Hak chi kwang* 10 (September 1916), 59.

90. Hyŏn Sangyun, "Kangnyŏk chuŭi wa Chosŏn ch'ŏngnyŏn," 43–49.

91. Koshū sei (Lonely Boat, one of Yi Kwangsu's pennames), "Chōsenjin kyōiku ni taisuru yōkyu," 51, reprinted in Hatano, *Kankoku kindai sakka tachi no nihon ryūgaku*, 138–40; and Hatano, *Ilbon yuhaksaeng chakka*, 171–77.

Yi Kwangsu tries to make it clear that he has no intention of challenging the legitimacy of Japan's colonial rule. Here his rhetorical strategy comes near to what Homi Bhabha calls "the discourse of colonial mimicry," the colonial subject's desire to copy his or her colonizers in order to access the latter's resources of power. Yet it is impossible for colonial subjects to become exactly the same as the colonizers as long as the colonial condition subsists. As a result, colonial mimicry is "constructed around an *ambivalence.* . . . [I]n order to be effective," it "must continually produce its slippage, its excess, its difference."[92] There is a similar slippage in Yi Kwangsu's words: while asking that Koreans be granted the same level of education as the Japanese on the premise that through proper education the former could become like the latter, he does not refute the very foundation that keeps the relationship between them inevitably unequal, namely, Japan's colonial rule.

As I discuss in chapter 5, a strong desire for social progress marks the figures of sensitive young men. However, these characters' "modern" desire is often shown through their negative emotions, intense inferiority complex, paranoia concerning the gaze of others, and nervous acts of looking at others. Such oversensitive figures would hardly have been imaginable without the system Japanese colonizers put in place in Korea, of which surveillance was just one element. Soon after the protectorate treaty in 1905, those dwelling in the capital city, Seoul (then called Kyŏngsŏng), were forced to follow meticulously itemized rules that regulated their daily conduct to an unprecedented degree. The Road Management Act (Karo kwalli kyuch'ik) is a good example. Enacted in 1906 at the behest of the newly appointed Japanese police affairs adviser, Maruyama Shigetoshi (1856–1911), this required people to stay on a designated side of the road, depending on whether they were walking or steering a cart. People were not allowed to move an oversized load without first obtaining an official permit from the police bureau. Littering on the road was forbidden. So was loitering in a public space.[93] On the pretext of investigating a violation of the innumerable statutes regarding sanitation, the police could inspect any household.[94]

92. Bhabha, *Location of Culture*, 122.
93. Yi Chongmin, "1910 nyŏndae kyŏngsŏng chumin ŭi choe wa pŏl," 101–2.
94. Chulwoo Lee, "Modernity, Legality, and Power," 21–51.

People faced incarceration, a fine, or even flogging for not observing these oppressive regulations.[95]

One must not forget, however, that beyond the ideological and legal spheres, modernity was manifesting itself physically prior to the rise of the domestic novel in the early colonial literary scene. Trains and streetcars, both of which began to operate in Korea in 1899, were already spreading a new sense of punctuality to major cities.[96] Beginning with domestic service in 1895, the Korean postal system joined the Universal Postal Union in 1900. By the time that the early colonial domestic novel had gained popularity among newspaper readers, the national postal system had come to serve as a well-established avenue for transnational communications. Compared to the figures of sensitive young men, the characters of the early colonial domestic novel are naïvely unsuspicious about the possible detrimental effect of modern apparatuses and technologies. As I discuss in the first four chapters of this book, modern/colonial institutions, technologies, and mass transportation do leave their marks on the early colonial domestic novel, in the forms of various elements such as characters, settings, imagery, and the chronotope. Technological advances are at times viewed with utter awe and wonder even though for the most part they constitute mute aspects of settings and imagery. The omniscient narrator of the domestic novel is frequently caught up in the imperative to valorize the new over the old—which often verges on a utopian vision. The modern school system magically turns an illiterate local girl into a national leader. Trains and steamships take characters from a war-ravaged Korean city to an advanced foreign land, offering them life-changing opportunities. The justice system seems to assure rational solutions to all social ills. The narrator and characters marvel at how much the modern postal and transportation systems help them overcome physical distance. None of the characters of the domestic novel internalize the social control aspects of these apparatuses the way that sensitive young men do through narrative voices often associated with modernist fiction: the first-person narrator, pathological perspectives, the subjective gaze, and the flâneur.

95. Yi Chongmin, "1910 nyŏndae kyŏngsŏng chumin ŭi choe wa pŏl," 101–2.
96. Cf. Friedman, *Tokyo in Transit,* 9.

I stress that domestic women's apparent lack of psychological complexity must not hold us back from listening to what these characters tell us about the primal scenes of Korean modernity. The significance of the figures of domestic women outstrips that of any other literary element in this genre precisely because reform-minded writers' aspiration for modernity takes on a complex and ambivalent form when it comes to the depictions of women as individual citizens. In the process of translating individuals as female characters not only under the pressure of reform but also up against the residual forces of the traditional gender and social hierarchy, early colonial Korean writers thus came up with a wide range of innovative images of female figures that one might not immediately associate with modern individuality. These female figures are important not because they resemble the sensitive young men or other types of individuals supposedly closer to the individual in nineteenth-century European literature, but, on the contrary, because they show us a type of individuality far removed from our contemporary fantasy about autonomous beings and secluded interiority.

In chapter 1 I identify the pivotal figure of the individual in the pioneering work of *sinsosŏl, Tears of Blood*. I call *Tears of Blood* a "domestic novel" in two different senses. First of all, as a coming-of-age story comparable to Victorian domestic novels such as Jane Austen's *Pride and Prejudice* and Charlotte Brontë's *Jane Eyre*, it follows a young Korean girl's maturation from war orphan to potential advocate of women's rights, while simultaneously tracing her individual growth through the process of becoming a wife of a reform-minded young man. This story about the genesis of a modern wife is juxtaposed with another narrative that revolves around her old-fashioned mother, who exemplifies the traditional faithful wife (*yŏllyŏ*): she remains chaste during the absence of her husband, who has moved to the United States to pursue an education. In casting these two conflicting narratives of domestic women as a symptom of male writers' ambivalent desires regarding women's liberation, I identify in this chapter the complexity of translating the individual into a female figure in early colonial Korean literature.

The early colonial Korean domestic novels, in which translating the individual and rewriting a traditional tale often go hand in hand, are examined in chapter 2. The two-volume work *Mt. Ch'iak (Ch'iaksan,* 1908,

1911) is particularly noteworthy, as it rewrites a premodern tale of female ghosts—"The Tale of Changhwa and Hongnyŏn" (Changhwa Hongnyŏn chŏn, n.d.)—as a story of a reform-minded domestic woman's defiant resistance of her in-laws' abuses. Traditionally, a female ghost was a culturally sanctioned literary device that offered some imaginative leeway for women to speak out against oppressive gender norms. In the process of rewriting "The Tale of Changhwa and Hongnyŏn" as a didactic tale of "civilization and enlightenment," the two authors of *Mt. Ch'iak* strip the supernatural elements from the traditional ghost story while creating what I call a "ghostly woman"—a female double who speaks for women's rights on behalf of a chaste *yangban* wife of a reformist man. I argue that ghostly womanhood offers an imaginary resolution to reformist male writers' conflicted desire to give women equal rights without forsaking the traditional gender norm of chastity.

I focus on two femme fatale figures who transgress traditional boundaries of gender and social status in my readings of two early colonial domestic novels, *A Coldhearted Flower* (*Pakchŏnghwa*, 1910) and *Peony Hill* (*Moranbong*, 1913), in chapter 3. The early colonial femmes fatales are unprecedentedly "unbound" individuals marked by their excessive and insatiable desires as well as their formidable power over men. In *A Coldhearted Flower*, the authority of the traditional patriarchy is undercut by a young and beautiful concubine of a rich old *yangban* man, as she not only runs off with a good-looking young steward a few times but also, after being dumped by her young lover, manages to return to her husband and avoid severe punishment. In *Peony Hill*, a shrewd outcast woman threatens the authenticity of patriarchal lineage by faking kinship ties with several *yangban* families and wielding influence over these families' futures. I suggest that, unlike the iconic cultural figures of *sinyŏsŏng* (new women) in the 1920s and 1930s, these women's defiance of traditional boundaries is not driven so much by the global discourse of the "new woman" as by the symbolic power vacuum left by the lack of male authority after the loss of national sovereignty but before the rise of new cultural elites.

If female characters in early colonial Korean literature often find their individuality in their domestic identities, those identities are ripe for interpretation by a radical dissident imagination. Chapter 4 is devoted to Kim Kyoje's *Flowers in the Mirror* (*Kyŏngchunghwa*, 1923), in which domestic women exercise their human rights by forming a radical form of

family: same-sex marriage. After breaking fre[...]
their old-fashioned marriages—including [...]
from getting an education and their in-laws [...]
mer wives of the same man manage to g[...]
American missionary and a Japanese entr[...]
regard patriarchal marriage as hopeless [...]
female alternative family. The story o[...]
multaneously with the story of thei[...]
fallen *yangban* family, who rises to b[...]
characters of this work—the two women and the[...]
individuals, as each of them struggles to exercise individual human agency
through the pursuit of a modern education, wealth, and happiness. Yet
their individuality does not rise above gender differences. The two female
protagonists express their conception of individual rights by creating a
home, which lives up to the ideals of equality and solidarity, whereas their
ex-husband embodies the myth of the self-made man.

Chapter 5 turns to another iteration of the individual, sensitive young
men. Instead of investigating how they "discover" their interiority, my
reading focuses on unraveling the ways in which these seemingly private
figures are subject to the force of nationalism, colonial surveillance, and
the ideology of progress. I first place Chang Ŭngjin's short story "Confession under the Moon" (Wŏrha ŭi chabaek, 1907) as a transitional work
between early colonial domestic novels and sensitive young men's narratives. In this story, an anonymous third-person narrator witnesses a depraved old *yangban* man's emotional confession of his sins in his last
moment prior to his suicide and interprets it not just as an individual's
personal story but also as the end of a chapter in national history. Whereas
the death of this emblematic figure of traditional society serves as an allegory of the demise of Korea as a nation in Chang Ŭngjin's short story,
neither old male patriarch nor national allegory find their ways in the
stories about sensitive young men in the late 1910s. In the sensitive young
men's stories, the protagonists do not have an unmediated tie with the
community that the old man of "Confession under the Moon" has. Instead, their experiences of the world are mediated by their private psyches.
In Hyŏn Sangyun's "Persecution" (P'ippak, 1917), an educated young man
internalizes colonial surveillance and the desire for progress in the form of
mental illness as well as debilitation. Yang Kŏnsik's "Sad Contradictions"

(Sŭlp'ŭn mosun, 1918) depicts a young male flâneur in Seoul who switches his gaze between inward and outward to internalize the ideology of progress as his private desire.[97]

These sensitive young men lose their unmediated ties with the world outside by receding into their inner space. At the same time, they tend to impose a more elitist tone upon individuality: now the latter is less about human rights collectively accomplished and defended and more of a highly intellectual and private attainment that is the province of a relatively small group of elites. The shift from domestic women to sensitive young men also suggests that access to individuality was not open to the same degree to each gender in early colonial Korea. However, one should neither conclude that the figure of a sensitive young man was the prototypical form of the individual, which women and nonelites would be directed to emulate in a more egalitarian society, nor assume the figures of domestic women to be a truer form of Korean individuality. Both domestic women and sensitive young men resulted from early colonial Korean writers' cultural interpretations under historical constraints. Neither is more authentic than the other, even though one of them may seem a little more familiar to contemporary readers than the other. Ri Hyŏngsik's "discovery" of his inner self in Yi Kwangsu's *The Heartless* is one of many forms of individuality. If the Korean translation of the individual, or *kaein*, remains a politically and culturally viable idea in contemporary Korean society, we might ask whether *kaein* has ever become the equivalent of the individual in Europe, more than a century after its initial introduction to Korea. The translation of the individual has been, and probably will be, constrained by historical conditions. The diverse images of individuals in early colonial Korean literature attest that individuality was indeed open to cultural interpretations and imaginations to a considerable degree. If that was the case in the early twentieth century, it is likely still true in the twenty-first.

97. Janet Poole shows us how this sense of progress no longer appeared attainable to Korean modernist writers who published under Japanese fascism during the last decade of colonial rule. See Janet Poole, *When the Future Disappears*.

CHAPTER ONE

Enlightened Daughter,
Benighted Mother

Yi Injik's *Tears of Blood* (*Hyŏl ui nu*, 1906) opens with a lady (*puin*) hysterically running across the corpse-strewn fields of P'yŏngyang under an intense afternoon sun.[1] Her dress is loose, almost falling off, though she does not notice; she is piercingly crying out "Ongnyŏn," the name of her seven-year-old daughter. During the P'yŏngyang battles of the Sino-Japanese War (1894–1895), she is accidentally split from her only child and her husband. As the reader soon learns, her husband has also been separated from their daughter. The family has been torn apart.

In this pioneering example of the early colonial domestic novel, mother, father, and daughter have all been wrested from their home at the very outset of the story, as though it were necessary that the home should be vacated before it begins to undergo a radical change. As I discuss in detail in this chapter, these opening lines illustrate the ongoing disintegration of a premodern family at the turn of the twentieth century with remarkable historical acuity.[2] As the story continues, the lady returns to their home a few days later, but her husband and daughter travel separately out of Korea and spend the next decade abroad, living modern lives in Japan while acquiring modern Western knowledge. Only in *Peony Hill* (*Moranbong*, 1913), the unfinished sequel to *Tears of Blood*, will

---

1. Yi Injik, "Hyŏl ŭi nu."*Mansebo*, July 20; Yi, *Tears of Blood*, 159. Quotations are mostly from W. E. Skillend's translation, with my modifications.
2. Yi Tuhŏn, *Han'guk kajok chedo*, 586.

husband and daughter return to their homeland, as though to highlight the newborn chasm between the old and the new.

It has been a truism that *Tears of Blood* promotes the modern reforms that many Korean intellectuals and leaders felt were vital to the survival of the nation at the turn of the last century. Readings of *Tears of Blood* focus almost exclusively on the lady's child, Ongnyŏn, who makes an unintended voyage to the "civilized" world and becomes an emblematic figure of enlightenment. In my discussion of the novel's opening above, however, I deliberately shift the focal point to Ongnyŏn's mother, Ch'unae, to call attention to its unique narrative structure, which has been overlooked by previous scholars.[3] Considering the story's unremitting propagation of the theme of "civilization and enlightenment," the novel gives too much space to this old-fashioned character, who clings to the old Confucian way of living throughout the story. Out of the fifty installments originally published in the daily newspaper *Mansebo* (Three Thousand Generations) from July 20 to October 10, 1906, twenty direct a spotlight on the mother, almost four times more than the number focusing on her husband, Kim Kwanil, and twice more than the number focusing upon her daughter's fiancé, Ku Wansŏ. More to the point, it is this woman's experience that carries the story up until the eighteenth episode, where Ongnyŏn's side of the story begins. If the mother is, as literary critics seem to presume, merely a minor character of no significance, why would the author give her such an extensive space—two-fifths of the entire volume?

One might be tempted to explain away this initial emphasis on the figure of Ch'unae in strictly literary terms, by ascribing the "lopsided" narrative structure to the author's failure to live up to the modern aesthetic standard. In spite of the author's aspiration to emulate the modern Western novel, some critics have hesitated to bestow the supposedly celebratory adjective "modern" on Yi Injik's fiction for the reason that it is

---

3. The first name "Ch'unae" is used exclusively during the framed story of her childhood in *Tears of Blood*. She is most often identified as *puin* (lady), a traditional title for a married woman of the upper class, along with a couple of variants, such as *Kim ssi puin* (Kim Kwanil's wife) or *Ch'oe ssi puin* (Madam Ch'oe, Ch'oe being her last name; Korean women keep their last names after marriage). Her first name does not appear at all in the sequel, *Peony Hill* (*Moranbong*, 1913) See chapter 3 of this book for my reading of this work.

still largely dominated by remnants of traditional narratives.[4] This approach is flawed, however, because it imposes a modern artistic norm upon a work written under different cultural and historical constraints, as if there were a universal aesthetic standard uniformly applicable to the multiplicity of literary productions that have come into being in different times and places. Rather than dismissing the mother's story as tangential to the novel's meaning, I contend that *Tears of Blood* is made up of two different genres of narratives: one, the domestic novel, follows a young girl's growth into a modern wife in accordance with the pattern of a coming-of-age story; the other rewrites the traditional biography about a virtuous woman (*yŏllyŏ chŏn*) with early colonial Korea as its background. Equally important, I suggest that not only the daughter's "modern" story but also the mother's old tale was shaped by the historical tensions between nation-building efforts, the ideology of "civilization and enlightenment," and colonialism, which put many reform-minded Korean intellectuals in a self-contradictory position.

Long considered a traitorous pro-Japanese collaborator, Yi Injik himself exemplified the ideological conflicts characteristic of early colonial Korea. While working as an aide to Yi Wanyong, the pro-Japanese prime minister who coordinated the Japan-Korea annexation treaty in 1910, he published a series of fictional works that did not necessarily harmonize with his political beliefs. In *Introduction to New Literature* (*Kaesŏl sin munhaksa*, 1939–41), the first in-depth study of the Korean "new novel" (*sinosŏl*), Im Hwa identifies Yi Injik as a contradictory figure who shows "no small distance" between his act of collaboration and the kind of Korean nationalist political idealism that strongly infuses some of his literary works.[5] Until recently, however, the political ambiguity of his literary works has tended to be overlooked by critics. Between the 1960s and the 1980s, when the history of modern Korean literature was examined from the viewpoint of anticolonial nationalism, many scholars from both sides of

4.   An advertisement for *Tears of Blood* reads, "This fiction imitates the manner of the *Western novel* (*sŏyang sosŏl*)," *Mansebo*, April 3–June 29, 1907. However, the contemporary literary scholar Kim Yŏngmin, for instance, argues that Yi Injik's literary works fall short of the mark of modern fiction, pointing to his characters' inconsistencies, unbalanced plots, frequent use of coincidences and traditional clichés, and Confucian gender ideology. Kim Yŏngmin, *Han'guk kŭndae sosŏlsa*, 203–65.

5.   Im Hwa, *Im Hwa sin munhaksa*, 170–71.

the cease-fire line considered it scandalous that the pioneering author of modern Korean fiction was pro-Japanese. As a result, Yi Injik and his literary achievements were completely erased from major North Korean histories of modern literature until 1986.[6] Though South Korean scholars did not go so far as to eliminate his historical presence, they often undermined his literary legacy by depicting his fiction as unabashed colonialist propaganda or, as in the case of Ch'oe Wŏnsik, by arguing that *Moss on a Peak* (*Chamsangt'ae*, 1906) by Yi Haejo (1869–1927) was the first new novel, not Yi Injik's *Tears of Blood*, even though this unfinished work is written in the mixed style that combines Chinese characters with the addition of vernacular verb endings and prepositional particles, unlike the majority of new novels.[7]

As the dawn of the new millennium saw a gradual amelioration of the dogmatically nationalist political climate, and the strict schism between nationalism and imperialism began to be held in abeyance, literary scholars started casting a more sympathetic eye on Yi Injik's political and literary legacy. Ch'oe Chongsun's recent monograph, for example, tries to separate Yi Injik's "pragmatic" and "realistic" political view from Japan's colonialist ideology, while claiming that Yi Injik allows a colonialist vision to be blended into his narrative not only to represent the social complexity of the turn of the twentieth century but also to avoid censorship.[8] In a similar vein, I maintain distance from rigid nationalist interpretations in order to seek an alternative understanding of Yi Injik's fiction. Still, it is not my intention to vindicate the author of the charge of being pro-Japanese with his literary works as the pretext. Rather, I try to articulate the ways that early colonial Korean political discourses— those of "civilization and enlightenment," colonialism, and nationalism— are uneasily integrated into the two sub-narratives of *Tears of Blood*, while asking what the tension between them tells us about the gender politics behind early colonial Korean translation of the individual.

The protagonist of the tale of a faithful wife, Ch'unae, occupies the dark terrain of the benighted, the opposite of the promising land of the

6.   Kim Yŏngmin, *Han'guk kŭndae sosŏlsa*, 162.
7.   Ch'oe Wŏnsik, *Han'guk kŭndae sosŏlsa ron*, 286–305; Ch'oe Wŏnsik, *Han'guk kyemong chuŭi*, 148–54.
8.   Ch'oe Chongsun, *Yi Injik sosŏl*, 307–11.

enlightened through which her daughter travels. The world of the latter tends to be more favorably portrayed than that of the former. And yet *Tears of Blood* is not exactly a clear-cut manifesto of the nation's embrace of "civilization and enlightenment." The dichotomy between the benighted and the enlightened is complicated by the fact that both Ongnyŏn and Ch'unae embark on paths that develop the images of "national" homes: through the transnational education of "civilization and enlightenment," Ongnyŏn becomes a prospective wife of a reform-minded Korean man and, in place of the status-based premodern family, is taught to create a new Korean home, one that purportedly will have horizontal relationships with other Korean homes and equal access to the emerging nation. Yi Injik's image of Ch'unae as an exemplary virtuous wife, on the other hand, invents a unified symbol of the nation's past by refurbishing class-bound *yangban* womanhood into a timeless tradition of a modern Korea.[9]

By articulating the complex political implications of not only the new but also the old-fashioned female character in *Tears of Blood*, I also hope to shed new light on a genere normally called, with some condescension, *kajŏng sosŏl* (the domestic novel), which flourished between 1906 and 1915 and continued to be published into the early 1930s. Predominantly written by reform-minded male writers, works in this genre typically orbit around conflicts among female characters over the issues of marriage, family, and home life. Because of their focus on domestic women, critics often treat these works as merely trivial diversions meant for women as opposed to "modern" literature, which engages in "serious" and "realistic" social concerns. For example, Im Hwa's *Introduction to New Literature* opts to list only a small number of "social novels" (*sahoe sosŏl*) as worthy of a critic's trained eye, while excluding even more works that he classified under the supposedly condescending category

9. Ch'unae could be compared to the female protagonist of another of Yi Injik's stories, "A Widow's Dream" (Kafu no yume, 1902). Published in the Japanese newspaper *Miyako shinbun* (Newspaper of the Old Capital) under the heading of *Chōsen bungaku* (Korean literature) four years prior to the serialization of *Tears of Blood* and notably targeted at the Japanese public, this short story portrays a sorrowful *yangban* widow with a highly aesthetic sensibility rather than a moral contemptibility. This was written by Yi Injik with the help of a Japanese writer, Chizuka Reisui (1866–1942). Yi Injik, "Kafu no yume" (A widow's dream) *Miyako shinbun*, January 28 29, 1902. For an analysis of this story, see Tajiri, *Yi Injik yŏn'gu*, 64–69, 275–78.

of "domestic novels."[10] His gender-based taxonomy of the genre classifies *Tears of Blood* as a typical social novel, and later scholars generally agreed with him on this point. Until recently the standard account has suggested that most of the new novels are distractions from the path toward the modern novel that *Tears of Blood* opened up, diversions created by writers who chose to cater to the vulgar tastes of uneducated women.

Against this dominant tendency, first of all, I suggest that we should classify *Tears of Blood* as a domestic novel, not to belittle its value but to reclaim it as the first work of an epoch-making genre, in which modern individuality was articulated through the issues of women's education and modern conjugal marriage. My reading contends that, as a coming-of-age story comparable to Victorian domestic novels such as Jane Austen's *Pride and Prejudice* and Charlotte Brontë's *Jane Eyre*, *Tears of Blood* translates the notion of the individual through a young Korean girl's maturation from a war orphan to a wife of a reform-minded young man and to a future advocate of women's rights. On the other hand, I also call into question what role the story of the mother—in which she lives as a traditional chaste wife during the absence of her husband, who has moved to the United States to pursue an education—plays in the coming-of-age story of the daughter.

Two Outlines

Tears of Blood is usually outlined as follows: in the midst of the Sino-Japanese War, a seven-year-old girl, Ongnyŏn, becomes lost and, when wounded by a gunshot, spends a night alone on Peony Hill.[11] Japanese

---

10. Im Hwa, *Im Hwa sin munhaksa*, 168–69, 181.

11. Between 1906 and 1940, three different versions of *Tears of Blood* came out in at least five different editions. The first version was serialized in *Mansebo* between July 20 and October 10, 1906, before it was turned into a separate volume (the second version) by the publishing house Kim Sangman sŏp'o in 1907, and again in 1908 by Kwanghak sŏp'o. The author revised the previous version in light of colonial censorship, and it was published by Tongyang sŏwŏn under the new title *Peony Hill* (*Moktan pong*) in 1912. In 1940 the literary journal *Munjang* (Composition) carried the Tongyang sŏwŏn edition,

soldiers find her the next morning and take her to the Japanese Red Cross. Major Inoue, a Japanese army surgeon, tries to help her find her parents, but since they are nowhere to be found, he decides to adopt her and sends her to his home in Ōsaka. Under his childless wife's warm care, Ongnyŏn learns the Japanese language and goes to elementary school just like a Japanese child. When Major Inoue dies in battle in a year or so later, however, things begin to change. Realizing that her adopted child will make it harder for her to find a husband, Mrs. Inoue comes to harbor a grudge against Ongnyŏn. Unable to take her stepmother's ill-treatment, she runs away from home. On a train she takes in an aimless flight from town, she chances to make the acquaintance of a young Korean man, Ku Wansŏ, who is stopping over in Japan en route to the West, and follows him to the United States to continue her education. When they arrive in San Francisco, however, Ongnyŏn and Ku Wansŏ feel lost, as they neither know anyone to turn to for help nor speak any English to get by. Ku Wansŏ manages to communicate using a written form of literary Chinese (that is, through brush-talk) with a luxuriously dressed Chinese man, who turns out to be a real historical figure, Kang Youwei. This reformist scholar and politician introduces Ongnyŏn and Ku Wansŏ to a Japanese-speaking Chinese man, who in turn makes arrangements for them to enroll in a school in Washington, DC. Ongnyŏn excels in high school and soon graduates with honors. Her remarkable story is even recounted in an American newspaper. It happens that her father, Kim Kwanil, who has been going to school in the United States as well, reads the article and finally manages to reunite with his daughter. In the presence of Kim Kwanil, Ongnyŏn and Ku Wansŏ promise to marry and to become the future leaders of Korea.

---

but this time again as *Tears of Blood* (Yi, "Hyŏl ŭi nu," *Munjang*, 224–58). It is not known whether *Tears of Blood* was published again as *Peony Hill*. What is now commonly known as *Moranbong* (Peony Hill) was initially written as a sequel to the Tongyang sŏwŏn version of *Tears of Blood*, namely, *Moktanbong* (*Moktan* and *moran* are two different readings of the same Chinese characters for "peony"; both are legitimate and are interchangeable in contemporary usage). According to Kim Yŏngmin, the *Maeil sinbo* version of *Peony Hill*, unlike the author's other novels such as *Tears of Blood* and *Voice of a Ghost* (1906–7) was not immediately turned into a volume after the initial serialization in 1913. Kim Yŏngmin, *Han'guk kŭndae sosŏlsa*, 197–200; Ham, "Hyŏl ŭi nu," 203–32; Yi Injik, *Moktanbong*.

Such a précis, however, discounts almost half of the story. Especially in the first eighteen installments of the original serialization, *Tears of Blood* centers on Ch'unae, the "lady" who "looks about thirty years old," while giving little clue to the fact that her seven-year-old daughter will turn out to be the real protagonist of the story. After introducing this panic-stricken woman in the opening scene, the novel continues with a series of adversities that she experiences. Wandering in the fields alone, she finds herself at the mercy of a lascivious peasant. Instead of letting him dishonor her, she decides to commit suicide. Luckily, some Japanese soldiers show up at that moment and scare him away with gunshots before taking her to safety at their headquarters. After being released the next morning, she begins waiting for her husband and daughter to return. Her patience runs out in fifteen days. Concluding they must be dead by now, she tries to drown herself in a river. This time her former servant's son saves her. Learning from her father, Ch'oe Hangnae, who has come from Pusan, that her husband has survived and gone abroad to further his education, she decides to remain at home until her husband's return. The reader also learns of Ch'unae's childhood, during which time she lost her own mother and suffered at the hands of a proverbially evil stepmother, who otherwise played a flawless role as her father's new wife.

The focus of the story shifts abruptly from the detailed account of Ch'unae to that of her daughter. Once Ongnyŏn's story begins, the author seems to have forgotten nearly everything he has written up about Ch'unae until that point. The advertisement for the first book edition of *Tears of Blood* provides the following summary: "This work of fiction, written in the pure national script, was serialized last fall in *Mansebo*. . . . Ongnyŏn, a little girl of Mr. Kim in North P'yŏngyang, suffered many hardships during the war between Japan and China . . . was uprooted to foreign lands, and got an education."[12] While outlining the work as the story of Ongnyŏn, the advertisement entirely fails to mention the mother. It introduces Ongnyŏn not as the daughter of Ch'unae but as that of Mr. Kim, even though the story tells us very little about him. Given that the advertisement was initially put out nine months after the end of the story's serialization, one might go so far as to say that such teasers like these contributed to the erasure of Ch'unae's experience in this novel's

12. Advertisement, *Mansebo*, April 3–June 29, 1907.

later critical reception. It seems more likely, however, that the copywriter of this particular advertisement omitted any mention of this female character for the same reason that critics have been indifferent to her for a hundred years since: Ch'unae appears to represent just the opposite of what the dominant ideology of "civilization and enlightenment" suggest women become: enlightened, educated, and successful like her daughter, Ongnyŏn, who will make a significant contribution to the nation.

In order to reclaim this old-fashioned woman from critical oblivion, I would like to call attention not only to the apparent contrast between mother and daughter in their respective stories but also to their similarities: both halves of the story revolve around kinship relations and domestic practices. I show how public concerns such as nation building, independence, and national education are closely interlaced into the story of Ch'unae as well as that of Ongyŏn. Based on this observation, I now more closely examine each part of *Tears of Blood* as a separate domestic novel.

Ongnyŏn's Story: Domestic Individuality

Throughout *Tears of Blood*, "home" emerges as the key metaphor of a society in transition. The opening scene witnesses a *yangban* lady of the inner quarter running outside her home in broad daylight, which aptly captures the trauma of an existing Chosŏn social order beginning to fall apart: rarely did upper-class women ever leave the confines of their homes unaccompanied by family members.[13] As the reader later finds out, the

---

13. Unlike the majority of earlier novels, *Tears of Blood* does not pronounce Kim Kwanil's social status from the beginning. Still, Kim's *yangban* status is shown to the reader when he is referred to by his official title "ch'osi," which is translated as "a First Grade official" by W. E. Skillend. See Yi Injik, "Hyŏl ŭi ru," *Mansebo*, August 7, 1906; Yi Injik, *Tears of Blood*, 174. Kim's father-in-law, Ch'oe Hangnae, is referred to by another *yangban* official title, "Chusa." Also, Ch'oe Hangnae's servant Maktong urges Ch'oe to take responsibility for the decline of the country by saying that "it is you gentry [*yangban*] who destroyed the country." Yi Injik, "Hyŏl ŭi ru," *Mansebo*, August 9, 1906; Yi Injik, *Tears of Blood*, 176–77.

entire family had been evacuated from their home and taken refuge in Peony Hill before being driven asunder by the fighting. Within three weeks, mother, father, and daughter have all returned home, but they do not cross paths and miss seeing one another. The home no longer functions as a place, as it once used to, to keep the family together.

What the war has damaged is not the physical space of home, but the dominant kinship structure of Korean society that a *yangban* household used to represent. In this respect, it is telling that this pioneering new novel is set during the Sino-Japanese War and its aftermath. Through the Kabo Reforms (1894–96), a modern restructuring of institutions carried out by the Korean political party that had aligned itself with the Japanese, the Korean government overhauled, among other things, the core legal provisions that had sustained its traditional kinship practices, including "early marriage," the ban on widows' remarriage, and probably most importantly, the hereditary social status system that forbade marriage across status boundaries. Although the long-standing institutions that had seeped into almost every corner of society did not immediately expire but rather gradually faded away over the next several decades, such official efforts at reform marked a significant milestone toward the modern leveling of society.[14]

In the story, too, it is as a result of the war that the young female protagonist loses kinship ties with her natal *yangban* family. Such a loss not only brings extraordinary hardship upon her; it also frees her from the standard restrictions imposed upon women from upper-class families. Through modern schooling, she could cultivate talents that would otherwise have remained undeveloped. As the story indeed informs us, "Throughout Korean history there is no record of a girl with the intelligence and talents of Ongnyŏn. *Korean women were locked up in a corner of the inner room* and not taught anything. So, even if there had been a woman as intelligent as Ongnyŏn, the world would have no way to know."[15]

After a rather embroidered accolade to Ongnyŏn's success, the narrator attributes Korean women's "lack of intelligence" to their age-old in-

14. Kyung Moon Hwang, "Citizenship, Social Equality," 355–87.

15. Yi Injik, *Tears of Blood*, 156–221; Yi Injik, "Hyŏl ŭi nu," *Mansebo*, August 25, 1906 (emphasis added); Yi Injik, "Tears of Blood," 187.

carceration in the inner quarter (*kyujung*). His observation, nonetheless, is not without prejudice. Numerous conduct books and household manuals written by and for women attest to the fact that women were not completely alienated from the world of letters during the Chosŏn dynasty.[16] Besides, it was unusual but not entirely impossible for a woman to gain the ability to read literary Chinese in Chosŏn society, if she was lucky enough to have open-minded male relatives. Even in the late Chosŏn period, when neo-Confucian gender segregation became stricter than ever before, women like Im Yunjidang (1721–93) and Kang Chŏngildang (1772–1832) managed to become erudite in the Chinese classics and to write Chinese poetry and commentaries in neo-Confucian philosophy, the kinds of writings that were the exclusive province of elite men.[17] The aficionados of fiction (*sosŏl*) in the eighteenth and nineteenth centuries were not unacquainted with the ideas of women's education and public achievement.[18] Stories of female heroes, such as *A Tale of Golden-Bell* (*Kŭm pangul chŏn*), *Three Jade Pillars* (*Sam'okju*), and *A Tale of Hong Kyewŏl* (*Hong Kyewŏl chŏn*), chronicle the lives of elite women who perfect their martial arts skills and render distinguished service to the state.[19]

Generally speaking, however, such historical and fictional images of educated women in the Chosŏn period do not so much transgress the conventional gender boundary as maintain, if not reinforce, the status quo. Whether written by men or women, conduct books were to inculcate in elite women Confucian gender norms. No matter how erudite women might be, they were neither educated outside the home nor asked to work for the state or to use their knowledge for the benefit of the public. Even the fictional characters of female warriors infiltrate the male domain only after they hide their "natural" sex by dressing up like men or even, as in case of Pang Hallim, by marrying a woman.[20] They are given back their stereotypical gender roles as wives and mothers once they

---

16. Deuchler, "Propagating Female Virtues," 142–69.

17. Yi Haesun, *Chosŏn cho hugi yŏsŏng*, 18–39.

18. For a brief history of the book-lending stores of the late Chosŏn period, see Ōtani, *Chosŏn hugi tokcha yŏn'gu*, 75–84.

19. Chŏng Pyŏnghŏn, "Yŏsŏng yŏngung sosŏl," 389–416.

20. Pak Hyesuk, "Yŏsŏng yŏngung sosŏl," 156–93; Chang Sigwang, *Chosŏn sidae tongsŏng hon*. See chapter four of this book for a more detailed discussion about *The Tale of Pang Hallim* (Pang Hallim chŏn, n.d.).

remove male attire. Even if they continue to hold the position after disclosing their "natural" sex, they neither wear women's garments on duty nor enact a "feminine" persona in the public space.[21]

The female protagonist of *Tears of Blood*, in contrast, has no need to veil her sexual identity to leave the confines of home and become seeped in the "advanced" knowledge available at the time. Such a change has more to do with the new idea of home than with the birth of a modern, bourgeois individual woman. Ongnyŏn appears to enjoy more freedom than her historical and literary female predecessors not because she consciously attempts to free herself from the traditional gender role but rather because, even though her identity is still deep-seated in the domestic space, the symbolic implication of home changes in *Tears of Blood*.

In the same vein, I would stress that Ongnyŏn's initiation into modern womanhood begins through a new kinship relationship into which she enters in Major Inoue's Japanese home. Although the narrator goes to great lengths to advocate for modern education for women and praises Ongnyŏn for her exceptional work at school, the home plays more of a seminal role in Ongnyŏn's transformation than any educational institution. As a matter of fact, the story gives little clue about her school-based education. Other than the fact that Ongnyŏn finishes elementary school during her stay in Japan, readers are not informed about what Ongnyon's school looks like, who the teachers are, what kinds of subjects she studies, how well she gets along with her Japanese schoolmates, or how the new learning transforms her. Instead, Major Inoue's home functions like a school. Ongnyŏn learns the Japanese alphabet, *kana*, and acquires a basic reading knowledge of Japanese not in school but at home from the live-in maid of the Inoues, Yukiko (Sŏlcha in the Korean reading).[22] Rather than Ongnyŏn's schoolteachers, it is the visitors and guests to Major Inoue's house who note her remarkably rapid progress in Japanese; and only six months after her first exposure to the language, her fluency makes them easily mistake her for a native-born Japanese child.[23] The Inoues' Japanese home also provides Ongnyŏn with an introduction to

21. Ku, *Hong keywŏl chŏn*.

22. The maid's name is written in Chinese characters, allowing the reader to pronounce it in both Japanese and Korean ways.

23. Yi Injik, "Hyŏl ŭi nu," *Mansebo*, August 25, 1906; Yi Injik, "Tears of Blood," 187.

modern domestic customs. In applauding Mrs. Inoue's decision to re-
marry, for example, the narrator condemns the age-old Korean pro-
scription against widows' remarriage: "There is no such evil custom—
moral crime, one might call it—in civilized countries, there is no shame
anywhere else in the world in a young widow marrying again."[24]

It might be tempting to read the female protagonist's absorption of
the Japanese language and customs as the author's covert promotion of
Japan's assimilation of Korea. Indeed, one cannot fail to notice the author's political allegiance, as Japan is generally portrayed as superior to
Korea or China throughout *Tears of Blood*. The narrator comments that
Ongnyŏn will survive her gunshot wound, for example, because it was
not a "poisonous" Chinese bullet but rather a Japanese bullet that
"pierced her left leg."[25] Nevertheless, it is not fair to say that Ongnyŏn
is dispatched to Japan to become Japanese. Her thorough immersion in
Japanese language and culture hardly effaces her "origin." When people
mistake her for a native-born Japanese girl, Mrs. Inoue always corrects
them by referring to her as a "Korean child."[26] Her "blood" becomes a
real issue when Mrs. Inoue, a few years after her husband's death, comes
to feel doubtful about raising "somebody else's child" (*nam ŭi chasik*) by
herself.[27] As the kinship tie with Mrs. Inoue dissolves, Ongnyŏn starts
a family-like relationship with a seventeen-year-old "Korean man"
whom she meets on the train that she has boarded after running away
from the Inoues.

The two itinerants, Ongnyŏn and Ku Wansŏ, see their fortuitous
encounter evolve into a deep bond on the basis of their common native
language and mutual compassion. When he spots a smart-looking "Japanese" girl on a train, Ku Wansŏ calls to mind the womenfolk of his own
country. He unwittingly spits out in Korean: "What a fine girl! She is

24. Yi Injik, "Hyŏl ŭi nu," *Mansebo*, August 29, 1906; Yi Injik, "Tears of Blood,"
189. The banning of remarriage of widows was enacted in the late fifteenth century and
enforced especially upon most *yangban* women for centuries, until it was lifted by the
Kabo Reforms.

25. Yi Injik, "Hyŏl ŭi nu," *Mansebo*, August 17, 1906; Yi Injik, "Tears of Blood," 181.

26. Yi Injik, "Hyŏl ŭi nu," *Mansebo.*, August 25, 1906; Yi Injik, "Tears of Blood,"
187.

27. Yi Injik, "Hyŏl ŭi nu," *Mansebo*, September 4, 1906; Yi Injik, "Tears of Blood,"
193.

clever, I'm sure. If you take our Korean girls [*uri nara kyejip*], girls like her just idle away all their time, but here girls like her all go to school, I believe."[28] The "Japanese" girl responds to this in fluent Korean, pretending to talk to herself: "I've got to find a place to sit down. I can't stand all the way."[29] Thanks to Ongnyŏn's retention of her native language after four years of living among the Japanese, Ku Wansŏ can recognize her as Korean. Although "her young body" is "steeped in Japanese custom," there is no hesitation in Ongnyŏn's response to Ku Wansŏ's hail: "Hello there! Are you a Korean [*Chosŏn saram*]?" "Yes, I am."[30]

The bonding is also emotional. At first, it impresses the young man, who has just left home in search of new learning in a foreign land, that this eleven-year-old girl has already finished elementary school in Japan. While Ku Wansŏ self-consciously deliberates on his lack of education, Ongnyŏn looks back on her life in a self-reflexive way. Ku Wansŏ's compliment saddens her because it reminds her that, unlike him, she has never intentionally striven for any of her achievement but let her "misfortune" lead her way. Her silent tears put an end to their conversation. Out of sympathy, Ku Wansŏ follows Ongnyŏn when, without enough money to continue her journey, she gets off at Ibaraki, even though it is not his destination. Once they are out in the street, however, Ku Wansŏ feels completely at a loss, whereas Ongnyŏn acts as if "she had been in Ibaraki several times."[31] He does not even try to hide from her how little he knows about Japan and how apprehensive he is about going alone to the United States. Ongnyŏn feels "like she has met not a fellow country man but *her real parent or brother*" and confides her story to him.[32] In return, Ku Wansŏ proposes that she study in America with him, and he generously promises to pay for her education.

28. Yi Injik, "Hyŏl ŭi nu," *Mansebo*, September 12, 1906; Yi Injik, "Tears of Blood," 198.

29. Yi Injik, "Hyŏl ŭi nu," *Mansebo*, September 13, 1906; Yi Injik, "Tears of Blood," 198.

30. Ibid.

31. Yi Injik, "Hyŏl ŭi nu," *Mansebo*, September 15, 1906; Yi Injik, "Tears of Blood," 200.

32. Yi Injik, "Hyŏl ŭi nu," *Mansebo*, September 16, 1906; Yi Injik, "Tears of Blood," 201 (emphasis added).

Ongnyŏn's pseudofamilial relationship with Ku Wansŏ explains why the story does not suggest that she assimilates into American culture as well as she does into Japanese culture in Ōsaka. Ongnyŏn and Ku Wansŏ in effect create a proxy home where she cultivates her "Korean" identity. Just as Yukiko teaches her *kana* to aid her entry into Japanese society, for instance, Ku Wansŏ helps Ongnyŏn learn the Korean alphabet, Han'gŭl.[33] Not that Ongnyŏn immediately converts her Japanese acculturation back into Korean; even five years after her departure from Japan, Ongnyŏn uses "a lot of Japanese expressions" as she is still "steep[ed] in Japanese customs."[34] Still, Ku Wansŏ keeps reminding her of her national origin by asking her to communicate with him "in the Korean way" and sharing his critical views of traditional customs of Korea with her.[35]

Symbolically, it is when Ongnyŏn decides to have a conjugal relationship with Ku Wansŏ that she most strongly asserts her Korean identity as well as her selfhood. During the marriage proposal scene, Ku Wansŏ makes a suggestion to Ongnyŏn that seems to conflict with his patriotism: they should not only discuss their marriage "in the Western way," namely, without having Ongnyŏn's father speak for her, but should also speak in English instead of Korean to keep their relationship from being defined by the relational hierarchy embedded in the Korean language.[36] Obviously his experience in the United States has made him more conscious of gender inequality. The attempt to imitate the Western conjugal norm exactly the way it is, however, is not necessarily incompatible with his patriotic ambition. He does not so much aspire to "become Western" as to introduce "civilized" marriage practice and an egalitarian form of the family to Korea. To his radical request, "Ongnyŏn replies neatly and tidily in Korean" even though "in English she is good enough to be his

33. Yi Injik, "Hyŏl ŭi nu," *Mansebo*, October 10, 1906; Yi Injik, "Tears of Blood," 219.

34. Yi Injik, "Hyŏl ŭi nu," *Mansebo*, September 21, 1906; Yi Injik, "Tears of Blood," 205–6.

35. Yi Injik, "Hyŏl ŭi nu," *Mansebo*, October 10, 1906; Yi Injik, "Tears of Blood," 206.

36. Yi Injik, "Hyŏl ŭi nu," *Mansebo*, October 4, 1906; Yi Injik, "Tears of Blood," 213–14.

teacher."[37] While confidently responding to her suitor just like Western women, she emphatically distinguishes herself from them by choosing her mother tongue. In so doing, Ongnyŏn not only safeguards her national identity as an individual but also implicitly takes up the role of defending the national identity of the family that she is about to create with her suitor.[38] I must emphasize that this is her individual choice, not something she follows on the basis of existing guidance.

Their marriage engagement, thus, signals the birth of a *modern Korean* family. Yet it does not involve a typical wooing. The relationship between Ongnyŏn and Ku Wansŏ is curiously lacking in romantic feeling from the beginning. From their first encounter on the Japanese train, Ku Wansŏ treats Ongnyŏn as little more than a child. He does not tell her that he is unmarried, though Ongnyŏn assumes otherwise. Not until the evening of her high school graduation does she find out that he is a bachelor. The fact that Ku Wansŏ sees only an asexual child in Ongnyŏn and that Ongnyŏn thinks of him as married, and therefore unavailable, does away with any room for possible romance to develop between them and thus ensures the "innocence" of their initial family-like relationship. Even when they start talking about marriage, the kind of affection that they have for each other remains closer to respect and appreciation than amorous passion. Their language sounds more like an avowal of patriotism than that of enduring love:

> Mr. Ku asked one thing, that he and Ongnyŏn should continue studying hard for several more years until they had all the education they wanted, before they went home and got married. Then Ongnyŏn could take upon herself the education of Korean women. When he showed his ambition, and when she heard what he proposed, she firmly made up her mind to educate Korean women, and contracted to marry Mr. Ku. . . . Ongnyŏn wanted to study hard, and after returning home, to broaden the knowledge of Korean women and help them to get equal rights with men, in-

---

37.   Yi Injik, "Hyŏl ŭi nu," *Mansebo*, October 4, 1906; Yi Injik, "Tears of Blood," 214.

38.   This scene resonates with Mrinalina Sinha's observation that "women are called to perform certain important nationalist tasks such as the preservation and transmission of the national language (the 'mother tongue' as it were) and the national culture." See Sinha, "Gender and Nation," 258.

stead of being oppressed by men, and then to educate them so that the women too would become useful people in the land and honored people in society.[39]

In this peculiar "marriage contract," Ku Wansŏ invites Ongnyŏn not so much into the private sphere but into the public realm of the newly arising nation. Ongnyŏn willingly accepts the invitation and decides to work for the public good as a future leader of Korean women. Though it may sound odd to modern-day feminists, Ku Wansŏ's marriage proposal encourages Ongnyŏn to think of Korean women's oppression and their equal rights with men. Ongnyŏn learns how to claim her human rights, in other words, by deciding to create a new home as the wife of a reform-minded man.

In its confusion of egalitarian marriage and patriotism, Ku Wansŏ's marriage proposal illustrates how the discourse of modern domesticity plays a pivotal role in "a leveling of society"—the process of bestowing the "equal rights, privileges, and duties in relation to the state" upon all the populace across social status, gender, and regional differences.[40] As Chosŏn society reproduced the status demarcation through class endogamy, the leveling of society involved removing the established hereditary barriers between families as much as between individuals within national boundaries. In *Tears of Blood*, significantly, neither party of the marriage engagement is concerned about the other's social status. Quite the opposite of traditional conjugal practice, wherein a male patriarch controls all the marriage affairs within the family, Ku Wansŏ initiates the proposal by insisting that the head of Ongnyŏn's family, Kim Kwanil, not speak on behalf of his daughter but allow Ongnyŏn to exercise the right to make her own choice in marriage. His subsequent demand that Ongnyŏn pledge herself to the nationalist cause before he asks for her hand in marriage symbolizes how marriage is no longer a matter of hereditary status-based kinship alliances but rather one of serving the nation and of cultivating a sense of citizenship.

39.   Yi Injik, "Hyŏl ŭi nu," *Mansebo*, October 4, 1906; Yi Injik, "Tears of Blood," 214.
40.   Kyung Moon Hwang, "Citizenship, Social Equality," 355–87.

Ongnyŏn's peculiar engagement to Ku Wansŏ thus vividly shows how the Western-influenced idea of home played a central role in propagating modern notions such as citizenship, individual rights, and the national community in early colonial Korean domestic novels. It is noteworthy that during this period the discourse of the new home revolved around the neologism *kajŏng*, the Korean reading of the Japanese term *katei*. According to Muta Kazue, *katei*, originally a Chinese term, took on a modern connotation in Japan as it was adopted as a translation of the Victorian concept of "home" in the 1880s. By the 1890s, it had come to symbolize a desire for a new type of family.[41] To my knowledge, no comprehensive study has yet attempted to draw an exact trajectory by which the term *kajŏng* came into use. My preliminary research suggests, however, that the term was imported from Japan toward the end of the nineteenth century and circulated widely in Korea through nationalist textbooks, newspapers, journals, and magazines in the protectorate period, when *Tears of Blood* was initially serialized.[42] Notably, one periodical that incorporated this term into its title, *Kadyŏng chapchi* (Home Magazine), was launched only a month before the serialization of *Tears of Blood* began.[43] Ongnyŏn's journey illustrates the global circulation of the discourse of modern domesticity. While leaving her native home allows her to experience the "civilized" world, her transnational education in "civilization and enlightenment" still keeps orbiting around family or family-like relationships and culminates at the moment that she receives a proposal of marriage from a reform-minded Korean compatriot. As the closing statement of the story suggests, she ultimately finds her way back to Korea.[44] When she actually does return, in the sequel, *Peony Hill*, she brings with her new ideas of family and home and becomes an agent of *kajŏng*, the new Korean home that will serve as a building block for the homogeneous national community. To the extent that it adapts the transnational discourse of home into literary language, *Tears of Blood* is a bona

---

41. Muta, "Meijiki sōgō zasshi," 12–25.

42. Yoon Sun Yang, "Nation in the Backyard," 35–46.

43. *Kadyŏng* is a regional pronunciation of *kajŏng*. Four surviving volumes of *Kadyŏng chapchi*, volumes 3 (August 1906), 4 (September 1906), 5 (October 1906), and 7 (January 1907), are reprinted in *Han'guk yŏsŏng kwan'gye charyojip*, 147–300.

44. "The reader may look forward to the return of the girl to her homeland in the sequel." Yi Injik, "Hyŏl ŭi nu," *Mansebo*, October 10, 1906.

fide domestic novel, participating in the global flow of ideas about modern domesticity and individuality, and responding to the political changes of turn-of-the-century Korea.

Inventing "Traditional" Ways of Living

Compared to Ongnyŏn, her mother may seem little affected by the new social order. During the entire time that Kim Kwanil and his daughter are learning new ways of life outside Korea, Ch'unae remains at home as before. That she remains unchanged amid dramatic social upheaval, however, does not mean that she is empty of meaning. On the contrary, she offers a no less subtle and complex symbol of the transition of turn-of-the-century Korea than her daughter. Of all the characters in *Tears of Blood*, Ch'unae most signifies hereditary *yangban* status. The narrator repeatedly points out that she is a "lady," "raised in the inner quarter," the section of a *yangban* house set aside for females.[45] More important, her social status is engraved on her body so that no one can detach it from her. Her "face, which is white as if it were pasted with four-o'clock flowers' powder," proves she has never been exposed to outdoor labor.[46] Her nobility is most evidently illustrated through the inappropriate bodily contact she accidentally has with a farm laborer:

> The man . . . ran to her and took hold of her to lift her up. But when she gathered herself together, she realized that the hand which had touched her hand was a farm laborer's hand as rough as a rope-end. The sudden shock and dread made her flesh creep . . . the man had been going about looking for his wife in the fighting . . . his woman was a farm laborer's woman, used all her life to working hard with a hoe, or a pestle, or a clothes paddle. The hand of the lady was as soft as silk, and she was wearing a skirt of the almost finest ramie cloth. The laborer would have been the sort of

---

45. Yi Injik, "Hyŏl ŭi nu," *Mansebo*, July 24, 1906 (this part is omitted in the English translation); Yi Injik, "Hyŏl ŭi nu," *Mansebo*, July 29, 1906; Yi Injik, "Tears of Blood," 167.

46. Yi Injik, "Hyŏl ŭi nu," *Mansebo*, July 22, 1906; Yi Injik, "Tears of Blood," 159.

man who had never in his life even had a peep in, never mind touched, the hand of anyone who wore clothes like this.[47]

In the gender-segregated and status-based Chosŏn society, it was a complete blasphemy for a lower-class man to touch an upper-class woman's bare skin. That a mere farm laborer could dare covet a *yangban* lady's body thus shows the extent to which the Sino-Japanese War had disturbed a social order based on the nobility of *yangban*. Ch'unae's "noble" body, nonetheless, resists any change. Just like an exemplary woman of Chosŏn Korea, she would rather choose death than let her chastity be defiled by the farmer's hands.

Indeed, Ch'unae resonates with the images of women abundant in traditional morality books such as *Biographies of Virtuous Women* or *Illustrated Guide to the Three Bonds* (*Samgang haengsilto*), various editions of which were published by royal authority throughout the Chosŏn dynasty.[48] Women in these works fulfill their lifelong duties as wives, mothers, and daughters-in-law in spite of their husbands' untimely deaths and willingly choose to die as virtuous women when forced to live otherwise. Once married, they are virtually subject to their husbands, so that widows often either commit suicide soon after their husbands' deaths or "postpone" their deaths until just after their children's marriages or their in-laws' bereavements. Ch'unae's suicide attempt can be understood in this context. The following scene rather blatantly shows how important her husband is to her: "Completely absorbed in her search for Ongnyŏn, she went on calling Ongnyŏn until she was hoarse and exhausted, without realizing that she had just lost *someone whom she cherished ten or*

---

47.   Yi Injik, "Hyŏl ŭi nu," *Mansebo*, July 24, 1906; Yi Injik, "Tears of Blood," 161.

48.   *Illustrated Guide to the Three Bonds* was published to propagate the Confucian codes of behavior, especially the three types of fundamental relationships—between ruler and subject, father and son, husband and wife—through illustrations and short narratives about exemplary episodes. Other than the first edition, which came out in classical Chinese in 1434, each episode in later editions is presented in both classical Chinese and a Han'gŭl translation along with an illustration, obviously targeting both the literate and illiterate populations. It has been observed that those editions published after Hideyoshi's invasion in the late sixteenth century tended to give more space to the section on virtuous women than the other sections. Chu Yŏngha et al., *Chosŏn sidae ch'aek*; Yi and Kim, *Han'guk ŭi yŏllŏ chŏn*. Also see Oh, *Engraving Virtue*.

twenty times more than Ongnyŏn: She plunked herself down on the hill-track. 'Where is my husband? He went down to the foot of the mountain to find Ongnyŏn.' Suddenly her mind shifts from Ongnyŏn to her husband."[49]

Certainly not only readers of the English translation but also contemporary Koreans would find such a comparison between the value of a husband and that of a daughter preposterous. Probably for this reason, W. E. Skillend's English translation omitted all references to the husband: "She was so absorbed in her search for Ongnyŏn that even if something thought to be ten or twenty times as important as Ongnyŏn had been lost, she would not have acknowledged that. She went on, just calling Ongnyŏn until she was hoarse, and then she squatted down, exhausted, on the hilltrack."[50] This strange sidenote in the original does not so much have to do with her callous calculation as with the Confucian belief that married women should be perceived as half-dead after their husbands' deaths. Thus, Ch'unae can put an end to her suicide attempts only when she learns that her husband is still alive and will return home in the future.

Ch'unae's image as a virtuous wife does not so much restore traditional Confucian morality in itself as bear unprecedented symbolic implications. This point has been made by Sin Ch'unja's study, one of the rare attempts to call attention to the political significance of this old-fashioned female character. Supposing a discrepancy between Yi Injik's patriotism and his pro-Japanese political career, she describes Ch'unae as the symbol of the fatherland (*cho'guk*) in crisis whose hope of reform helps her endure her harsh reality.[51] On the other hand, No Sangnae and Sin Misam reach the opposite conclusion, when they claim the female protagonist in Yi Injik's earlier short story, "A Widow's Dream," is excluded from the newly arising domain of the nation.[52] For them, the author's refusal to acknowledge the widow as a part of the nation attests to his alignment with colonialism, which led him to give up the project of nation building and collaborate with the Japanese. Their opposing conclusions notwithstanding, both studies equally view old-fashioned female

49. Yi Injik, "Hyŏl ŭi nu," *Mansebo*, July 22, 1906 (emphasis added; this part is omitted in the English translation).
50. Yi Injik, "Tears of Blood," 160
51. Sin Ch'unja, *Kaehwagi sosŏl yŏn'gu*, 32–50.
52. No and Sin, "Yi Injik sosŏl," 467–94.

characters as the determinate figures—it is their fates that show whether the "pro-Japanese" pioneer of modern Korean literature was a colonialist or a nationalist. To put it differently, they both view the old-fashioned character as the "authentic" body of Korea, untouched by modern changes, although Sin Ch'unja claims that Yi Injik takes her as the true foundation of the nation while No Sangnae and Sin Misam say that he leaves her out of the nation.

In place of imposing a fixed political reading of the old-fashioned woman, I would suggest that, due to the historical and textual complexity of *Tears of Blood*, this seemingly one-dimensional premodern character vacillates between being a remnant of the uncivilized past and acting as an emblem of the nation's sacred past. On the one hand, Ch'unae does appear to embody what "civilization and enlightenment" should prevail over. She represents, in a way, the kind of woman that Ongnyŏn would have grown up to be, had she stayed home. When the narrator laments that "Korean women were locked up in a corner of the inner room and not taught anything," therefore, one may assume that Ch'unae is simply classified as an emblem of the uncivilized state of Korea.[53] On the other hand, as a casualty of the war between two neighboring countries, the mother does not seem to evoke so much criticism of Korea's backwardness as sympathy for the nation in crisis. Not even once, as a matter of fact, is she directly identified as "unenlightened" or "uncivilized" in *Tears of Blood*.

These demeaning labels are, however, retrospectively associated with Ch'unae by other male characters, especially when they metonymically equate her with Korea in distress. Instead of holding the warring parties responsible for the calamity, Kim Kwanil lashes out at the victims—ordinary Koreans: "Our people want to think only of themselves. . . . Whether others fail or succeed, they seek to satisfy only their own desires."[54] By erroneously ascribing the cause of the international war to common people's selfishness, Kim Kwanil obscures Japan's imperialist desire, which had taken a tangible form through the Protectorate Treaty a year prior to the initial serialization of *Tears of Blood*. Considering the political climate of the Protectorate period, it is not a stretch to paraphrase

53. Yi Injik, "Hyŏl ŭi nu," *Mansebo*, August 25, 1906; Yi Injik, "Tears of Blood," 187.

54. Yi Injik, "Hyŏl ŭi nu," *Mansebo*, July 28, 1906; Yi Injik, "Tears of Blood," 166.

Kim Kwanil's words as follows: Korea lost its diplomatic sovereignty not because of the imperialist expansion but because of its own shortcomings—its incapacity to fulfill the ideal of "civilization and enlightenment." Behind the belief that the innocent people of Korea suffer because "Korea is not strong enough" lies a *colonialist* perspective that holds not the intruders but the victims accountable for colonial rule.[55]

This metonymic displacement, however, does not entirely remove the gap between Ch'unae and "uneducated Korean women." She is evidently "educated"—to a degree. Though lacking in knowledge of classical Chinese, she is literate enough in the vernacular, Ŏnmun (a former condescending title for Han'gŭl), to leave a suicide note on her bedroom wall before throwing herself in the Taedong River. She exchanges letters with her husband in Ŏnmun during the whole time he is away from home.[56] In the closing scene, more symbolically, she *reads* a letter that her daughter has sent from the United States through the modern mail system. The vernacular letters help the old-fashioned woman maintain or restore her ties to her family members, who grow apart from her while they are on the other side of the national border.[57] Whereas women's writing of vernacular letters was an everyday practice in Chosŏn Korea, Ch'unae's epistolary communication, assisted by international postal networks, displaces her from the old society and into the modern nation that has been incorporated into the global world, even as a colony. At the turn of the century, the vernacular became the national script, a core instrument to bring into being the imagined, homogenous unity among people of different regional origins, genders, and social statuses.[58] In spite of herself, she passes into the nation. The colonialist portrayal of her thus does not completely succeed in suppressing such a nationalist appropriation of the old-fashioned woman's image. As a result, the virtuous woman is placed in a modern tension between nationalism and colonialism.

When examining Ch'unae's intrinsic association with the nation, I should add that I do not subscribe to Sin Ch'unja's primordialist

55. Ibid.

56. Yi Injik, "Hyŏl ŭi nu," *Mansebo*, September 30, 1906; Yi Injik, "Tears of Blood," 212.

57. Yi Injik, "Hyŏl ŭi nu," *Mansebo*, October 10, 1906; Yi Injik, "Tears of Blood," 219,

58. Anderson, *Imagined Communities*, 24–36.

assumption that "Korea" has continually existed in the same mode throughout history. On the premise that the nation is a product of modernity shaped in part by "collective identities in premodern eras," I am more interested in looking into the ways in which the "old-fashioned" female character in *Tears of Blood* serves to create the "new" communal sense of the nation.[59] In this sense, Ch'unae reminds me of what Fredric Jameson calls the "vanishing mediator." According to Etienne Balibar's succinct explanation, the vanishing mediator is "the figure . . . of a *transitory* institution (or force, community, or spiritual formation) that creates the conditions for a new society and a new civilizational pattern, albeit in the horizon and the vocabulary of the past, and by rearranging the elements inherited from the very institution that has to be overcome."[60] Similarly, Ch'unae sets up "the condition for the new nation" by turning the *yangban* womanhood of the Chosŏn period into a timeless tradition of the emerging community. The image of old-fashioned womanhood that she evokes is no longer bound to a status-based premodern household, but to the "traditional" Korean home that was often signified by the word *ka* at the turn of the century. At that time, the usage of the term *ka* was modified, based on the Japanese word *ie*. The form of patrilineal family specific to the former samurai class, *ie*, was modified by the drafters of the Meiji Civil Code as the universal household system that would be uniquely and distinctively Japanese.[61] Similar to *ie*, *ka* promoted the new idea that a form of family peculiar to the nation has continuously existed from time immemorial, screening the historical fact that the status-based society of Chosŏn Korea made a distinction between upper-class lineage and that of the lower class. The idea of the traditional home was thus the illusion necessary for the genealogy of the nation, an erroneous history that evened out the murky reality for the sake of a unified spirit.

Thus, whereas Ongnyŏn learns to exercise her rights abroad while cultivating a relationship with a reform-minded man as well as a sense of her national identity as Korean, Ch'unae plays a double role as a vanishing

59.   Anthony Smith, "Origins of Nations," 106.

60.   Jameson, *Ideologies of Theory*, 2: 3–34; Balibar, *We, People of Europe?*, 233.

61.   Hong, "Singminji hojŏk chedo," 167–205; Ueno, *Kindai kazoku no seiritsu*, 69–74; Toshitani, "Kazokuhō no jikken," 99–118.

mediator of the emerging nation on the one hand and as a vestige of the uncivilized past on the other. Behind the split narrative lies the dilemma of turn-of-the-century reformist intellectuals, who cultivated the aspirations of modern nation building at the same time that colonizing discourses seemed to demonstrate that their homeland did not meet the standard of modern civilization.[62] Daughter and mother appear to be pushed in opposite directions: one represents the civilized, the other the uncivilized. At other times they both seem to fit seamlessly into the national paradigm: one embodies the new home (*kajŏng*), while the other embodies the traditional (*ka*). One cannot pinpoint why the split seems more salient and crucial between women than between men without considering the ambivalent desires of Yi Injik, who, as a male reformist writer of the time, went against the grain of his own Confucian upbringing to advocate gender equality.[63] While Ongnyŏn pursues the new egalitarian image of a wife, Ch'unae invites the hierarchical gender norm back into the realm of the national imagination by proposing the faithful wife as an image of the persisting past.

The two women's identities, shaped by their relationships with the national community and the domestic space are, however, not so much stable, as precarious. Ambiguity is embedded in the character of Ch'unae. At any moment in the narrative she could be taken as either an emblem of the nation's still-vigorous past or a harmful vestige of the past. The marriage between Ongnyŏn and Ku Wansŏ is put off for the future; so is their plan to devote their lives to nation building. Neither knows much about her or his own country. After recounting how Ongnyŏn and Ku Wansŏ celebrate their "patriotic" engagement vows, the narrator points out their naïveté:

> There is nothing in the world so enjoyable as to set one's own goals. Ku Wansŏ and Ongnyŏn moved abroad when they were young. With no idea how barbarous and incapable Koreans are, they both thought that when

62. As for the literary appropriation of the idea of *katei* and its tension with *ie* during the Meiji period, see Ito, *Age of Melodrama*; Ragsdale, "Marriage, Newspaper Business," 229–55.

63. Little is known about Yi Injik's personal life, but it is fair to assume that, born in 1862, Yi Injik had not been exposed to reformist values until he reached at least his early thirties.

the day arrive[d] for them to return to Korea, there would be many ambitious people in Korea who would listen to the words of educated and learned people, and approve of them so that everything would turn out as Mr. Ku planned, and that, as Ongnyŏn planned, women of Korea would all be educated by her, and that everywhere many people would arise with an education like hers. . . . Their feelings came from the state of minds of youthful students [*sonyŏn haksaeng*] who had studied abroad.[64]

In this passage the narrator calls our attention to the gloomy future that lies ahead of the young reformists while advising readers not to take it as an accurate reflection of Korean reality. Thus, *Tears of Blood* introduces an unprecedented sense of uncertainty to the narrative. One can understand the peculiar ending of *Tears of Blood* in this vein. Instead of the conventional closure of premodern fiction, which celebrates the prosperity of the protagonist's offspring, the novel ends when Ongnyŏn's letter reaches her mother at her natal home in P'yŏngyang. As if trying to impress readers with the speed of the international mail system, the narrator specifies the exact dates that the letter was sent from the daughter in the United States and received by the mother.[65] A postscript is added to announce the sequel: "The sequel is slated to recount the story after the schoolgirl returns to her homeland. The Volume 1 is over [*sang kwŏn chong*]."[66] As I discuss in chapter 3, part of which focuses on the 1913 sequel to *Tears of Blood*, *Peony Hill*, Ongnyŏn's dreams of creating a new reformed family and of playing a role in nation building never come to realization. It is not until the beginning of *Peony Hill* that she fully internalizes the uncertain future of the community. Her individuality remains inextricable from the collective ideals. Nonetheless, her individuality is far from stereotypical or prescribed, just as the future of the community is nothing but unpredictable.

64.   Yi Injik, "Hyŏl ŭi nu," *Mansebo*, October 5, 1906; Yi Injik, "Tears of Blood," 214–15.

65.   The dates follow the lunar calendar in the original. According to the Gregorian calendar, the letter was sent on August 14, 1902, and received on September 9, 1902. Yi Injik, "Hyŏl ŭi nu," *Mansebo*, October 5, 1906; Yi Injik, "Tears of Blood," 220.

66.   Ibid.

CHAPTER TWO

From Female Ghosts
to Ghostly Womanhood

No matter how ironic it may sound, the writers of early colonial Korean domestic novels frequently turned to traditional forms of fictional narrative while marketing their own works as "new," "adhering to the style of the Western novel," and "different from old-fashioned fiction (kusosŏl)." With regard to early colonial domestic novels, a series of questions is posed to literary scholars by the fact that the hybridization between the old and the new, despite the intentions of the writers, was closer to the norm than the exception. What pre-twentieth-century narrative elements survived in the early colonial domestic novel? Which ones became extinct? What might have caused some literary components to outlive the form of fiction to which they had initially belonged? Did the surviving narrative elements remain more or less the same as before or change to a certain degree? To explore these questions, I call attention to the two-volume domestic novel *Mt. Ch'iak* (*Ch'iaksan*, 1908, 1911), which rewrites a traditional ghost story, "The Tale of Changhwa and Hongnyŏn," by portraying a reform-minded *yangban* woman who goes against Confucian conduct codes and challenges her abusive in-laws.[1] Such a fantastical ghost-like figure was at odds with the reformist belief in the universality and the political validity of "civilization and enlightenment" (*munmyŏng kaehwa*). Therefore the writers of *Mt. Ch'iak* made it explicit that they

1. The first volume of *Mt. Ch'iak* was authored by Yi Injik, the second by Kim Kyoje. Yi Injik, *Ch'iaksan*, vol. 1; Kim Kyoje, *Ch'iaksan*, vol. 2.

characterized a supposedly obsolete figure in this novel for the purpose of criticizing the "uncivilized" female subculture of folk religion and shamanism. However, they hardly marginalized such a figure; instead, they conjured up an iconoclastic aspect of a premodern female ghost to create one of the most unique literary iterations of the individual in early colonial Korea, which I call a "ghostly woman." To see exactly what changes *Mt. Ch'iak* made to the traditional ghost story, a close look at "The Tale of Changhwa and Hongnyŏn" is in order.

The Return of Repressed Women's Voices: "The Tale of Changhwa and Hongnyŏn"

"The Tale of Changhwa and Hongnyŏn" is allegedly based on a criminal case from the Ch'ŏlsan district of P'yŏngan province around the early 1650s.[2] Other than the ever-increasing corpus of contemporary editions, which ranges from children's stories and theatrical productions to television dramas and horror films (including the recent global hit *A Tale of Two Sisters*, which was remade by DreamWorks as *The Uninvited* in 2009), over fifty different versions of the story are extant in wood-block prints, undated manuscripts, editions printed using metal movable type, and editions using lithography written in vernacular Korean, literary Chinese, or mixed script.[3] As is usually the case with folktales, the source is lost to history. It is impossible to determine exactly when and in what language it was initially written, or how closely existing versions reproduce the criminal case that served as the basis of the story.[4] Scholars seem to agree, however, that at least one early vernacular version of the story existed sometime between the 1650s and 1797. In this essay I predicate my discussion upon the most succinct and oldest verifiable version, a Chinese edition from 1818, while occasionally comparing it with the undated vernacular edi-

2. Chŏng Chiyŏng, "Changhwa Hongnyŏn chŏn," 422–41.
3. Kim Jee-Woon, *Changhwa, Hongnyŏn.*
4. For an overview of the different editions of "The Tale of Changhwa and Hongnyŏn," see Cho Hŭiung, *Kojŏn sosŏl ibon mongnok*, 597–604; Sŏ Hyeŭn, "'Changhwa Hongnyŏn chŏn,'" 387–418.

tion, *Chyanghwa Hongnyŏn chyŏn*, a wood-block printing of twenty-eight leaves made in Seoul (*Kyŏngp'an 28 changbon*).[5]

According to the 1818 Chinese edition, the story goes as follows: Pae Sigyŏng, head of the local government advisory committee (*chwasu*) in the Ch'ŏlsan district office, has two daughters, Changhwa and Hongnyŏn, from his first marriage. After his beloved wife's premature death, he re-marries and has two sons, P'iltong and Ŭngdong, by his second wife. He deeply adores his daughters, so he decides to marry them off only after careful and prolonged deliberation. This is when his vicious second wife begins planning to murder her stepdaughters: she does not want to lose money on their weddings. One day, when Pae Sigyŏng is out of town, she skins a rat to make it look like a human fetus and puts it on Changhwa's sleeping pad. After spreading its blood on her clothes, she wakes her step-daughter up to accuse her of having a stillborn baby out of wedlock. A few days later, when Pae Sigyŏng returns home, the wicked woman shows him the dead rat as proof of Changhwa's illicit behavior and suggests that they should kill her to save the family's reputation. In a fury, he takes his wife's advice and orders P'iltong to drown Changhwa in a nearby pond. The very night of Changhwa's death, Hongnyŏn dreams of her beloved sister, who tells her how she died. No sooner does she confirm her sister's tragic death, than Hongnyŏn kills herself by jumping into the same pond.

Having turned into ghosts (*wŏn'gui*), the two sisters find their way to a local magistrate of the Ch'ŏlsan district to implore him to redeem Changhwa's honor and take revenge on the offenders, only to witness him dying from shock. All those appointed as magistrates to the town for the next eight years either pass out or die before the ghosts finish telling their story to them. The successive deaths of magistrates, along with recurrent droughts, devastate the whole Ch'ŏlsan district and ultimately arouse the concern of the royal court. The king appoints as magistrate Chŏn Tonghŭl, the former governor of the Hŭngdŏk region, who is known for his strong will and sound sense of judgment. The new magistrate not only confronts the ghosts without fear and listens to their full story, but opens

5. Chŏn Kirak, "Changhwa Hongnyŏn chŏn," 95–100. I also consulted Chŏn Sŏngt'ak's modern Korean translation of the original Chinese text: Chŏn Sŏngt'ak, "Changhwa wa hongnyŏn," 4–8. For the vernacular version, see "Chyanghwa Hongnyŏn chyŏn," in *Han'guk pangak pon sosŏl*.

a murder investigation and eventually punishes Pae Sigyŏng with exile and decapitates his wife and P'iltong for their crimes. The people of Ch'ŏlsan finally find peace again. As a sign of the heavenly reward for his virtue, Chŏn Tonghŭl later achieves the rank of T'ongjesa, commanding officer, one of the highest honors in military service.

The question of female sexuality is at the very center of "The Tale of Changhwa and Hongnyŏn." Throughout the story, female virtues—especially that of chastity—play a pivotal role in defining the sisters' identities. The story emphasizes Changhwa's and Hongnyŏn's flawless and desirable feminine conduct: "they bear elegant demeanors, have beautiful writing skills, are dexterous at sewing and weaving, conduct perfect ancestral rites, exercise impeccable courtesy toward their parents, and display extraordinarily gentle manners toward guests."[6] Changhwa's alleged lack of chastity gives her loving father a good enough reason to kill her, and thus the ghosts are less concerned with condemning the cruelty of intrafamilial homicide than with proving Changhwa's chastity.

This point is distinctly illuminated in the trial scene. Chŏn Tonghŭl summons the suspects, Pae Sigyŏng and his wife, and asks them to explain how their two daughters died. Showing the skinned rat as proof, Pae Sigyŏng's wife tells the magistrate that Changhwa committed suicide due to her guilt over having a stillborn baby out of wedlock and that Hongnyŏn killed herself soon afterward, ashamed of her sister's behavior. The magistrate sets them free without further interrogation, as if women of loose morals did not deserve either a good life or a fair trial. The ghosts show up again that night, advising Chŏn Tonghŭl to open up the belly of the "corpse" of the stillborn baby. Only when he sees rat feces inside does Chŏn Tonghŭl find Pae Sigyŏng and his wife guilty. In other words, the ghost of Changhwa receives redemption by proving her bodily chastity. Given that in the 1818 edition Changhwa is killed a few days after her stepmother initially accuses her of having a stillborn baby, one may ask why Changhwa did not try to prove her innocence through the judicial system while she was alive. To answer this question, it is helpful to take a look at the age-old state practice of "the cult of chastity."

The cult of chastity, initially originating in China, is the institutionalized worship of chaste widows who devote their lives to serving their late husbands' families without remarrying. Although chastity had already

6. Chŏn Kirak, "Changhwa Hongnyŏn chŏn," 95.

been considered in China one of the key female virtues for many centuries, the celebration of female chastity intensified considerably during the Song dynasty (960–1279).[7] In 1304, the Yuan court began offering chaste widows official recognition via "imperial testimonials of merit" (Chinese, *jing bao*; Korean, *chŏngp'yo*), a practice continued by the Ming regime (1368– 1644). Those who committed suicide after rape or attempted rape and those who were killed during sexual assault were posthumously recognized as well. The chastity cult reached its culmination during the Qing dynasty (1644–1911), when the state began commemorating as a martyr "[any] woman whose betrothed died prior to the consummation of marriage but who moved in with her parents-in-law to serve them and refused to marry any other man."[8]

In Korea, it was not until the eighth year of King Sŏngjong's reign (989) during the Koryŏ dynasty (918–1392) that the state began commemorating chaste women for the purpose of propagating Confucian values.[9] The chastity cult was even more systematically inflicted upon upper-class *yangban* women during the Chosŏn dynasty: in 1477 a new legal code prohibited remarried widows' descendants from sitting for the civil service examination.[10] In the latter half of the Chosŏn period, when "The Tale of Changhwa and Hongnyŏn" appeared, the promotion of female chastity reached such a level of fixation that even the false rumor of the bride having had illicit sex could allow the groom's family to legitimately call off the engagement. When wrongfully accused of having illegitimate sexual relations, a woman's only recourse to redeem her honor in public was to take extreme measures—self-injury, starvation, and suicide—because her words were not taken as a legitimate defense of her innocence. Exemplary women were typically married or betrothed and remained faithful to their husbands or fiancés in the face of trials and temptations. However, biographies of virtuous women also include some stories of maidens who ran the risk of death to prove their chastity against false accusations.[11] Once vindicated through such reckless behavior, they were canonized as paragons of female virtue.[12]

7.   Du and Man, "Competing Claims on Womanly Virtue," 219–47.
8.   Sommer, "Uses of Chastity," 78–80.
9.   Pak and Kim, "Han'guk ŭi munhwa," 394, 400.
10. Deuchler, "Propagating Female Virtues," 160–61.
11. See Yu, "*19 segi yŏsŏng pŏmchoe*," 159; Kang Myŏnggwan, *Yŏllyŏ ŭi t'ansaeng*.
12. Yi and Kim, *Han'guk ŭi yŏllŏjŏn*, 106–11.

Changhwa's helplessness against the false accusation is far from atypical. This is not to say, nonetheless, that Changhwa takes extreme action to counter the false charge as did canonized women. Other than Changhwa's immediate, emotional reaction to the accusation—"terrified, she was just shedding tears"—the reader does not know what is going on in her mind while her father comes to his final verdict.[13] Does she give up all hope of life right away? Or does she brace herself for an expected interrogation by her father? For three days, Changhwa continues to be a virtuous daughter. She complies with her father's command to "visit her maternal uncle who longs to see her," although she at first refuses to do so, saying, "Women should not heedlessly leave the women's quarter, not to mention at this late night hour."[14]

In the vernacular text, however, the time gap between the stepmother's accusation and Changhwa's death disappears: the very night that the stepmother sets her up with a skinned rat dripping blood, Changhwa is taken out of the house, completely unsuspecting of the false charge against her. She does drown herself in a pond—making it a suicide rather than a murder—but not to demonstrate her chastity in public. She does so because, when learning of the stepmother's false accusation from her half-brother, she realizes that "an attempt to vindicate her innocence would be fiercely challenged by the stepmother" and also because "she could not defy her father's order." The vernacular edition more emphatically dramatizes Changhwa's will to maintain her dignity as a virtuous woman. Her last words, addressed to her half-brother, emphasize her undying adherence to the principle of filial piety: "Take pity on lonely Hongnyŏn and give her proper guidance so that she won't sin against our parents."[15]

However, upon returning to the world of the living as a ghost, Changhwa seems to deviate from the path of an exemplary *yangban* woman. By the standard of the traditional Confucian practice that forbade elite women from contacting men other than their close relatives, the Pae sisters' face-to-face visits with government officials are unquestionably contemptible behavior. Furthermore, the ghosts no longer remain silent

---

13. Chŏn Kirak, "Changhwa Hongnyŏn chŏn," 95.
14. Ibid.
15. "Chyanghwa Hongnyŏn chyŏn," in *Han'guk panggak pon sosŏl chŏnjip*, 20. In the vernacular edition, the brother's name is Changsoe, different from that of the 1818 Chinese edition, P'iltong.

about the wrongful accusation. They not only persuade the state authorities to accept their version of the story as truth but also intervene in the investigation of the case by providing the magistrate with the decisive clue to solve it. Without their advice, the magistrate would not have slit open the alleged stillborn baby's belly to discover it was just a rat.

According to Ch'oe Kisuk, a scholar of premodern Korean literature, female ghosts are more threatening to society than their male counterparts as presented in short unofficial accounts called *yadam*, especially those that appeared in collections from the eighteenth to the nineteenth century.[16] The majority of male ghosts return to the world of the living to fulfill unfinished familial and social duties such as teaching their sons, taking care of their families, marrying off their children, or maintaining relationships with their surviving friends. By contrast, female ghosts are rather rancorous, as they come back to take revenge against those responsible for their deaths. Boudewijn Walraven traces the cultural roots of female ghosts' vengeful nature to popular folk religion during the Chosŏn period, in practices that persisted among women in the form of private rituals in the inner quarters, which were segregated from male elites' official ancestor worship. In contrast to the state-sponsored cult of chastity, popular religion perceived chaste women as potentially dangerous, as their disgruntled sprits could return to threaten the well-being of the living.[17]

Likewise, the ghosts of Changhwa and Hongnyŏn appear to threaten the survival of the entire community by causing devastating droughts and, though unintentionally, by inflicting deadly heart attacks upon local magistrates. More problematic is that, while trying to restore Changhwa's honor, the ghost sisters run the risk of condemning their own father along with their wicked stepmother. Needless to say this would be a serious violation of filial piety, the most fundamental moral principle in Confucian society. However, the ghosts do not go so far as to cast doubt on the patrilineal foundation of society but rather compromise their desire for retribution according to Confucian morality. In the 1818 edition of the story, they ask the magistrate to apply a lesser degree of punishment to Pae Sigyŏn. Their leniency toward their father reflects their firm adherence

16. Ch'oe Kisuk, "Pulmyŏl ŭi chonjaeron," 313–55.
17. Walraven, "Popular Religion in a Confucianized Society," 190–91. I would like to thank Theodore Hughes for bringing my attention to Walraven's essay.

to the Confucian principle of filial piety, despite the graveness of his sin. In fact it is hard to think of him as less an accomplice than his son P'iltong: even though Pae Sigyŏn did not plot against his daughters' lives, it is he who ordered the killing of Changhwa without carefully examining the accusation. What is more, instead of holding a grudge against their father, the ghosts grieve over the sentence imposed upon him at the end, even though it has been significantly reduced.

In the vernacular edition, Changhwa and Hongnyŏn even more emphatically exonerate their father: they plead to the magistrate not to prosecute him at all, saying that "our father is a kindhearted person" but "hoodwinked by the malicious woman's ingenious trick, could not tell black from white."[18] As if to confirm their unconditional devotion to their father, the ghost sisters are later reborn to him and his third wife as twin sisters. "The Tale of Inhyang," a variant of "The Tale of Changhwa and Hongnyŏn," resolves the conflict between filial piety and the cult of chastity through the untimely death of the father. Torn between the social obligation to punish his unchaste daughter and his parental affection toward her, the father falls ill and dies of extreme emotional distress before the ghosts of Inhyang and her sister, Inhyŏng, pay their first visit to a local magistrate.[19]

Changhwa's and Hongnyŏn's ghosts combine two competing identities, one informed by patrilineal social norms and the other by popular religion. In both versions of "The Tale of Changhwa and Hongnyŏn" discussed here, the benevolent representative of the state does seem to succeed in pacifying the female ghosts' vindictive and restless identities by listening to their otherwise repressed voices. From our contemporary standpoint, their demand hardly seems radical: they do not try to correct the discriminatory patrilineal moral code, just lament the unfair price that they had to pay in spite of their rigorous observance of these rules. And yet it is important to remember that only by turning into the fearful figures of ghosts can the victimized women in "The Tale of Changhwa and Hongnyŏn" seek public recognition of their innocence. It is this im-

---

18.   "Chyanghwa Hongnyŏn chyŏn," in *Han'guk pangak pon sosŏl chŏnjip*, 41.

19.   Yi Sŭnggyu, ed., *Inhyang chŏn*, 21. Yi Sŭnggyu appears as an author and publisher (chŏjak kyŏm palhaengja) on the copyright page, not on the front book cover.

age of the emboldened female ghost that becomes integrated into the iconoclastic figure of a reform-minded woman in *Mt. Ch'iak.*

A Domestic Woman's Civilizing Mission

Like a number of early colonial domestic novels, volume 1 of *Mt. Ch'iak* not only responded to a need for social reform and national strength but was also produced commercially to make a profit in the burgeoning modern publishing market. The following ad—which was initially run by One and Only Publishing House (Yuilsŏgwan) in *Hwangsŏng sinmun* (Capital Gazette) on November 8, 1908, and regularly reappeared until August 6, 1909—attests to the dual intentions driving the creation and promotion of this work: "*Mt. Ch'iak* (Mr. Kukch'o Yi Injik) (List price forty chŏn): This novel [*sosŏl*] was written by Mr. Yi. Over a decade he put a lot of energies into this novel to amend our nation's unsavory family morals. It not only helps elevate the moral sense but also occasionally serves up superb entertainment. Hurry and get one."[20]

While stressing the intent to promote the idea of renovating domestic customs, the ad is carefully designed to grab readers' attention by placing the pen name (Mr. Kukch'o) as well as the real name (Yi Injik) of the luminary author at the beginning and by using an unusually large font to print the title of the novel. Calling into question the prevalent assumption that early colonial domestic novels like *Mt. Ch'iak* were intended to cater only to uneducated female readers' old-fashioned tastes, this ad was not merely published over nine months in a newspaper targeted toward male elites but also was written in the hybrid script that mixes classical Chinese with the vernacular Han'gŭl—the style that *Hwangsŏng sinmun* adopted to serve its targeted audiences, male elite readers—even though *Mt. Ch'iak* itself was written in the unmixed form of the vernacular script, the style that Yi Injik had adhered to for his novels since 1907.

By the time the first volume of *Mt. Ch'iak* was published in July 1908, Yi Injik had already serialized two novels, *Tears of Blood* (*Hyŏl ŭi nu*, 1906)

20.   Advertisement in *Hwangsŏng sinmun*, November 1, 1908–August 6, 1909.

and *Voice of a Ghost* (*Kui ŭi sŏng*, 1906–7), as well as two short vignettes: "Short Story" (Sosŏl tanp'yŏn, 1906) and "A Widow's Dream" (Kafu no yume, 1902), which was written in Japanese. For reasons unknown, the second volume of *Mt. Ch'iak*, published three years later, was written by a relatively new figure in the fiction publishing market, Kim Kyoje, whose novel, *A Peony* (*Moktanhwa*), had come out earlier that year. Considering that the two volumes were written by two different writers within different social milieus—the patriotic reformist zeal right after the Protectorate Treaty and the aftermath of the 1910 annexation—it would be hard to read the two volumes of *Mt. Ch'iak* as a coherent whole and ignore the discrepancies and gaps that keep each volume at a distance from the other. Yet it is equally difficult to treat them as completely separate pieces, since volume 2 continues major elements of volume 1. A comprehensive comparison between the two works is a topic for a separate study. For now it is sufficient to say that volume 2, though taking up the motif of a female ghost, does not retain the most peculiar aspects of the female characters that appear in volume 1. For this reason I will mostly focus on *Mt. Ch'iak*, volume 1, in drawing my key points on the modern alteration of the traditional female ghost, though I will still include some aspects of volume 2.

In the opening passage of volume 1, the third-person narrator derogatorily describes Mt. Ch'iak as an emblem of moral depravity: "Mt. Ch'iak is the toughest mountain in the vicinity of Wŏnju, Kangwŏn Province. With no bright color or distinctive peak, it is merely covered in dull pitch-black darkness. . . . One could say Mt. Diamond is civilized [*munmyŏng han san*], Mt. Ch'iak barbarous [*yaman ŭi san*]. As the heart of Mt. Ch'iak swarms with tigers even during daytime, it often occurs that huntsmen who try to prey on animals end up being tigers' prey."[21] The contrast between Mt. Diamond and Mt. Ch'iak segues into the feud between Madam Yi and Madam Kim. The female protagonist, Madam Yi, is the only daughter of Yi P'ansŏ, a Seoul-based government official known for his strong support of political reform. She has recently married Hong Ch'ŏlsik, the only son of Hong Ch'amŭi, a conservative local bureaucrat in Wŏnju. Hong Ch'ŏlsik's stepmother, Madam Kim, stands for what makes the old Korea barbarous and destructive by

21.   Yi Injik, *Ch'iak san sangp'yŏn*, 1.

being a proverbial evil stepmother (and stepmother-in-law), on the one hand, and practicing superstition and shamanism, on the other. As is the case with a number of early colonial domestic novels, *Mt. Ch'iak* displaces the political dispute between Minister Yi and Hong Ch'amŭi onto the clash between two domestic women, namely, the one's daughter and the other's wife. The following episode rather explicitly illustrates this dislocation.

On a moonlit night, Madam Yi and her beloved handmaid, Kŏmhong, openly complain about the hardships that Madam Kim and Namsun—Madam Kim's eleven-year-old daughter and Hong Ch'ŏlsik's stepsister—inflict upon them. Madam Yi shares with her maid her secret wish to leave her in-laws' house for her natal home and even cries while saying she feels envious of the moon that, from high above, can easily see her mother, who lives in Seoul. To raise her mistress's spirits, Kŏmhong says, "Once Madam Kim passes away, would there be any reason for you to suffer? As for your husband Mr. Hong, you know how much he cares about you, don't you?" Madam Yi turns her attention to another person who has been giving her and Kŏmhong a difficult time: her sister-in-law Namsun. "Beside Madam Kim I also cannot stand Namsun," she says, without knowing that her little sister-in-law has been eavesdropping on their conversation. Always more outspoken than her mistress, Kŏmhong goes on to add: "She must be a fox mistakenly born as a human. How sly a ten-year-old can be!" Once they realize that Namsun has been listening in on their complaints the whole time, however, Madam Yi and Kŏmhong are startled and return to their room to wait anxiously for Madam Kim's railing and ranting to begin. The political subtext comes fully to the surface when Madam Kim brings up Madam Yi's family background while berating her for her disrespectful behavior: "So, is it okay for a Seoul minister's daughter to treat her mother-in-law and sister-in-law like dirt?" Later, she grumbles about Madam Yi: "Having an *enlightened* daughter-in-law has already paid off. Have I not heard her insulting me? Have I not listened to her cursing me? . . . If not one of the enlightened, why would she have the nerve to have such an attitude toward me?"[22]

To contemporary readers, Madam Yi may seem to differ only slightly from a traditional woman victimized by patrilineal marital custom, which

22. Ibid., 4–8, 33.

restricts married women from frequently visiting their natal homes. Compared to Pae Sigyŏng's virtuous daughters—or, more precisely, the living versions of them—however, Madam Yi does stray from the ideal conduct code: though a daughter-in-law in a *yangban* family, she does not shy away from speaking out about the stepmother-in-law's ruthless behavior toward her. Still it would be fair to say that Madam Yi's identity as a "civilized and reformist" woman derives less from her rebellious spirit than from her family's affiliation with the reformist party. She is the only daughter of a reform-minded politician and, more importantly, the wife of Hong Ch'ŏlsik, a young man ready to dedicate himself to moving the nation forward. One can argue that one of her main roles in the reform movement is to enable her father to make a political coalition with the only male heir to a conservative bureaucrat. Without this marital tie, Yi P'ansŏ, a reformist politician without his own male heir, would not be able to exert political influence on a young man like Hong Ch'ŏlsik, and Hong Ch'ŏlsik for his part would not dream of pursuing costly "new learning" (*sin hangmun*) in Japan without Yi P'ansŏ's unstinting financial support.

Madam Yi's ancillary yet crucial contribution to the reform movement distinguishes her from other "traditional" Korean women. She eagerly supports Hong Ch'ŏlsik's decision to pursue new learning in Japan, though she knows that his absence will make her life even more miserable. "Darling, please don't worry about me. If you rest your heart on a trivial matter like family, what can you achieve as a man?" Her selfless attitude, according to Hong Ch'ŏlsik's playful remark, stems from the reformist political stance that her family advocates. "Certainly *a reformist's daughter* is different from others. She tells me what to achieve or not. She's much better than I. I should learn new knowledge lest I be looked down upon by my wife."[23] Hong Ch'ŏlsik goes on to say that, in contrast with his wife, other Korean women are too consumed with their own interests to pay attention to the ongoing national crisis. At times his supposedly reformist view verges on a colonialist gaze: "Our countrymen set a high price on their bodies, parents, wives, children, houses, and wealth but do not care whether their country is dying out or thriving. After ruining their country by their own hands, they are upset and resentful, complaining they don't want to be ill-treated and have

23.　Ibid., 21 (emphasis added).

no way to live. They will just bring down the country [even further]. How foolish!"[24]

Hong Ch'ŏlsik praises Madam Yi for, unlike other Koreans, sharing his vision of reform: that only the pursuit of new knowledge will help Koreans regain their sovereignty. His criticism against "other women" soon moves to a critique of a series of military uprisings organized by the righteous army (*ŭibyŏng*) in protest against the Protectorate Treaty. According to Hong Ch'ŏlsik, these anticolonialist protesters are simply "foolish," because the loss of sovereign rights are caused most of all by Koreans' lack of moral and intellectual prowess. His emphasis on new learning as the only way of reforming Korea is consonant with the political rhetoric that Japan had already been using to forge unequal treaties with Korea: Japan intended to "help" Korea to progress toward civilization. Therefore Japan would only colonize Korea until it became prosperous and strong. This colonialist narrative advises Koreans to strive for wealth and power in a way that does not question or challenge Japan's role as their guide, even though it means that Koreans accept their secondary status in Japan's empire and that resumption of self-government would be deferred to the indefinite future.

It is not hard to find flaws in Yi Injik's portrayal of Madam Yi as an advocate of reform values. While transporting reformist ideas from one man to another, Madam Yi does not release herself from traditional gender roles and family obligations, nor does she go overseas to get a modern education like her husband. It is as if the thought never occurs to Hong Ch'ŏlsik or Minister Yi—or even to Madam Yi herself—that she, too, might benefit from modern schooling. Many scholars indeed have found it perplexing that Yi Injik depicts a wife of an enlightened man in such an old-fashioned way barely two years after the serialization of *Tears of Blood*, in which he introduced readers to the iconoclastic female figure of Ongnyŏn, who acquires a modern education first in Japan, then in the United States, and eventually assumes the role of a future leader who works for Korean women's liberation.

Nevertheless, there seems to be greater emphasis on Ongnyŏn's and Madam Yi's roles as wives in a new home (*kajŏng*) than on how much education they have. Indeed, for many reform-minded intellectuals of the

24. Ibid., 25.

1900s, a home was often thought of as a viable educational venue for the majority of Korean women. For instance, the preface of *Self-Study for Women and Children*, one of three extant women's textbooks published in Korea in 1908, reads:

> Men and women are the same human beings, the most precious among all living creatures. Why would only men study but not women? Comparing our women with American women and the women of European countries, it is shameful to call ours the same human beings who have bodies and souls. We wrote this book to help those who cannot afford to go to school and women in their twenties or thirties whose housework keeps them from learning so that they can *study at home on their own.*[25]

In this preface, the author Kang Hwasŏk (1868–1929) suggests that the self-study primer will help children from poor families and domestic women to study without leaving their homes. Kang's version of gender equality was imbued with a nationalist overtone, considering women's education mainly as a means to raise the nation's level of civilization. The radical call for universal education for all women of the nation, regardless of their age and financial situation imposed an unprecedented degree of political significance upon the gendered space of home. The following quote from another of these textbooks, *Women's Primer*, unequivocally identifies women's place in the nascent nation: "Women will be *mothers of the people* [*paeksŏng*]. Only after women's education becomes fully developed can they raise good persons. To teach women is, that is to say, to improve child-rearing practice [*kajŏng kyoyuk*], which in turn will guide citizens [*kungmin*] to the right path of learning."[26]

Whereas the preface to *Self-Study for Women and Children* envisions the home as the main site where women gain access to elementary education, *Women's Primer* suggests that educated women can exert influence over the nation through their domestic roles as mothers. It should be noted that the metonymic displacement of women into "mothers of the nation" is hardly unique to early colonial Korea. For instance, it resonates with what was called "Republican motherhood" during the Revolutionary era

25. Kang Hwasŏk, *Puyu toksŭp*, 277 (emphasis added).
26. Chang Chiyŏn, *Nyŏja tokpon*, 1 (emphasis added). Page citations are to the reprint edition.

in U.S. history (1763–83), the attempt to integrate women into the Revolution on the premise that "in their capacity as mothers women exercised a determining power over the fate of the Republic in the values that they taught boys who would grow up to lead the nation."[27] It also echoes the ideology of "good wives and wise Mothers" (*ryōsai kenbo*), a modern concept coined in Japan during the early Meiji era to impose upon domestic women the public role of contributing to the advancement of the nation.[28]

In the same vein, one can draw a parallel between Madam Yi in *Mt. Ch'iak* and the heroines of mid-nineteenth-century American domestic fiction, who fulfill the duty of buttressing the nation's morality through the exertion of their feminine sentiment over the domestic sphere. Although Madam Yi may not step out of the home to become a modern schoolgirl, she still contributes to the nation's civilizing mission by supporting the spread of reformist ideas, enduring the hardships imposed upon her during her husband's absence, and ultimately helping her in-laws, especially the women, to realize the harm in their outmoded way of life and to embrace the values of civilization and enlightenment. According to Amy Kaplan, nineteenth-century American domestic fiction resonated with the imperialist rhetoric of the time, which supported U.S. rapid expansion of its territory through its wars against Mexico and Spain, and proposed that domestic women's Christian influence could reach racial minorities, foreigners, and "heathens."[29] Similarly, Madam Yi's task of civilizing the home not only complements Hong Ch'ölsik's efforts to bring civilization to the nation from Japan but also covertly endorses his colonialist justification of Japan's imperialist infringement upon Korea as the predestined expansion of civilization to uncivilized terrains.

Vanishing Premodern Ghosts

Unlike her nineteenth-century American counterpart, however, the civilized woman of *Mt. Ch'iak* projects the image of the uncivilized not upon her racial "others" but upon her fellow citizens, especially women who

27. Romero, *Home Fronts*, 14.
28. Choi Hyaeweol, "Wise Mother, Good Wife," 1–33.
29. Kaplan, *Anarchy of Empire*, 23–50.

have yet to embrace reformist ideals. The story unfolds along the division between civilized Korean women and their uncivilized counterparts, represented by Madam Yi and Madam Kim, respectively. After Hong Ch'ŏlsik's departure to Japan, Madam Kim becomes more abusive toward Madam Yi and eventually abandons her on Mt. Ch'iak—a mountain famous for its steep valleys and rocky trails—in the hope that she will fall prey to wild animals. Soon thereafter, the daughter-in-law's "ghost" begins haunting the Hong house. Out of fear, Madam Kim, who believes deeply in superstitious folk religion, starts pouring money into exorcisms. Nevertheless, the effort to banish the ghost turns out to be unsuccessful because there was no real ghost in the first place: Kŏmhong was pretending to be a ghost the whole time to take revenge on the stepmother-in-law of her mistress.

The figure of a female ghost helps distinguish good people (the civilized) from the morally corrupt (the uncivilized)—or those aware of the falsehood of a ghost cult from those enthralled by it. Thus, the attitude toward ghosts in *Mt. Ch'iak* stands in stark contrast to that of "The Tale of Changhwa and Hongnyŏn." In "The Tale of Changhwa and Hongnyŏn," Chŏn Tonghŭl's ability to face the female ghosts and listen to them attests to his ethical and intellectual superiority to those simply overpowered by them. *Mt. Ch'iak*, on the contrary, assumes that all "witnesses" to a ghost are morally flawed and "uncivilized." It is the least-educated woman of the Hong family—Oktan, the female servant of Madam Kim—who first brings up the idea of a ghost. Oktan is also the one who gets Madam Yi into trouble: she lies to her mistress, Madam Kim, and tells her that Madam Yi is having an affair with another man. Not surprisingly, her untruthful words add fuel to Madam Kim's hostile feelings toward Madam Yi: "What a bitch! Isn't she from a *yangban* family too? How dare she do such a thing and damage the reputation of my family? Does the bitch still call herself a minister's daughter? Her husband has gone to Japan just for a few days, but it looks like she already desperately wants to sleep with another man. I'll definitely pay her back for damaging my family reputation, even if that means I have to feed her poison."[30] Oktan creates this unfounded and deadly rumor about Madam Yi as part of a plot to kidnap her for Ch'oe Ch'iun, a prodigal son of a wealthy man in Songdo.

30.   Yi Injik, *Ch'iak san sangp'yŏn*, 75.

What Oktan really needs is an excuse to take Madam Yi out of the house so that she can hand her over to the depraved man who has an undue desire for a married *yangban* woman.

Now the world Madam Yi lives in appears little different from the one that the innocent girls are subject to in "The Tale of Changhwa and Hongnyŏn." In spite of her reformist family background, Madam Yi remains confined to the inner quarter to follow the social norms of elite women of Chosŏn Korea. Being removed from home does not mean being free from oppressive male dominance but rather the loss of the patriarchal protection of her body. This world is also guided by false beliefs. The cult of ghosts is one of them—as we can see from the scene in which Oktan discourages her mistress from killing Madam Yi outright and instead proposes they abandon Madam Yi in the heart of Mt. Ch'iak as prey for tigers: "It would be a mistake. For what she did, she may well deserve to die, but if you kill her with poison, *her ghost—the malicious ghost of a youth—will come back to have her revenge on you.* Listening to this, Madam Kim felt a little bit of a chill."[31]

This passage can be interpreted as a satirical reading of "The Tale of Changhwa and Hongnyŏn." The parody of the traditional story of a vengeful female ghost loses its moralizing undertone when it is retold by a dishonest, low-born character who is trying to manipulate circumstances. This character's lack of reliability puts into doubt the authenticity of her story of a ghost and therefore raises a question that never comes up in the earlier ghost story: Are ghosts real? In *Mt. Ch'iak*, a ghost no longer belongs to the transcendental realm of the dead but moves to the modern world of rationality. The scene where the "ghost" appears for the first time draws attention to the illusory vision of those who witness it: "On the night of New Year's Day, the wind started to whistle over the rooftop above Madam Yi's room. Hearing it from the main room, Madam Kim shuddered. Namsun threw herself into her arms and says, with her eyes widening, 'Dear me! What's that sound? Is it sister-in-law's ghost?' Upon hearing this, Madam Kim feels chills all over her body and is completely overtaken by fear."[32] No sooner do Madam Kim and Namsun hear the sound of mysterious noises from the roof above the room previously

31. Ibid. (emphasis added).
32. Ibid., 179–80.

occupied by Madam Yi than they "realize" in horror that her ghost has returned. The unintelligible sound is sufficient to convince Namsun and Madam Kim of the return of Madam Yi's ghost—suggesting that the false perception is in fact caused by their guilt.

By shifting the focal point from the ghost's voice to the mental reaction of those who believe in ghosts, *Mt. Ch'iak* heralds what I would call a "psychological turn" in modern literary representations of ghosts, a new trend in twentieth-century Korean fiction characterizing ghosts as psychological effects such as delusion, oversight, dream, madness, and guilt. For example, the short story by the leftist writer Yi Kiyŏng, "The Poor" (Kananhan saramdŭl, 1924) overlays the image of a ghost upon a woman who endures economic hardships and her husband's abuse without complaint, while making it clear that the ghost is nothing but the husband's hallucination, resulting from his guilt and shame at his inability to support his family.[33] In "A City and a Specter" (Tosi wa yuryŏng, 1928), one of the modernist writer Yi Hyosŏk's earlier works penned under the influence of the proletarian literary movement, the first-person narrator/protagonist mistakes a crippled beggar woman for a ghost, only to conclude that class discrepancy has created many "deathly" lives in society, including his own.[34]

In both short stories, the main characters are awakened to the dire social reality through the dual processes of seeing a ghost and then realizing that it was in fact an illusion. The process of their self-awakening is portrayed without a patronizing undertone, which the third-person narrator of *Mt. Ch'iak* has toward the women of the Hong family while describing how they "witness" the ghost of Madam Yi. The narrator soon extends this attitude to the entire village, when the "ghost" of Kŏmhong begins haunting the Hongs' neighbors. The people of the village are no less terrified than the women of the Hong family when the Hongs' dog is found dead on the rooftop of the house, and the roof tiles are rearranged to form the Chinese character *mang* (亡, to ruin). The entire village loses its nerve at an appearance of "ghost fire" (*tokkebi pul*) which is followed by a spiteful ghost's sobbing voice from an open field of the village in the middle of the night. Later, the allegedly "rational" narrator explains:

33. Yi Kiyŏng, "Kananhan saramdŭl," 59–85.
34. Yi Hyosŏk, "Tosi wa yuryŏng," 106–21.

people are scared only because of their illusory conviction in the super-natural power of a ghost. The narrator laments: "How deeply country bumpkins believe in ghosts!"[35] One should recall that in "The Tale of Changhwa and Hongnyŏn," it is Chŏng Tonghŭl's ability to listen to the dead girls' ghosts and trust their words that makes him superior to other magistrates. The narrator of *Mt. Ch'iak*, on the other hand, questions the epistemological basis of "The Tale of Changhwa and Hongnyŏn" by claiming that a ghost is nothing but an illusory artifact of a feeble mind.

This part of *Mt. Ch'iak* might be also read as a warning to readers: Do not believe in ghosts, no matter how credible they may seem. The nar-rator's attempt to "civilize" readers verges on a colonialist viewpoint to the extent that, just as Hong Ch'ŏlsik blames average Koreans for having lost their national sovereignty, he holds the women's and villagers' be-nighted minds responsible for keeping them from seeing the truth. The narrator considers himself superior to these characters, assuming that there should be a clear-cut distinction between an inferior type who be-lieves in ghosts and an awakened person who understands what a ghost actually is. As I discuss below, *Mt. Ch'iak* shows that, in spite of the nar-rator's effort to banish them, female ghosts eventually find their place in early colonial Korean literary imagination.

Ghostly Womanhood

Instead of replacing folk religion with a rational way of thinking, *Mt. Ch'iak* creates its own version of a female ghost, as Kŏmhong does not simply play the ghost of Madam Yi but revives the premodern image of a subversive ghost woman by doing what Madame Yi would have done if she had died and turned into a ghost: she takes revenge on her mistress's in-laws and says what her mistress could not spell out. More often than not, the narrator sounds self-contradictory as he tries to suppress the folk belief in ghosts while endorsing traditional female ghosts' roles in giving critical voices to wrongfully accused women.

35. Yi Injik, *Ch'iak san sangp'yŏn*, 191.

Thus the significance of Kŏmhong's role goes much beyond what one might expect from a minor character. From the very beginning, Kŏmhong stands out among the maidservants of the Hong family. The narrator introduces her as "a fifteen- or sixteen-year-old with a lovely, roundish face" and so attractive that, "if she had been living even somewhere close to Seoul, she would have wanted to quit her job as a handmaid and find a better life"—that is, she is someone whose nominal social status does not appear to fit her.[36] Whereas other domestic servants like Oktan and Ch'uwŏl strive to be released from slavery or to make a fast buck by fawning over their owners, Kŏmhong never shows any desire to achieve such social mobility. Instead, she maintains an unusually close relationship with her mistress, Madam Yi, accompanying her everywhere like a shadow and frequently echoing her feelings. When she overhears in her sleep that Madam Yi will soon send her husband off to Japan, for example, Kŏmhong weeps in sympathy for her mistress. Madam Yi in turn relies on Kŏmhong emotionally, seemingly taking Kŏmhong to be an indivisible part of herself. The morning of her husband's departure, Madam Yi tearfully tells Kŏmhong: "My husband will be going abroad for study. Kŏmhong! If he leaves, who else would help *us*?"[37]

The relationship between Madam Yi and Kŏmhong echoes the close sisterly bond that Changhwa and Hongnyŏn have. Just as Changhwa expresses anxiety concerning her younger sister's future while facing her own death, so does Madam Yi think of Kŏmhong when, after giving up any hope of surviving alone on the mountain with her chastity intact, she decides to commit suicide. Before jumping into an abandoned well in the mountain, she says: "Going to my deathbed, I cannot stop thinking about one thing. It is not the debt of gratitude I owe to my parents, not my husband's affection, not bitter feelings against my parents-in-law. . . . Awake or asleep, I always vividly see that Kodusoe was ruthlessly stomping on Kŏmhong with his feet. Poor Kŏmhong. . . . Are you dead or alive? If you have died, I will see you in the underworld."[38]

36. Ibid., 4.
37. Ibid., 27, 29 (emphasis added).
38. Ibid., 166. See also "Chyanghwa Hongnyŏn chyŏn," in *Han'guk pangak pon sosŏl*, 18–21.

The scene Madam Yi recalls in this passage epitomizes Kŏmhong's role as her ghostly double. Kŏmhong is "stomped on" by a brutal male servant while protesting against Madam Kim's decision to send Madam Yi back to her natal family (even though Madam Kim's actual plan is to have Madam Yi abandoned on Mt. Ch'iak as prey for tigers). Whereas Madam Yi, though shocked, complies with her mother-in-law's order, Kŏmhong fearlessly pressures her mistress to demand that her in-laws should give a reason for throwing her out. Madam Kim, in fury, orders Oktan's husband, Chang Kodusoe, to "rip her mouth apart and chain her to a post."[39] Madam Yi helplessly listens to the sound of Kŏmhong being brutally beaten by Kodusoe as palanquin bearers carry her away from the house. That is to say, Kŏmhong runs the risk of being killed in order to *speak for* her mistress.

Given that Kŏmhong is prone to behaving like an iconoclast, unafraid of infringing upon the strict social hierarchy that places *yangban* far above the outcast, even before she begins "haunting" the Hong household, we can read her as another iteration of the individual in early colonial Korean domestic novels. Kŏmhong's transgressive behavior reminds us of Nancy Armstrong's definition of the individual: a person who "surmount[s] the limits of an assigned social position."[40] At the same time, her individuality appears peculiarly out of the ordinary because, paralleling Madam Yi, she tends to limit her role in helping her mistress claim her rights. While vocally criticizing how unfairly Madam Yi is treated by her in-laws, Kŏmhong remains reticent about the discriminatory social hierarchy that keeps her from searching for her own freedom or selfhood. Kŏmhong acts as Madam Yi's double but nothing else. One can compare the relationship between Madam Yi and Kŏmhong to the intimate sisterhood between Changhwa and Hongnyŏn. No one doubts Hongnyŏn's chastity. Yet she not only kills herself but also, in the form of a ghost, audaciously transgresses the social expectations set for *yangban* women in order to take revenge on those who have wrongfully inculpated her sister. As Hongnyŏn's ghost freely crosses the boundary between the world of the living and that of the dead to vindicate her sister's honor, so Kŏmhong not only cuts

---

39. Yi Injik, *Ch'iak san sangp'yŏn*, 124.
40. Armstrong, *How Novels Think*, 4.

across the barrier between social statuses but also supplements her double's identity without holding a separate selfhood. Viewed in this light, it does not appear as a mere coincidence that the name Kŏm*hong* shares the character *hong* with Changhwa's younger sister *Hong*nyŏn—more accurately, the ghost of Hongnyŏn.

Then, why does the identity of Madam Yi need to be supplemented by her ghostly double? By waging tough battles against the "uncivilized" on behalf of her mistress, Kŏmhong allows Madam Yi to keep her traditional womanly identity intact. Together they create a hybrid female figure—a ghostly woman—who challenges the vice of the uncivilized without completely flouting traditional gender norms rather rigorously imposed upon upper-class *yangban* women. Despite her allegiance to reform, Madam Yi mostly remains confined to the inner quarter so that she "does not even know how the main gate of Hong Ch'amŭi's house looks [like] from outside."[41] Her limited knowledge about the mundane world outside the women's quarter makes her "noble," evidence that she has abided by the gender norms of Chosŏn Korea. Madam Yi's residual identity as an elite *yangban* woman becomes more noticeable during her exile on Mt. Ch'iak. After losing her family's protection, Madam Yi is unable to ward off a series of threats to her chastity, which is a *yangban* woman's symbolic asset. From that point on, Madam Yi's story focuses on her struggles to maintain her chastity in the face of strange men's attempts to kidnap or rape her. Several times she verges on committing suicide.

On the other hand, relatively unimpeded by the upper class's fixation on chastity and its norms of womanly behavior, Kŏmhong easily transgresses the cultural segregation between men and women. At one point she even uses her sexual appeal to get what she wants. A month after her mistress's disappearance, she embarks on a quest to find Madam Yi, although she has not yet recovered from Kodusoe's violent beating. With her good looks and glib tongue, she at first convinces one of the palanquin bearers to tell her where he abandoned Madam Yi. The palanquin bearer, overjoyed by the rare opportunity to have a face-to-face conversation with such a beauty, guilelessly lays bare the facts that he has gathered from Kodusoe, who became his drinking buddy after their joint trip to Mt. Ch'iak. Her failure to find Madam Yi notwithstanding,

41.   Yi Injik, *Ch'iak san sangp'yŏn*, 164; Yi Injik, *Ch'iak san hagwŏn*, 23.

Kŏmhong not only survives several days of searching on a mountain teeming with beasts and lustful drifters, but also manages to collect sufficient evidence to conclude that her mistress must be still alive. After exhausting all means for continuing her search, she makes her way to Minister Yi's home in Seoul (without, like her mistress, taking an extreme measure, such as a suicide attempt). With his help, she carries out a vengeful plot against the women of the Hong household, in which she plays the role of leader of a group of male peddlers. Ultimately, Kŏmhong leads the war against the "uncivilized."

A similar example of ghostly womanhood is found in Yi Haejo's *The Blood of Flowers* (*Hwa ŭi hyŏl*, 1911), an early colonial domestic novel that rewrites the famous *p'ansori* fiction *The Tale of Ch'unhyang* (*Ch'unhyang chŏn*). In the original story, Ch'unhyang, the gifted and beautiful daughter of a local female entertainer in Namwŏn in Chŏlla province, marries a magistrate's son without his parents' knowledge or permission and, even after his reluctant relocation to the capital city due to his father's transfer, remains faithful to him in the face of a newly appointed magistrate's violent attempt to make her serve him as his concubine. After being brutally tortured by the evil magistrate, she is saved by her husband, who has passed the civil service examination and returned to Namwŏn as a secret royal inspector. In some variants of the story, the king, impressed by her admirable womanly virtue, legitimizes her marriage to a man whose status is superior to hers and bestows upon her the status of a *yangban* wife.

Similar to Ch'unhyang, the female protagonist of *Blood of Flowers*, Sŏnch'o, is the talented and charming daughter of a female entertainer in another city in Chŏlla province, Changsŏng. Unlike the former, Sŏnch'o is a female entertainer herself but, following Ch'unhyang's footsteps, determines to keep her chastity intact until the right man comes along. Unfortunately, she ends up not with an amorous son of a local magistrate but with a charlatan: a corrupt secret inspector brings a wrongful charge against her father and blackmails her into accepting his marriage proposal in order to save her father from being executed. After spending the night with her, he withdraws his marriage proposal and runs away.

Akin to *Mt. Ch'iak*, *Blood of Flowers* conjures up a traditional female ghost to repudiate the "uncivilized" practice of folk religion on the one hand and to empower a woman to fight injustice on the other. The narrator of *Blood of Flowers* begins by relating a series of strange events that occurred after Sŏnch'o's death. Her ghost begins haunting the inspector. His three sons and grandchildren lose their lives, one after another. On the very same day as her suicide, a drought begins, as if the whole town was under the vengeful power of Sŏnch'o's ghost. Later, the narrator gives rational explanations for each incident: the ghost is merely an illusion on the part of the inspector stemming from his guilt; his personal tragedy has nothing to do with what he did; the drought is only a coincidence. Most important, what appears to be the ghost of Sŏnch'o is in fact her younger sister, Moran, who acts like her dead sister to take revenge on him.

As in the case with Kŏmhong, the figure of a vengeful female ghost gives Moran the authority to fight for justice. After her sister's death, Moran trains herself as an entertainer against her parents' will and takes a job as a professional dancer and singer at a Seoul-based entertainment house. When she spots the inspector during a high-brow social gathering where she was invited to dance, she acts as if she were possessed by Sŏnch'o's ghost and divulges the inspector's corrupt behavior and wrongdoings to her guests, who consist of important government officials, luminaries, and foreign ambassadors and consuls. After this incident, the inspector falls into a downward spiral. By assuming the form of her dead sister's ghost, in other words, Moran gains the otherwise inaccessible power to punish a *yangban* man and to put an end to his career.[42]

Considering that works like *Mt. Ch'iak* and *Blood of Flowers* were written by reform-minded male writers who were most likely not exposed to anything close to an egalitarian gender norm for the first time until well into their adulthoods, it seems peculiar that the leading male characters in both stories remain incompetent, regardless of their political positions, while the main female characters are waging a heated battle against the uncivilized. This is particularly striking when we take into account the strong influence both male family heads and local magistrates exercise over women's lives in *The Tale of Ch'unhyang* and "The Tale of Changhwa and Hongnyŏn." In *Mt. Ch'iak* the political opposition between Minister Yi and Hong Ch'amŭi never develops into a dramatic scene. The tension between the conservative father and his reform-minded son ends with the latter's departure in the earlier part of *Mt. Ch'iak*, and

42.　Yi Haejo, *Hwa ŭi hyŏl*.

is significantly mitigated, if not gone entirely, toward the end of the second volume, when Hong Ch'ŏlsik finally reappears in the story after a long hiatus. As the reader is briefly informed, he has not only managed to mend his broken relationship with his father while studying at Waseda University in Japan but also has been receiving sporadic financial support from him.[43] These male figures play no more than trivial roles whenever they are enmeshed in the conflict between the civilized and the uncivilized. Hong Ch'amŭi is curiously spared the wrath of his daughter-in-law's ghost. Instead of drawing on his supposed political power to have a search conducted for his missing daughter, Yi P'ansŏ limits his role to giving financial support to Kŏmhong for her act of revenge. Hong Ch'ŏlsik does not return to Korea until the battle between the uncivilized and the civilized in his family has reached its denouement. Unlike in "The Tale of Changhwa and Hongnyŏn," no state authorities are involved to resolve the series of criminal cases, including kidnappings and attempted murders and rapes. Similarly, in *Blood of Flowers*, Sŏnch'-o's father remains helpless throughout the story. The royal inspector, whose job is to investigate corrupt local officials, is himself no less corrupt. The state's power is not completely invisible, but, still, state intervention seems no more effective in stopping him from trying to regain his social position than Moran's theatrical act as her dead sister is.

One might be tempted to interpret the curious ineptitude of Korean male authority in *Mt. Ch'iak* and *Blood of Flowers* as a symptomatic response to Japan's seizure of state power and its control over the burgeoning public sphere in Korea. The first volume of *Mt. Ch'iak* was published during a time when Korea was moving from a semicolonized state to Japan's colony. Both the second volume of *Mt. Ch'iak* and *Blood of Flowers* came out a year after the annexation. Colonial censorship was informally put into operation as early as the outbreak of the Russo-Japanese War (1904–5), when the Japanese authorities started imposing prepublication screenings upon Korean newspapers on the pretext of ensuring military security and public safety. A series of new laws, such as the Security Law (Poan pŏp, 1907), the Newspaper Law (Sinmunji pŏp, 1907), and the Press Law (Ch'ulp'anpŏp, 1909), constrained people from openly participating in political activities and expressing political opinions either in public

43. Kim Kyoje, *Ch'iaksan sangp'yŏn*, 91.

or through print media.[44] Colonial power allowed little to no room for reform-minded writers to portray what a new civilized nation-state would look like, the way the political novelists in Japan and China did. Therefore, writers of early colonial domestic novels envisioned the domestic sphere as the main site for the movement of civilization and enlightenment and put forth domestic women at the frontiers of that movement while at the same time trying not to compromise their traditional male superiority.[45] These conflicting male desires are "imaginarily resolved" through the literary device of the ghostly female double, which integrates two incompatible characters—the civilized woman and the virtuous wife—into one person.[46] I should stress that I am not seeking to define a "purely objective" form of masculinity or gender that supposedly exists independent of narratives. My point is rather that it is through the literary device of ghostly womanhood that male reformists' attempt to renovate traditional womanhood is revealed to be in conflict with their residual adherence to elite *yangban* sexual norms. Ghostly womanhood offers an imaginary conciliation of the incoherent desires that a yangban woman can become an individual and hence the standard bearer of modernity while retaining her pristine traditional sexuality and womanly virtue.

The ghostly woman's departure from traditional gender norms thus results from the new social and symbolic role assigned to women by male reformists. Given that a woman like Madam Yi also spouts the colonialist rhetoric of the "civilizing mission," we may not be able to rejoice wholeheartedly at the emergence of this new female figure. However, her politically dubious position should not stop us from identifying her symbolic importance in early colonial Korean literature. Unlike the main characters of Yi Kwangsu's *The Heartless* or European realist novels, Madam Yi does not strive for interiority or attempt to view the world through a firm sense of selfhood. Nor is she modeled after what Indra Levy calls "Westernesque" women—the femmes fatales in modern Japanese fiction who have little in common with actual Western women but

44.   Robinson, "Colonial Publication Policy," 84, 326.

45.   About how Korean reformists and social commentators redefined masculinities at the turn of the century, see Tikhonov, "Masculinizing the Nation," 1029–65.

46.   Claude Lévi-Strauss analyzes the structure of a myth as the imaginary resolution of a real contradiction in Lévi-Strauss, *Structural Anthropology*, 217. See also Jameson, *Political Unconscious*, 77.

still play the role of the embodiment of "Japan's cultural assimilation with the modern West."[47] The identity of the ghostly woman goes against the premise that the modern novel reproduces, in various forms, "one mind per body and one body per mind."[48] Once characters with secluded interiority became central figures in Korean fiction in the late 1910s, the efforts to reconcile incompatible desires were more likely to take the form of individuals' inner struggles. The ghostly woman attests to the noncontemporaneous aspects of early colonial domestic novels: the transition from premodern literature to modern literature did not move in a straight line. More important, her ambiguity points to both the possibility and the limits of a male-centered translation of women's rights and individuality. Short-lived and largely overlooked by modern literary scholarship, the ghostly woman, thus, represents a unique iteration of the translation of the individual.

47. Levy, *Sirens of the Western Shore*, 5–9.
48. Armstrong, *How Novels Think*, 24.

CHAPTER THREE

Unbound Desire:
"Femmes Fatales"
in the Fin-de-Siècle Scene

The further the nation falls down, the muddier public morality has become. As a result advocates of *kaeinjuŭi* [individualism] are arising in the fields of politics, education, and industry. . . . Those folks are unaware of the relationship between the individual and the nation. They believe the nation's rise and fall have nothing to do with individuals. How frustrating! They are advocating *kaeinjuŭi*. Therefore, no matter how harmful it is to their village, they are happy as long as it produces their individual benefit. No matter how harmful it is to their prefecture, they advocate it as long as it produces their individual benefit. No matter how harmful it is to their nation, they encourage it as long as it produces their individual benefit.

—*Taehan maeil sinbo*, November 21, 1909

About a year prior to Japan's official colonization of Korea, *Taehan maeil sinbo*, known for its pointed criticism of Japanese colonialism, published the editorial "Don't Live by Individualism" (Kaeinjuŭi ro saeng ŭl salji maljiŏda) in the hybrid-style edition and a slightly modified version, "Don't Strive to Live Selfishly" (Chagŭi ilsin ŭl wihaesŏ salgi rŭl kuhaji maljiŏda) in the vernacular edition. The vernacular title renders the Sino-Korean translation *kaeinjuŭi* of the English word "individualism" as a synonym for "selfishness" or "self-centeredness." In early colonial Korea, living according to the principle of "individualism" was often "translated" as the selfish act of putting one's own interest ahead of that of the community. The editorial opines that the blind quest for individual benefit was not just detrimental to the prosperity of the community but could also jeopardize the very basis of one's own happiness. At one point, *kaeinjuŭi* is even singled out as the main cause of the crisis of the nation:

"What made our people's [*tongp'o*] lives so miserable? There are many reasons, but the number-one reason is *kaeinjuŭi.*"[1]

The derogatory translation of individualism derived from the early colonial Korean print media's pressing concern about the issues of survival as a collective and of solidarity among citizens. Social pundits often pointed to *kaeinjuŭi* as directly responsible for the erosion of the nation's moral foundation. What future would there be for the nation if each Korean focused only on her or his own rights and desires and nothing else? The embrace of individualism was viewed with particular alarm when it came to the question of women's pursuit of desire. Early colonial domestic novels such as Yi Haejo's *A Coldhearted Flower* (*Pak chŏng hwa*, 1910) and Yi Injik's unfinished novel *Peony Hill* (*Moranbong*, 1913) represent the prevailing anxiety over unbridled individualism through female characters that I call early colonial Korean "femmes fatales." *A Coldhearted Flower* relates a scandalous extramarital affair between an old *yangban* man's beautiful concubine and her virile young lover. In *Peony Hill*, a money-driven outcast woman subverts the authority of *yangban* patriarchy by feigning the identity of an elite *yangban* woman at liberty but also by forging fake kinship ties with several *yangban* families. The division between the enlightened (new and constructive) and the benighted (old-fashioned and stalled) becomes even more tenuous with the *femmes fatales* in *A Coldhearted Flower* and *Peony Hill* than with the domestic women in *Tears of Blood* and *Mt. Ch'iak*. Though offhandedly classified as *kuyŏsŏng* (old-fashioned women) as opposed to *sinyŏsŏng* (the new woman), these female characters indeed have affinities with the enlightened to the extent that the early colonial *femmes fatales* undermine the authority of *yangban* patriarchy in favor of new moral values. Given that they show no interest in the advancement of either the nation or their personhood, however, they are not so much the productive standard-bearers of reform as their doppelgangers: they are destructive forces that turn former ruling-class *yangban* men into abject figures. These figures, in other words, "translate" the notion of the individual into an agent of depravity marked by transgression of the traditional social norms on the one hand, and by the unbound pursuit of their desires. As iconoclasts, they boldly try to reverse gender and class hierarchy, but instead of striving to modernize kinship relations

1. *Taehan maeil sinbo*, November 21, 1909.

and domestic space, they are often content with the fading forms of a traditional domestic identity: one character spends the rest of her life as a liminal figure of the domestic woman—a concubine no longer loved by her husband, while the other has no identity outside her deceptively forged relationships with *yangban* families.

The Adulteress and Her Faithful Husband: "A Coldhearted Flower"

A Coldhearted Flower is exposé fiction, a genre that trafficked in accounts of contemporary scandalous affairs to be consumed by the prurient public.[2] It was initially serialized in the vernacular in a short-lived newspaper known for its political satires, *Taehan Minbo* (People's Daily of Great Korea, 1909–10), only a few months before the annexation, based on the account of a sex scandal involving a young concubine of a man identified as Major Pak (Pak Ch'amryŏng).[3] Published a few weeks prior to the serialization of *A Coldhearted Flower* came out, the scandal appeared in a gossip section of *Hwangsŏng sinmun* (Capital Gazette) called "Exploring a Bizarre World" (Pyŏlgye ch'aet'am), with the title in the form of a Chinese couplet: [A] young steward steals a young beauty; an old major cries over his old love" (So Sijong t'usinhyang, No Ch'amryŏng ŭpguyŏn; "A Young Steward" hereafter).[4]

---

2.   The venue for the original serialization of *A Coldhearted Flower*, *Taehan Minbo*, also frequently featured political satires in various forms—such as cartoons, short stories, and the new novel—while openly promoting itself as a newspaper "relentlessly criticizing flatterers and [the] corrupted among high-ranking minsters." *Taehan minbo*, November 23, 1909, reprinted from Yi Yumi, "Kŭndae kyemonggi tanp'yŏn sosŏl ŭi wisang," 145.

3.   "Pyŏlgye ch'aet'am," *Hwangsŏng Sinmun*, February 20–25, 1910. This account was written in the house style of *Hwangsŏng Sinmun*, which mixed Chinese vocabulary and phrases with vernacular verb endings and prepositions. Unlike other pieces from this newspaper, this story incorporated some vernacular Chinese vocabulary (*baihua*), which rarely appeared in writings of Korean literati. A few Korean writers, such as Yi Haejo, experimented with vernacular Chinese in the writing of their novels in Korean.

4.   Han Kiyŏng deserves credit for determining that *A Coldhearted Flower* was based on "A Young Steward." Han Kihyŏng, *Han'guk kŭndae sosŏlsa ŭi sigak*, 157–96. Han

A Coldhearted Flower can be characterized as a Korean iteration of late Qing exposé fiction, a genre that Lu Xun calls *qianze xiaoshuo* (*kyŏnch'aek sosŏl* in Korean) or "tales that chastise or excoriate" in his *A Brief History of Chinese Fiction* (*Zhongguo xiaoshuo shilüe*, 1925).[5] The author Yi Haejo (1869–1927) was known for his avid readership of late Qing Chinese fiction, and as Sŏng Hyŏnja attests, his earlier novel *The Sword That Exorcises Superstition* (*Kumagŏm*, 1908) was inspired by the late Qing exposé *The Broom That Sweeps Away Superstition* (*Sao mi zhou*, 1903).[6] According to David Wang, this late Qing Chinese genre "aim[s] at revealing social abuses and indicting political corruption," and is "characterized by topical urgency, vigorous cynicism, and a compulsive need to laugh at everything high and low."[7] The world of this genre is "peopled by charlatans, impostors, con artists, clowns, tricksters, dupes, hypocrites, quacks—all reveling in the impending downfall of the imperial system." Just as late Qing exposé writers often did, so Yi Haejo found the source material of *A Coldhearted Flower* in a sensational contemporary story that may or may not have been true. The pen name he used for the serialization of this work in *Taehan Minbo* seems to hint at his possible self-identity as an exposé fiction writer: "Sumunsaeng" (Rumor scribbler).

Though "A Young Steward" was cast as a "true story," it is marked by little journalistic objectivity, instead being replete with undoubtedly fictional imagery.[8] The all-knowing narrator not only gives specific details of the triangular love affair—what the lovesick steward does in order to seduce Major's Pak's beautiful, twenty-something concubine,

Kiyŏng's main emphasis is to show that the new novel was built upon not only the tradition of premodern vernacular fiction (*han'gŭl sosŏl*) but also that of premodern literary Chinese fiction (*hanmun sosŏl*). He also conjectures that "A Young Steward" was based on a rumor about a pro-Japanese politician's relative. In his recent book-length study of Yi Haejo, Pae Chŏngsang reaches a similar conclusion. See Pae Chŏngsang, *Yi Haejo munhak*, 229–39.

5. Wang, *Fin-de-Siècle Splendor*, 183.

6. Sŏng Hyŏnja, "Sinsosŏl e mich'in manch'ŏng," 89–93; Chang and Owen, eds., *Cambridge History of Chinese Literature*, 458.

7. Wang, *Fin-de-Siècle Splendor*, 183.

8. I would like to thank Amber Navarre, Hsiao-chih Chang and Weijia Huang for helping me decipher the idiomatic vernacular Chinese terms in "A Young Steward." I also appreciate the assistance of Si Nae Park and Sun Joo Kim with the translation of passages from this text into English.

how he secretly moved her from Suwŏn to Inch'ŏn to keep Major Pak from finding her, and exactly what Major Pak does to bring his unwilling concubine home—but also recounts the characters' thoughts. In the following scene, for example, the concubine, who is referred to as "the beauty" (*miin*), inwardly compares her old husband with the young steward: "This beauty ponders: even though Pak is supporting my parents, he is weak and feeble from his age and nothing but a nasty old thing. Yi is a young man with refined tastes [*p'ungyu sonyŏn*]. He will satisfy my sexual needs [*chŏngyok*] for the rest of my life. I can also confidently depend on him for at least a hundred years because, as a minister's son, he has both wealth and social standing."[9] The concubine measures what each man offers in a surprisingly upfront way. As both men are rich, high-ranking officials, the only thing that distinguishes one from the other is their sexual prowess. She is ahead of her time not only in seeing herself above all as a sexual being but also in being enthralled by a rudimentary form of consumer culture. Her fascination with the latest cultural fads helps the steward to seduce her: he offers her an exotic and expensive Western beverage, coffee (*kabae ch'a*), as well as a free ticket to a performance at Yŏnhŭngsa, a new-style commercial theater for *ch'anggŭk*.[10] She finds his "taste in the arts" (*p'ungryu*) appealing.[11]

A number of exposés published during the early colonial period utilized performance theaters such as Yŏnhŭngsa, Hyŏprulsa (later Wŏngaksa), and Tansŏngsa as settings. Though founded between 1902 and 1908 to modernize the supposedly "depraved" traditional theaters, they became better known as scenes for unseemly sex scandals involving members of high society, incidents emblematic of the decline of public morality. In its May 29, 1909 edition, *Taehan maeil sinbo* laments that new theaters like Yŏnhŭngsa and Tansŏngsa no longer live up to their initial purpose of renovating social manners (*p'ungsok kaeryang*) but are

---

9. "Pyŏlgye ch'aet'am," *Hwangsŏn Sinmun*, February 22, 1910.

10. Andrew Killick describes *ch'anggŭk* (literally, "musical performances," a modified form of traditional Korean opera) as hybrid-popular drama, emphasizing that it is not so much traditional Korean one-man opera, *p'ansori*, but a new genre combining traditional performance with modern theatrical elements. Killick, *In Search of Korean Traditional Opera*, xxvii, 60.

11. "Pyŏlgye ch'aet'am," *Hwangsŏn Sinmun*, February 22, 1910.

merely "encouraging debauchees to waste their money."[12] An article published in *Taehan maeil sinbo* in February 5, 1909, "A Scandal from the Women's Society" (Yŏgye ch'umun), divulged the full names of the politicians involved in the scandals: the politician Min Pyŏngsŏk's secondary wife, "Jade" (Pich'wi), invited Governor Yun Kappyŏng's concubine to performances at Yŏnhŭngsa.[13] They took turns sleeping with four male *ch'anggŭk* performers. Upon discovering this, Governor Yun broke up with his concubine. At the end, the story reports that Yun's concubine is now begging Jade to help her patch things up with her husband. Two days later, the same newspaper reported that the police were trying to find out the identities of the performers.

As "A Young Steward" suggests implicitly, social depravity was frequently blamed on women and their ill-advised adoration of the Western style of life. An editorial in *Taehan maeil sinbo* from July 27, 1910, "Regarding the Survey of Unlicensed Prostitution" (Mil maeŭm ŭl chosa hanŭn il e taehayŏ), attributes the increase in illegal prostitution squarely to women's slavish fascination with foreign trends (*oeguk p'ungjo*), in particular, "equal rights" (*kwŏlli kyundŭng*): "Facing the massive inflow of Western trends, utterly ignorant and illiterate women recklessly claim equal rights between men and women—even though they have no idea of what roles men should play, what women's duties are, and what rights are, or what equality is."[14]

Yet this editorial does not explain why prostitution, a two-party practice typically involving both a female prostitute and a male client, is blamed on the former only. Nor does it show how "Western trends" or the spreading notion of men and women enjoying equal rights might corrupt otherwise morally upright women. What is rather prominent in this editorial is male reformists' anxious attempt to control the translation of the European term of "the individual" within their own purview. The negative translation of individualism—*kaeinjuŭi*—is a catchall for other interpretations of this term that do not jibe with the male-centered reformist principle. Like morally delinquent female figures that some of early colonial Korean exposés condemn by using the supposedly derogatory

12. *Taehan mail sinbo*, May 19, 1909.

13. The same article was published under a slightly different title, "Ugly Behaviors" (Ch'uhan haengsil), in the vernacular edition. It also appears in Han Kihyŏng's *Han'guk kŭndae sosŏlsa ŭi sigak*, 186–87.

14. "Mil maeŭm ŭl chosa haŭn il e taehayŏ," *Taehan maeil sinbo*, July 27, 1910.

term *"kaeinjuŭija"*—a Korean translation of the English word "individualist"—the concubine in "A Young Steward" succumbs to the seduction of an attractive young man who boasts of his refined tastes for Western consumer products. Her lack of respect for the gendered moral code and blind pursuit of her own monetary and sexual desire invite us to read her as an early colonial literary iteration of *kaeinjuŭija*. Literary and historical narratives from Chosŏn Korea commonly portray women as facing the constant menace of relentless male sexual desire, with the most recounted situation being a woman defending her chastity from brutal rape attempts. However, it is not accurate to say that stories about women embracing their sexual desires are rare: recall the explicit love scenes between the young lovers in the *p'ansori* fiction *The Tale of Ch'unhyang* and the passion of a court lady (*kungnyŏ*) for a man other than the prince to whom she is already committed in the eighteenth-century love story *The Tale of Unyŏng*.[15] A number of love poems allegedly written by *kisaeng* (female entertainers) such as Hwang Chini and Hong Rang also address this topic. In the character of an impoverished lower-class female vagabond, Ongnyŏ, in the *p'ansori* script *The Song of Pyŏn Kangsoe*, female sexual desire takes the form of a grotesque force that threatens not only manhood but also the human race itself. Most men drop dead after sleeping with Ongnyŏ, overwhelmed by her sexual force. As her energy is decimating the male population in three neighboring provinces in the northern region of the state, she is thrown out of her community.[16]

In Chosŏn Korea, the principle of female chastity—that a woman should remain a virgin until entering into the sole sexual relationship she will have in her life—was forcefully imposed upon *yangban* elite women.[17] Women of royal or upper-class families were harshly punished for acting on their desire for anyone other than their legal husband. In 1480, King Sŏngjong sentenced Ŏ Udong, a woman from a reputable *yangban* family, to death for having extramarital relationships with a number of men.[18]

---

15. Pak Hŭibyŏng, *Han'guk hanmun sosŏl hyohap kuhae*, 333–85; *Unyŏngjŏn*; *Unyŏng-jŏn: A love affair*.

16. Sin Chaehyo, *Pyŏn Kangsoe ka*.

17. Deuchler, *Confucian Transformation of Korea*; Deuchler, "Propagating Female Virtue in Chosŏn Korea."

18. Chŏng Chiyŏng, "Munhak sok ŭi sahoesa," 357; National Institute of Korean History, "Chosŏn Wangjo Sillok: The Annals of the Joseon Dynasty," http://sillok

According to Sun Joo Kim and Jungwon Kim, beginning in the early sixteenth century, the legal apparatus of Chosŏn Korea punished adulterers differently depending on the gender and status of the culprit. A *yangban* woman was given the most severe penalty—a death sentence—for adultery, whereas a commoner woman was enslaved for the same offense. It was "acceptable by law for a husband to kill an adulteress on the basis of hearsay or suspicion alone."[19] Considered as belonging to either a prince or a king, court ladies were strictly forbidden to have sexual intercourse with other men. A violator of this law was immediately decapitated unless she was pregnant.[20]

Even the literary imagination scarcely releases female figures of *yangban* background from the patriarchal control of their sexuality. The namesake female character of *The Tale of Unyŏng* commits suicide out of guilt when the royal prince whom she serves as court lady finds out about her affair. Another court lady in a seventeenth-century love story, "A Record of Lovesick Town" (Sangsadong ki), Yŏngyŏng, ultimately evades punishment for an extramarital affair by keeping it a secret during the prince's lifetime. Even after the three-year-long mourning period after the prince's death is over, Yŏngyŏng does not even dream of eloping with her lover.[21] Only after her lover is almost dead from lovesickness (*sangsa*), and, after a special pardon is granted to her by the dead prince's first wife—who becomes a devoted Buddhist after her husband's death—can Yŏngyŏng finally be with him. According to the historian Chŏng Chiyŏng, the most sexually liberated female figure in the literature of Chosŏn Korea, Ongnyŏ in *The Song of Pyŏn Kangsoe*, is not yet completely exempt from the constraint of Confucian gender norms. After settling down with Pyŏn Kangsoe, a male drifter possessed of a monstrous virility, this outcast woman with a lethal sexuality not only remains faithful to him but also, when Kangsoe dies, is expected to live the rest of her live as a chaste widow. On his deathbed, Kangsoe makes Ongnyŏ promise to be faithful to him even though neither of them was *yangban*. Even after death,

---

.history.go.kr, key word search for "Yu Kamdong" and "Ŏ Udong," accessed on March 29, 2016.
19. Sun Joo Kim and Jungwon Kim, *Wrongful Deaths*, 23–24.
20. Sin Myŏngho, *Kungkwŏl ŭi kkot kungnyŏ*, 258–69.
21. Yi Sangsu, *17-segi aejŏng chŏn'gi*, 292–306.

his spirit tries to force *yangban* sexual morality upon her by gluing his dead body to the back of whoever tries to sleep with her.[22]

These legal, historical, fictional, and performance narratives located the principle of female chastity at the core of the moral values of Chosŏn Korean society. Thus, the concubine's uninhibited pursuit of her own sexual pleasure in "A Young Steward" suggests that Confucian moral values no longer have absolute authority over individual people's lives: the concubine not only runs off with her young lover but, more importantly, shows little remorse regarding her pursuit of sexual pleasure even after she is brought back to her husband—as if female chastity were utterly foreign to her. One can also detect the absence of a Confucian perspective on the part of the narrator, who, unlike the omniscient narrator of traditional fiction, maintains a nonchalant and nonjudgmental attitude toward this adulterous wife. We can say the same thing about the concubine's mother. She helps Major Pak find her daughter not because she adheres to the traditional moral principle of female chastity but of her assumption that Major Pak will be a more reliable provider for her and her husband: "[When] she is no longer beautiful and falls out of his favor, one cannot be sure whether his [the steward's] love will die. At that point, how can we expect him to care about her old parents?"[23] The narrator does not pass any moral judgment on the mother, either, but, on the contrary, points out how "adroit" (成精) she is at solving problems.[24] Neither the concubine nor her mother nor the narrator seem to view the world through the lens of the Confucian moral principles that had guided Korean society for centuries.

The fading away of moral principles inevitably compromises the authority of the male patriarch. Called an "honest" or "gullible" person (老實人), Major Pak neither punishes his concubine for her infidelity nor tries to take revenge on the young steward.[25] Once the concubine is returned to him, he pours all of his energy into regaining her love, to no avail: "All she sees is Yi's appearance. All she hears is Yi's voice. There is no way she can stop it. The more she sees old Pak's rooster-like skin, the more she loathes it." He does not so much enforce the exclusive ownership of

22. Sin Chaehyo, *Pyŏn Kangsoe ka.*
23. "Pyŏlgye ch'aet'am," *Hwangsŏn Sinmun*, February 25, 1910.
24. Ibid.
25. Ibid.

his concubine's body and sexuality as beg her to love him back like a heart-broken romantic hero. Eventually he does decide to file a lawsuit against his concubine (possibly against the steward as well); however, this is an act of frustration over his unrequited love rather than an avenue by which to reestablish his authority.[26] A five-character quatrain verse that appears at the end of the story as a postscript underscores Major Pak's anguish:

> The spring moon shines for nine nights
> A lady flower is too coldhearted
> Down to Mt. Ki moves a single phoenix
> An old man feels empty and dejected.

Just as the opening couplet portrays Major Pak as an emotional man who "cries over his old love," so the closing quatrain of the story highlights his sorrow and distress. If the concubine claims emotional self-authority through her unbound desire for the young steward, the major's sentimental response is not only to the loss of his lover but also to the waning influence of his patriarchal authority and that of Confucian moral values.

Reworking "A Young Steward" as a longer vernacular novel, the author of *A Coldhearted Flower* makes it clear that the concubine's sexual transgression is an integral aspect of the moral depravity of Major Pak's household and that of the larger community. It is a hopelessly topsy-turvy world that has lost its moral compass. Not so much a romantic hero as a lustful old man, Major Pak wastes his youth with numerous adulterous relationships before settling on one concubine—OO-chip.[27] Since, because of his age, he has been feeling insecure about his relationship with his young and beautiful concubine, Major Pak reacts to OO-chip's first elopement with violent fury. Too quick to assume that the concubine's young servant, Chŏngwŏl, is keeping her mistress's whereabouts from him, he brutally thrashes her almost to the point of death.[28] He is not the only one who completely succumbs to materialistic desires in *A Coldhearted*

---

26. Ibid.

27. *Chip* means "home," "house," or "family." Attached to the name of a region, it is also used to refer to a female adult from that region. OO-chip means a woman from the OO region. The book edition of the novel, *The Mountain, the River, Grasses, and Trees* (*Sanch'ŏn ch'omok*, 1912), replaces the name OO-chip with Kangnŭng-chip, a woman from Kangnŭng.

28. Sumunsaeng, *Pak chŏng hwa*, *Taehan Minbo*, April 10, 1910.

Flower. In fact, none of the characters in this novel strive to uphold any moral principle. Unlike that of "A Young Steward," the narrator does not spare anyone, either high or low, from his pointed sarcasm and mockery. Everyone acts only according to their own interests, both the main figures such as Major Pak, Steward Yi, and OO-chip; and the minor characters such as Shin mama, a group of marriage brokers whom Pak mobilizes to find his runaway concubine, and Major Pak's live-in maid, who attempts to murder him as OO-chip's accomplice. The book edition of *A Cold-hearted Flower*, published in 1912, adds Major Pak's servants to the list of characters who are morally depraved. When Major Pak is beating up Chŏngwŏl, none of his servants tries to save her because, as the narrator caustically notes, "the servants serving a master or mistress closely are commonly despised by other fellow servants" and "they have always attacked Chŏngwŏl anyway as she was, as [the concubine's] child servant, treated to slightly better food and clothing than they were."[29]

OO-chip resides at the core of a world awash with vice. In the first place, it is her insatiable sexual desire that brings to light the immorality of the rest of the character. Yet her moral depravity far exceeds that of any other characters in *A Coldhearted Flower*. After she is forcefully brought back to Major Pak by her parents, she tries to kill her husband with poisoned dumplings. When her attempt at murder fails without raising Pak's suspicion, she once again runs off with the steward. Unlike in other love stories, even Steward Yi does not help her justify her transgressive behavior with the promise of eternal love. Their passionate affair turns out to be only a transient fling. When it becomes clear that he no longer loves her, she shamelessly makes her way back to Major Pak. The male patriarch's oddly lenient response to her unruly conduct seems to confirm our suspicion that the principle of female chastity is losing its power. Upon her return from her first escape, he greets her with nothing but obsequious affection. Even odder, he accepts her when she comes back to him the second time—even though he knows by then that she has tried to poison him. He gives her a room in his house and continues to provide for her even though he eventually gives her the permanent silent treatment—a strangely light penalty for a homicidal adulteress.

Why does Major Pak forgive his concubine so easily? The narrator ascribes Pak's peculiar clemency toward OO-chip, quite unexpectedly,

29. Yi Haejo, *Sanch'ŏn ch'omok*, 37.

to the major's character: "Major Pak is not a merciless person" (*maŭmi yŏngakch'i mottan t'ŏira*). This is hardly convincing, though, because he has already proven himself to be harsh and ruthless by beating up OO-chip's child servant. I suggest that his leniency in fact testifies to the disappearance of the moral foundation on the basis of which male patriarchy was given the right to control female sexuality. A comparison of Major Pak with the male patriarchal figure—Pae Chwasu—in the premodern folktale "The Tale of Changhwa and Hongnyŏn" (discussed in chapter 2) is useful here. Pae Chawsu is portrayed as a warmhearted person and as a devoted father in the beginning. However, his benevolent character does not stop him from agreeing to put his daughter Changhwa to death when he is convinced, albeit mistakenly, that she had premarital affairs. His foremost duty, as family head, is to protect the reputation of his family. His decision therefore represents the unquestioning confirmation of the authority of the moral law, according to which anyone who transgresses the boundaries of female sexuality must be removed from family and society. In the world of *A Coldhearted Flower*, in which Confucian morality no longer has relevance, Major Pak pardons his concubine for infidelity not because he is more benevolent than the father in "The Tale of Changhwa and Hongnyŏn" but because he is no longer able to impose the old moral principle of female chastity upon his concubine. Major Pak is an accomplice of the morally empty world epitomized by his adulterous concubine. OO-chip can thus indulge her unbridled sexual drive without fear of severe punishment, an act that early colonial social critics often identified as an expression of *kaeinjuŭi*.

The Crazy Girl and the Female Con Artist: "Peony Hill"

The world of *Peony Hill*—the 1913 sequel to *Tears of Blood*—witnesses not only the crumbling of the Confucian moral foundation but also the dissolving of the earlier reformist vision for the nation's future.[30] The novel

---

30. There are two separate sequels to *Tears of Blood*. Before serializing *Peony Hill* in 1913, Yi Injik published an eleven-installment sequel to *Tears of Blood* in *Cheguk sinmun* in 1907. The 1907 sequel focuses on Ongnyŏn's mother, Ch'unae, and her three-week-long

recounts what happens to an "enlightened" girl, Kim Ongnyŏn, after her engagement to her reform-minded partner Ku Wansŏ. An emblem of the future of the nation, however, Ongnyŏn remains isolated from all the laughable aspects of colonial Korea *Peony Hill* puts on display. The focus of the story eventually shifts to a femme fatale figure, a low-born con artist whose real name is not revealed throughout the story; she is referred to at first as "thief of heaven" (*hanŭl pap toduk*) and later as Sŏ Sukcha, a Japanese-style modern name (read as Yoshiko in Japanese). Like Major Pak's concubine in *A Coldhearted Flower*, thief of heaven/Sŏ Sukcha transgresses social boundaries to satisfy her worldly desires. One may consider her to be more malicious than OO-chip, as, for example, she breaks up an engaged couple whose union would signal the arrival of modern marriage in Korea. Whereas Kim Ongnyŏn embodies the forward-looking vision of the individual as an agent of national reform, thief of heaven/Sŏ Sukcha acts in accordance with the selfish spirit of *kaeinjuŭi*, thus helping to scuttle reform. In other words, both female figures are in part shaped by the question: What is the individual?

Like its prequel, *Tears of Blood*, *Peony Hill* also portrays Kim Ongnyŏn's individualism as being critical for her journey toward becoming a modern wife. She is more than just an emblematic figure, though, as she becomes a psychologically complex, round character in the first part of the novel, a character that presages the sensitive young man to come. The story opens in a thickly wooded park in a modern American city, San Francisco. The narrator emphasizes the bustling surroundings of the park, which is teeming with people spending a Sunday morning of leisure. A church bell calmly resounds. A photographer keeps pressing the shutter of his camera, which is pointed at people on the move, without drawing much attention from them. The narrator uses the term *yŏlyo* (vibrancy) three times in the opening paragraph to emphasize the lively ambience of the park before zooming in on Kim Ongnyŏn, away from the crowd, lost in thought by a pond. Kim Ongnyŏn's physical detachment from the outside stresses her psychological isolation. What follows is her internal monologue:

---

visit with Ongnyŏn, Kim Kwanil, and Ku Wansŏ, who are going to school in Washington, D.C. Her trip to a Western country, though accompanied by her father Ch'oe Chusa, makes her much more modern than the way she is portrayed in the 1913 sequel. Yi Injik, "Hyŏl ŭi nu ha p'yŏn," *Cheguk sinmun*, May 17–June 1, 1907.

Is this Ongnyŏn who was shot and fell under Peony Hill? Is this the Ongnyŏn who was carried to a military hospital on a stretcher? Is this the Ongnyŏn who was resurrected by the hands of her father, the army surgeon Inoue? Is this Ongnyŏn who was studying in Washington, D.C., with Ku Wansŏ's help? I am glad to see her. Even Ongnyŏn is so glad to see Ongnyŏn's shadow. I am the Ongnyŏn who is standing outside the water. You are Ongnyŏn standing on her head in the water. I have something to ask you. Are you a corporeal object? If so, let me welcome you by holding your hand. Are you formless? If so, who are you that lies before my eyes? You will evaporate once I leave the water's edge. Once I die, remorse and distress in my mind [*han mank'o saryŏchŭng mantŏn maŭm*] will evaporate as well. Some say the soul is immortal, but unknowable are human affairs.[31]

Also serving as a recap of pivotal scenes from *Tears of Blood*, the first half of the passage not only details Kim Ongnyŏn's summing up of her past but also stresses the gap between her present selfhood and the previous one. In the second half, the recollection of her personal journey expands into a theoretical question about the nature of selfhood. Bordering on Cartesian skepticism, her solitary inquiry postulates selfhood as transient, "formless," and "unknowable." To understand the novelty of her inner complexity, one need only recall that in *Tears of Blood* she rarely seems uncertain about who she is, even while undergoing dramatic life changes, from a war orphan to an adoptee of a Japanese family, from runaway girl to American schoolgirl, and from honor student to potential national leader. Even a possibly subjective attribute such as her "talent" is depicted as self-evident to everyone.

To the extent that Kim Ongnyŏn muses on her own "growth" over the previous decade while asking the question of individual selfhood—"Who am I?"—the opening scene of *Peony Hill* brings her close to being like the sensitive hero of a bildungsroman or, more specifically, the protagonist of a female coming-of-age story. However, Kim Ongnyŏn's bildungsroman quickly comes to an end in the first part of the story. Once she returns to Korea after putting her marriage to her fiancé on hold, she loses her psychological depth, and her development as a civilized modern woman eventually ceases. The rest of the story revolves around the

31. Yi Injik, "Moranbong," *Maeil sinbo*, February 5–6, 1913.

wealthy pseudoreformist Sŏ Ilsun's infatuation with Ongnyŏn and his schemes to marry her against her will. This disjuncture between the earlier coming-of-age story and its shift to a comical marriage tale should not prevent us, however, from reading *Peony Hill* as a more complex and problematic work than a simple *yŏmjŏng sosŏl* (a distasteful and low-brow love story), the derogatory label that scholars have given to *Peony Hill*.[32]

Broadly speaking, the transition from a protagonist's experience of personal growth to marriage is the norm rather than the exception in coming-of-age stories. According to Franco Moretti, in the classic bildungsroman, such as Goethe's *Wilhelm Meister* or Jane Austen's *Pride and Prejudice*, growth is melded into the marriage plot: a young protagonist's "perfect marriage" functions not merely as a sign of the hero's "maturity" but also as a "metaphor for the social contract." In later examples of bildungsroman, like George Eliot's *Middlemarch* or Stendhal's *The Red and the Black*, however, marriage no longer symbolizes the happy synthesis between "free" individual growth and social constraints, but the impossibility of such a synthesis.[33] Susan Fraiman suggests that marriage complicates or even thwarts the process by which a girl becomes a woman in Victorian coming-of-age stories such as *Jane Eyre* and *The Mill on the Floss*.[34] Then, the marriage plot of *Peony Hill* is not so much evidence of this novel's vulgarity as an integral part of Ongnyŏn's coming-of-age story: her proposed "perfect" marriage with a reform-minded man pauses her progress, and the "uncivilized" Korean man's courtship reads as a threat to her growth into a civilized woman.

The two marriage plots draw on the rhetoric of civilization. In one of her monologues, Kim Ongnyŏn contrasts her relationship with the reformist Ku Wansŏ with conventional marriage, the only openly permitted heterosexual relationship in the Chosŏn period: "The emotional bond between husband and wife is mostly driven by blind passion, but the one between Ku Wansŏ and me comes from integrity and friendship. Unknowingly we have become deeply fond of each other as we came to know

---

32. Chŏn Kwangyong, "Sinsosŏl yŏn'gu: Moranbong," 233–50. Kim Yŏngmin even more bluntly discounts this work: "There is no particularly noticeable theme [in "Peony Hill"]. . . . If anything, it can be classified as a vulgar love story [*chŏ'gŭp yŏmjŏng sosŏl*]." Kim Yŏngmin, *Han'guk kŭndae sosŏlsa*, 208–9.

33. Moretti, *Way of the World*, 22–24.

34. Fraiman, *Unbecoming Women*, 1–31.

each other's attitude and character and also as we share the same wishes. It is noble and humble affection cutting across the separation between man and woman."[35]

Ongnyŏn's companionship with Ku Wansŏ is not merely an important step toward her maturity but also a challenge to the norms of marriage in Chosŏn Korea—where family heads exercise the right to choose conjugal partners for their children, regardless of the latter's feelings or preferences.[36] She experiences the new practice of premarital male-female companionship with anxiety and uncertainty rather than a sense of liberation, however:

> May this night never end! At the break of day I should say good-bye to Ku Wansŏ. I will be sixty thousand *li* away from him for ten years. Instead, may time go by quickly! Ku Wansŏ will return to Chosŏn in only three thousand six hundred days. The greatest of all the grievances in my life is that *I was not born a man. If I were a man, Ku Wansŏ and I would close our eyes to social manners or others' attention.* We would meet up ten times a day if we wanted. We could live together if we wanted to see each other day and night.[37]

This monologue takes place right after Ku Wansŏ's short visit to her hotel room, the night before her departure for Korea. No overt sexual intimacy is described in that scene, but such a private meeting of a young unmarried couple would have appeared as deviant behavior to those subscribing to the traditional gender norm that forbade boys and girls over the age of seven from even sitting together. Kim Ongnyŏn defies the spatially delineated traditional gender segregation, only to

---

35. Yi Injik, "Moranbong," *Maeil sinbo*, February 5–6, 1913.

36. It would be inaccurate to say that "free love" or "free marriage" never existed in Chosŏn Korea. Even though legitimate wives were chosen by family heads, men could choose their sexual partners "from the heart," either from among professional female entertainers, *kisaeng*, or among lower-class women such as domestic servants. However, those who sought recognition for their version of "free marriage" neither openly defied the legitimacy of existing sexual norms nor attempted to introduce a new sexual norm for the entire community as Kim Ongnyŏn does in this novel. See Pak Hyesuk, "Yŏsŏng yŏngung sosŏl," 156–93; Pak Ilyong, *Chosŏn sidae ŭi aejŏng sosŏl*; Pak Hŭibyŏng, *Han'guk chŏn'gi sosŏl ŭi mihak*; Pak Hŭibyŏng and Chŏng Kilsu, *Sarang ŭi chugŭm*.

37. Yi Injik, "Moranbong," *Maeil sinbo*, February 5–6, 1913 (emphasis added).

accept a new set of gender norms. Upon seeing Ku Wansŏ coming into her room, she feels "her cheeks flame and her heart pounding," "as if she had done something bad to him."[38] While rejecting the traditional restriction on heterosexual interactions, she internalizes the regulation of sexuality. It becomes solely a matter of her willpower whether or not she will fall into "the abyss of extramarital sexuality."[39] Ongnyŏn's following line allows us a glimpse at her inner struggle to control her desire for intimacy: "If I were a man, Ku Wansŏ and I would meet up ten times a day if we wanted."[40]

For the rest of the novel, however, the relationship between Kim Ongnyŏn and Ku Wansŏ remains arrested. Ku Wansŏ does not appear in the remaining episodes, which take place entirely in Korea. Ongnyŏn does not seem to experience psychological struggles anymore, once she is put in the position of defending her "free marriage" from an external threat: Sŏ Ilsun's courtship. Marriage with him would bring to naught the progress she has made since she was orphaned at seven. This threat is foreshadowed through her double, who happens to have the exact same given name as Kim Ongnyŏn: Chang Ongnyŏn. A crazy girl, Chang Ongnyŏn runs into Kim Ongnyŏn's house in P'yŏngyang a moment ahead of the latter's return. The narrator introduces Chang Ongnyŏn while listing the striking similarities between the two girls—same surname, same birthplace (P'yŏngyang), beautiful appearance, and closeness in age (one is seventeen, the other sixteen). Chang is thus Kim's mirror image, except in one crucial respect: the two have contrasting fates. Whereas Kim Ongnyŏn, at least while she was in San Francisco, is integrated into the modern world by putting new conjugal norms into practice in the form of premarital heterosexual companionship, Chang Ongnyŏn is still living in the "depraved" traditional world characterized by the sexual double standard that allows husbands to have multiple partners yet exacts strict compliance with the cult of chastity from wives.

Embedded as a frame tale, the story of Chang Ongnyŏn's past modifies the premodern narrative pattern of the rivalry between the good first wife and the vicious concubine by substituting a tragic ending for the usual happy ending—the restoration of family harmony through the

38. Yi Injik, "Moranbong," *Maeil sinbo*, February 8, 1913.
39. Fraiman, *Unbecoming Women*, 7.
40. Yi Injik, "Moranbong," *Maeil sinbo*, February 11, 1913.

victory of the virtuous. Chang Ongnyŏn's mother commits suicide after being falsely accused by the concubine of adultery. Upon realizing that her mother cannot vindicate her faithfulness even at the expense of her life, Chang Ongnyŏn leaves her house in the dark to drown herself in the Taedong River as her mother had done but, overwhelmed by the fear of rape, permanently loses her senses before reaching the river. Thus her strong adherence to the cult of chastity turns her into "a retarded creature less useful than a dead body" (*chuk ŭn sityeman mothan pyŏngsin*).[41]

Chang Ongnyŏn is, to a degree, comparable to Bertha Mason in Charlotte Brontë's *Jane Eyre* (1847). Rochester's crazy first wife from Jamaica, who is locked in the attic of Rochester's house, Mason haunts the story of Jane's love affair with Rochester. In their classic work of feminist literary criticism, *The Madwoman in the Attic*, Sandra Gilbert and Susan Gubar interpret this white Creole woman as Jane Eyre's "imprisoned hunger, rebellion, and rage" derived from a woman writer's fear and anxiety about entering the male-dominated realm of authorship. Gayatri Chakravorty Spivak's postcolonial feminist reading suggests that Bertha Mason is Europe's "not-yet-human-Other," a figure "produced by the axiomatics of imperialism," which also condition Jane's upwardly mobile entry to the English bourgeois family and her self-making process.[42] If we view Chang Ongnyŏn as a victim of the "uncivilized" Korean marriage system—as an emblem of the less-than-human state of the colony—her otherness is rather obscured in comparison to that of her Jamaican counterpart. She is not the shadow of a bourgeois woman of the European empire, but that of an equally colonized, though more "civilized," Korean woman. Chang Ongnyŏn shows that, being founded upon an unstable social basis, Kim Ongnyŏn's progress is at the risk of being revoked. Kim Ongnyŏn puts into words her symbolic relationship with Chang Ongnyŏn at one point, when her mother tries to talk her into marriage to Sŏ Ilsun: "Since Chang Ongyŏn has gone insane, what makes you think Kim Ongnyŏn wouldn't? Would I have any other choice but to go insane if my parents were acting insensitively?"[43]

---

41. Yi Injik, "Moranbong," *Maeil sinbo*, February 21, 1913.

42. Gilbert and Gubar view her as the female protagonist's dark "psychological double." Gilbert and Gubar, *Mad Woman in the Attic*, 360; Spivak, "Three Women's Texts," 243–61.

43. Yi Injik, "Moranbong," *Maeil sinbo*, April 29, 1913.

When Kim Ongnyŏn confronts the threat of being turned into a wife of an uncivilized man—or possibly into her doppelganger, Chang Ongnyŏn, the story shifts its focus to thief of heaven/Sŏ Sukcha. A shrewd maidservant of Sŏ Ilsun's money-hungry friend, Ch'oe Yŏjŏng, she is driven solely by insatiable sexual and material desires. No less adulterous than OO-chip in *A Coldhearted Flower*, she attempts to seduce Sŏ Ilsun even though she is married. She agrees to help Sŏ Ilsun devise a scheme to coerce Ongnyŏn to marry him, hoping to profit by it. What is most distinctive about her identity is her extreme malleability, which allows her to penetrate *yangban* families (which are no longer considered ruling class but still worthy of respect) as well as a family civilized by modern standards. That her name remains unknown throughout the story is emblematic of her plastic identity. Before she begins inserting herself into different families, she "empties out" her remaining domestic identity as a wife by "marrying off" her imbecile husband to a beggar woman—as if presuming that insofar as she belongs to no one, she is ready to join any family. She first gives herself a new name, Sŏ Sukcha, in order to be perceived as Sŏ Ilsun's "sister."[44] With her exceptional social skills, she is able to build enough trust with Kim Ongnyŏn to pledge sisterhood with her, later poses as a distant relative of Ku Wansŏ's paternal aunt's late husband (whose family name happens to be Sŏ), and finally lays claim to being a member of Ku Wansŏ's family.[45] Thus, she succeeds in forming fictive kinship ties with the three upper-class families to which Kim Ongnyŏn, Ku Wansŏ, and Sŏ Ilsun belong. By insinuating herself into a spectrum of families, from the most reform-minded (as exemplified by Kim Ongnyŏn and her Western-educated father) to the least (as exemplified by Ku Wansŏ's old-fashioned father, Ku Chŭksan), she poses as a "representative" of the larger community made up of all these families: the colonial community of Korea.

In the following dialogue, Sŏ Sukcha and Ku Chŭksan make this point clearer: they try to define their relationship by using the term *tongp'o*, used frequently to refer to the homogenous national community, or cosmopolitanism, in turn-of-the-century Korean newspapers.[46]

---

44. Yi Injik, "Moranbong," April 2, 1913. The Chinese characters of Sŏ Sukcha appear in parentheses in this installment.

45. Yi Injik, "Moranbong," *Maeil sinbo*, April 20, 1913.

46. Kwŏn Yonggi, "Tongnip sinmun e nat'anan 'tongp'o' ŭi kŏmt'o," 229.

SŎ SUKCHA: "Don't worry about the money. I don't think of my aunt [Ku Chŭksan's widowed sister] as a relative but as my mother. Isn't my mother's side of the family also my own? Too bad you don't recognize me that way and call me a guest each time you open your mouth."

KU CHŬKSAN: "Well said! People say all mankind are brethren [*tongp'o*]. I wish we could call ourselves brothers [*hyŏngje*], but who cares about a mother's side uncle like me?"

SŎ SUKCHA: "You wouldn't have said so if you thought of me as Kap-sun's sister [*hyŏng*]?"[47]

According to Kwŏn Yonggi, *tongp'o* (*tongbao* in Chinese; *dōhou* in Japanese), which literally means "of the same womb," is attested in *The Veritable Record of Chosŏn Dynasty* (*Chosŏn wangjo sillok*) as early as the fifteenth century to refer to siblings with the same father, more frequently to those in need of royal benevolence, and, after the eighteenth century, even to people living within the border of Chosŏn as a single ethnic group, regardless of their differences in terms of hereditary social status. The new connotations of "equal comradeship" among Koreans and "cosmopolitan-ism" were added to this term by the editors and contributors of *Tongnip sinmun* (*The Independent*, 1896–99). Around the time of the Russo-Japanese War, *tongp'o* became a synonym for *minjok* (ethnic nation), *kungmin* (national citizens), *min* (people), and *sinmin* (new people).[48]

From this rather farcical exchange between Sŏ Sukcha and Ku Chŭksan emerge two meanings of *tongp'o*: cosmopolitan community and patrilineal kinship. Ku Chŭksan first uses it in the broadest sense ("all mankind are brethren") and then switches it to mean "patrilineal family" by asking a rhetorical question: "Who cares about a mother's side uncle like me?" Ku Chŭksan's ingenuous switch between the different definitions of the term may make him seem unintelligent. And yet one can also read his second definition of *tongp'o* as his unwitting attempt to keep Sŏ from infiltrating his *yangban* family: the most authentic form of family is based on patrilineal linage; everything else is secondary. On the other hand, Sŏ Sukcha's family is solely formed by "fictive" mediums—a fake name,

47. Yi Injik, "Moranbong," *Maeil sinbo*, May 17, 1913.
48. Kwŏn Yonggi, "Tongnip sinmun e nat'anan 'tongp'o' ŭi kŏmt'o," 229–60. Also see Kwŏn Podŭrae, "Tongp'o ŭi susahak," 267–87; Kwŏn Podŭrae, "Tongp'o ŭi yŏksa chŏk kyŏnghŏm kwa chŏngch'i sŏng," 97–125.

a homonymous last name, a verbal pledge, and false beliefs—reminding us of what Benedict Anderson calls "imagined communities."[49] Anderson claims that "all communities larger than primordial villages of face-to-face contact (even perhaps these) are imagined" in the sense that even though "they will never know most of their fellow members, meet them, or even hear of them," in the mind of each lives the image of their communion. The building of a new community then involves not merely introducing new measures to imagine it but rejecting the old ones.[50] Like many agents of nation-building efforts, Sŏ Sukcha undermines the authority of the traditional hereditary class hierarchy. However, this is not to create a community founded upon the principle of a "horizontal comradeship," "sovereignty," and the sense of boundary. Instead of promoting a community patterned after a modern nation, she maintains parasitic relationships with the former ruling class to serve her unruly desires. For this reason, she remains no better than those of whom she makes sport and takes advantage.

I should make it clear that the colonial community depicted in *Peony Hill* is far from an accurate representation of the "historical" community of Korea during the colonial period. The type of colonial community Sŏ Sukcha embodies is molded by a colonialist standpoint: Korea cannot be reformed and therefore "deserves" to be colonized. Sŏ Sukcha tries to entice the highly educated reformist woman Kim Ongnyŏn into marrying the rich *yangban* playboy Sŏ Ilsun instead of her fiancé, the U.S.-educated reformist Korean man Ku Wansŏ. Insofar as the union between Kim Ongnyŏn and Ku Wansŏ can be read as symbolizing the reform of the nation, Sŏ Sukcha's attempt can be described as "antireformist." Unlike a number of female figures in early colonial domestic novels, Sŏ Sukcha does not identify herself according to blood or marital family affiliations. Even her real name is unknown to the other characters as well as to the reader. As I discussed earlier, her lack of a stable identity allows her to freely penetrate into various *yangban* families and to forge fictive family ties with all the families of the main characters of the novel. By forming fictive kinship ties, Sŏ Sukcha coalesces otherwise separate families into one big group, a "community." For Anderson, the community tie is fictively created in a modern nation. I call this community "colonial" because

49. Anderson, *Imagined Communities*.
50. Ibid., 6.

it is not built on the memory of its glorious past but is formed by a drifting low-born woman who is uneducated, antireformist, and money driven. It is a topsy-turvy world dominated by a sense of disorientation—where the former value system (symbolized by traditional *yangban* families in this novel) has collapsed, but a new one has yet to emerge.

The latter part of *Peony Hill* (where Sŏ Sukcha essentially becomes a protagonist) reminds us of late Qing exposé fiction (and early colonial Korean exposé fiction *A Coldhearted Flower*) as these works feature figures who challenge established social values only to turn themselves into objects of mockery. David Wang explains the narrative paradigm characteristic of the work of late Qing exposé writers as follows:

> The exposé writers are inconsistent literary practitioners; they can hold neither to the cynic nor to the moralist stance. If they are not the total moralist, who would claim to know what life should be, they are not the total cynic either, who would assume an end to "false consciousness" of what life really is. Precisely because they no longer feel obliged to abide by established ways of thinking and seeing the real, late Qing exposé writers showed much less inclination to link a certain form of representation to a moral capacity.[51]

In other words, late Qing exposé fiction criticizes or makes fun of existing values but at the same time refuses to consistently apply its moralism or mockery to what it criticizes. Consequently, the world portrayed in this genre is one marked by perpetual disorder. One can detect a similar narrative pattern in the latter part of *Peony Hill*: the outcast woman only temporarily destabilizes the *yangban* patriarchal authority, but is incapable of presenting an alternative new vision.

In contrast to *A Coldhearted Flower* as well as to late Qing exposé fiction, however, the latter part of *Peony Hill* does exempt one group of figures from mockery or criticism: the Japanese. Together with her accomplice Ch'oe Yŏjŏng, Sŏ Sukcha stops over in Inch'ŏn, a port city and transport hub with a large population of Japanese and other foreigners, on the way to visit Ku Chŭksan in Seoul. To the eyes of Japanese and Western people, Sŏ Sukcha and Ch'oe Yŏjŏng appear awkward and

51. Wang, *Fin-de-Siècle Splendor*, 218.

ridiculous. The narrator makes fun of their lack of steamship etiquette, contrasting them with the Western passengers, who have polished and confident demeanors. Whereas "Western people who are tall and have a big nose not only look upright [*kkutkkut*] and tidy [*mitmit*] but also move in a lively way," Sukcha and Yŏjŏng stand with "confused" looks (*ŏrit ŏrit hago*) on their faces, naïvely questioning whether they can trust steamship porters with their luggage.[52]

While putting a derisive spin on whatever Sŏ Sukcha and Ch'oe Yŏjŏng do, the narrator does not portray Japanese figures as ridiculous when they make foolish mistakes. A Japanese errand boy at a nearby inn does not come in for criticism when speaking to Sŏ Sukcha and Ch'oe Yŏjŏng in an almost incomprehensible Korean. The Japanese innkeeper suspects them of being "Russian spies" and reports them to the Japanese military police, yet the narrator places the blame squarely on Sŏ Sukcha and Ch'oe Yŏjŏng for their suspicious behavior. Though not a married couple, they are traveling together; they stay in separate rooms at night, but spend all day chatting with each other in one of the rooms; whenever anyone else is near them, they stop talking even though none of the Japanese clerks at the inn understand their language; and they are spending an obscene amount of money. It becomes even more obvious that the narrator views Sŏ Sukcha and Ch'oe Yŏjŏng through colonial eyes in a scene in which they are interrogated by the Japanese military police, an institution emblematic of Japan's imperialist expansion. Utterly disarmed by the authority of a Japanese military policeman, Sŏ Sukcha and Ch'oe Yŏjŏng guilelessly disclose every detail of what they have been doing as well as their future schemes. The Japanese policeman cannot stop laughing.

This encounter with Japanese figures seems to provide a clear identity for Sŏ Sukcha's ever-growing, topsy-turvy family: the "colonial community." Consisting of old-fashioned *yangban*, pseudoreformists, crazy girls, tricksters, and con artists, the colonial community has no memory of the glorious past, hope for the future, or ability to understand the fast-changing modern world. The Japanese characters' condescending gaze only confirms the stereotypical distinction between the colonizer and the colonized. Certainly, the Japanese figures in *Tears of Blood*—Japanese soldiers, Major Inoue, Mrs. Inoue—assert their superiority to Koreans.

52. Yi Injik, "Moranbong," *Maeil sinbo*, May 2, 1913.

And yet they lend a helping hand to Koreans in the latter's efforts to "move forward" and demonstrate civilized norms—whereas those in *Peony Hill* make fun of Koreans for their gauche attempts to become modern. Given that *Peony Hill* was written under the much closer scrutiny of colonial censorship than Yi's previous novels, one wonders if the mocking gaze resulted from integrating the perspective of the colonial censor into his authorial perspective. The serialization of *Peony Hill* began less than two years after its prequel—the most successful work by Yi Injik—was banned by the Japanese government general in June 1911, and about two months after the redacted edition of the novel was released by Tongyang sŏwŏn (Oriental School), a publishing house specializing in fiction. The author gave it a new title, *Peony Hill*, which eventually became the title of its sequel as well. The preface to the serialization of the sequel *Peony Hill*, dated in February 7, 1913, explains the reason as below:

> This novel [*sosŏl*] is about Ongnyŏn whose story was acclaimed by book lovers from all over the country several years ago. This time I have revised the entire piece. As it vexed me that the title of *Tears of Blood* verges on pessimism [*pigwan*], I changed the title to *Peony Hill* and wrote volume two, dedicating it to those keen to know about Ongnyŏn's final days. . . . *Peony Hill* has two volumes, but each volume can be read separately. The first volume consists of episodes about Ongnyŏn's hardships beginning when she was seven years old. It may be read without volume two. The second volume recounts Ongnyŏn's life from the age of seventeen on. It may be read without volume one.[53]

Thus, Yi Injik ascribes his commercially questionable decision to replace the already well-known title of his bestseller with an unfamiliar one to his sudden aversion to the "pessimistic" tone of the original title. Seen from the perspective of the colonized, *Peony Hill* seems not only more pessimistic than the original *Tears of Blood* but also, by focusing on the least respectable types, demeaning to Koreans. As Kyeong-Hee Choi reminds us, Korean literature was written for Japanese censors as much as for Korean audiences during the colonial period.[54]

53. Yi Injik, "Moranbong," *Maeil sinbo*, February 7, 1913.
54. Kyeong-Hee Choi, *Beneath the Vermilion Ink*.

And yet Sŏ Sukcha neither internalizes the colonial gaze nor strives to separate herself from the stereotypical image of the colonized, as is the case with the majority of female characters in early colonial domestic novels. As if not understanding what made the Japanese police laugh at her, Sŏ Sukcha continues to persist with her preposterous scheme. Thus, as with most of her sister figures in early colonial Korean domestic novels, she does not strive to find a separate selfhood outside her fictive family and community. Whereas Ongnyŏn, in *Tears of Blood* and in the earlier scenes in *Peony Hill*, locates her identity as an individual under the umbrella of the ideal of a modern egalitarian home and that of a civilized nation, the female trickster in the latter part of *Peony Hill* inadvertently crushes lingering hopes for future reform.

The serialization of *Peony Hill* ends at the point when Sŏ Sukcha tries to convince Ku Wansŏ's parents that Kim Ongnyŏn has had an affair with Sŏ Ilsun. On July 8, 1913, after putting the serialization of *Peony Hill* on hiatus for a month, *Maeil sinbo* published an announcement: "Owing to the author's personal circumstances, we have no choice but to suspend the publication of the novel *Peony Hill* for a while." The serialization never resumed, despite the suggestion of a possible continuation.[55] An incomplete work like *Peony Hill* leaves us with unresolved questions: How would it have ended if the author had completed it? Will Sŏ Sukcha break up Kim Ongnyŏn and Ku Wansŏ? Or will Ongnyŏn and Ku Wansŏ overcome the obstacles to their marriage? Will that marriage make Kim Ongnyŏn a bourgeois wife or an old-fashioned one?

Taking Yi Injik's entire oeuvre into account, however, one will notice that the incomplete ending in *Peony Hill* seems to be the rule, rather than the exception: most of his novels are left unfinished or close with

---

55. Several scholars, including Chŏn Kwangyong, Ch'oe Wŏnsik, and Tajiri Hiroyuki, attribute the unexpected discontinuation of *Peony Hill* to the exceptional popularity of *A Dream of Long Regret* (*Chang han mong*), Cho Ilche's adapted translation of the Japanese novelist Ōzaki Kōyō's melodramatic domestic fiction *The Gold Demon* (*Konjiki yasha*). However, it is not clear exactly how *The Gold Demon*'s popularity discouraged Yi Injik from finishing his novel. For about three weeks, from the first installment of *A Dream of Long Regret* in May 13, 1913, to the last installment of *Peony Hill* in June 3, 1913, the two works appeared simultaneously in *Maeil sinbo*. Chŏn Kwangyong, "Sinsosŏl yŏn'gu," 104–23; Ch'oe Wŏnsik, *Han'guk kŭndae sosŏlsa ron*; Tajiri Hiroyuki, *Yi Injik yŏn'gu*, 39.

an unresolved ending. *Tears of Blood* ends with the anticipation of a sequel: "The reader may look forward to the return of the girl to the homeland in the sequel."[56] The 1917 sequel to *Tears of Blood*, serialized in *Cheguk sinmun*, was halted only after eleven episodes.[57] Yi Injik left the second volume of his *Mt. Ch'iak* unfinished; it was completed by another writer, Kim Kyoje.[58] *Silver World* (*Ŭnsegye*, 1908) appears to end abruptly in the middle of conflict: a martyred reformer's two U.S.-educated children are being taken prisoners by the righteous army (*ŭibyŏng*), the volunteer militia that organized to resist Japanese imperialist forces, while their terrified mother is praying to Buddha to save them.[59] Fredric Jameson claims that closure, or the narrative ending, not merely "project[s] some sense of a totality of experience in space and time" but also marks the "boundary or limit beyond which thought cannot go."[60] In the same vein, I am tempted to suggest that the incomplete ending of *Peony Hill* might be enough to show both the "totality" and "limit" of Yi Injik's colonialist imagination, a moot point attained by Yi Injik's colonialist reform. Stalled at a moment where an outcast woman tries to break up a modern marriage between Ongnyŏn and Ku Wansŏ, in the second half of the novel *Peony Hill* repeatedly hints at the dark potential of building a modern nation. From the fact that the narrative came to a standstill even before the serialization of the novel was abruptly discontinued, we might infer that Yi Injik might not have been able to envision the future of Korea beyond revealing its ills even if he had completed *Peony Hill*.

There are tantalizing similarities between the *femmes fatales* in *A Coldhearted Flower* and *Peony Hill* and the literary figure of the modern girl, which appears in, for example, Yŏm Sangsŏp's "Sunflowers" (Haebaragi, 1923) and Kim Tongin's "The Tale of Kim Yŏnsil" (Kim Yŏnsil chŏn, 1939). For both early colonial femmes fatales and the modern girls in the 1920s and 1930s are unruly "individualists" driven by insatiable desires and characterized by chameleon-like identities. But there is a clear distinction between them. According to the feminist literary historian Yi Hyeryŏng, the unruly modern girls of the fictional narratives of the

56. Yi Injik, *Hyŏl ŭi nu, Mansebo*, October 10, 1906; Yi Injik, "Tears of Blood," 220.
57. Yi Injik, "Hyŏl ŭi nu ha p'yŏn," *Cheguk sinmun*, May 17–June 1, 1907.
58. Yi Injik, *Ch'iak san*; Kim Kyoje, *Ch'iaksan*.
59. Yi Injik, *Ŭnsegye*, 141.
60. Jameson, "Progress versus Utopia," 147–58.

1920s and 1930s tend to highlight the moral superiority of male elite figures.[61] On the contrary, *A Coldhearted Flower* and *Peony Hill* couple their
femmes fatales with abject *yangban* males while casting them both as em-
blems of fin-de-siècle Korea—a hopelessly depraved, colonized community. The ways in which young elite male writers tried to overcome their
abjection and regain their symbolic power is the main topic of chapter 5.

By the mid-1910s, the early colonial domestic novel was no longer
taken seriously by young elite writers, nor did it attract editors and publishers of up-and-coming journals, newspapers, and magazines. Even
though mostly published as "second-grade" sixpenny fiction (*yukchŏn sosŏl*)
afterward, it kept evolving by incorporating the latest cultural and political discourses into its narratives. Before moving to the figures of sensitive young men in chapter 5, I will discuss in chapter 4 how the early
colonial form of the domestic novel was combined with radical feminist
imagination in the early 1920s, when various issues related to women's
sexuality were intensely debated in the print media.

61.   Yi Hyeryŏng, *Han'guk kŭndae sosŏl.*

CHAPTER FOUR

Sapphic Marriage
and Radical Domesticity

Let us take our vows. We shall grow old single and not be slaves
of love. We would rather fulfill our greatest duty, to develop
women's society, which has been left benighted over a thousand
years. If you agree, I will pledge sisterly love [*chamaeae*] with you.

—*Flowers in the Mirror*, 1923

The female protagonists in the early colonial Korean domestic novel
I have examined so far learn to claim their place in the nation and
their individuality while embracing, rather than renouncing, their domestic identities as wives, daughters, daughters-in-laws, and mothers. They
pose questions, though often haltingly rather than coherently, about Confucian gender norms, conjugal practices, superstitious beliefs, and discrimination against women in accessing education. Their iconoclastic
stances notwithstanding, the fact that they still hold their identities as
domestic women often leaves them vulnerable to the criticism that they
are complicit with the gendered project of nationalism—which includes
women to the realm of the nation only to limit their roles to domestic
space and ultimately to subordinate them to their male compatriots. For
this reason, it is commonly assumed that modern Korean fiction had not
placed patriarchy under scrutiny until female writers began relating stories at least partially based on their own experiences and adopted the realist narrative techniques familiar to today's audiences. In the previous
chapters, I have brought to light subtle moments where an alleged hierarchy between women and men becomes ambiguous in the early colonial
domestic novel, in order to suggest that the female figures of these novels
frequently unsettle the gendered project of nationalism rather than neatly
fitting into it. In this chapter, I take this point one step further and

propose that the identities of domestic women were also ripe for inter-pretation by a radically dissident imagination. There is no other work that better attests to this point than Kim Kyoje's 1923 novel, *Flowers in the Mirror* (*Kyŏng chung hua*), in which domestic women's call for rights takes a surprisingly radical form: same-sex marriage.[1]

The epigraph to this chapter is from a scene where one of the female protagonists, Ch'oe Sunjŏng, responds to the proposal made by her ex-husband's second wife, Hong Kŭmsŏn—whose marriage has also ended with a split-up—that they should enter into a lifelong relationship of "sisterly love." Sunjŏng spells out her terms for the "marriage" contract: their sisterly bond must not remain private but contribute to the ad-vancement of women in society by helping other women claim their right to freedom. Each woman has paid a dreadful price for her "old-fashioned" marriage to the same teenage boy, Yi Pŏmch'il. Sunjŏng's marriage was over because she disobeyed her in-laws' demand to drop out of school. Kŭmsŏn suffered from her in-laws' abusive treatment, was wrongfully accused of having an affair with another man, and was abducted by a vi-cious family servant. As is often the case with female characters in early colonial Korean domestic novels, both women experience turns of good fortune. Sunjŏng manages to go to college with the help of the widow of an American missionary, Mrs. Hulbert, after graduating from the school that the missionary founded. After going through a series of life-changing incidents—a false accusation of illicit sex, abduction, a threat of being raped—Kŭmsŏn is rescued by a Japanese international trader, is adopted by him, and becomes an educator and advocate of women's rights for education. It is after completing college degrees abroad and having bright futures ahead of them that the two ex-wives of Yi Pŏmch'il meet for the first time. Since they see no hope in traditional heterosexual marriage, they decide to form an all-female alternative family and dedicate their life to women's education in Korea.

Certainly strong-willed women are not uncommon among early co-lonial domestic novels, including those published by the author of *Flow-ers in the Mirror*, Kim Kyoje. Similar to Ch'oe Sunjŏng, the main female character in Kim's earlier work *A Peony* (*Moktanhwa*, 1911), Yi Chŏngsuk, is cast out of her anti-reformist in-laws' family because she would not give

1.   Kim Kyoje, *Kyŏng chung hwa*, 75–148. As is often the case with many writers of early domestic novels, little is known about the Kim Kyoje's (1883–1955) personal life.

up on going to school. As I examined in chapter 2, *Mt. Ch'iak* volume 2 (1911) portrays a reform-minded *yangban* woman who saves her old-fashioned in-laws from their benighted belief in folk religion. Kim's novel *Microscope* (*Hyŏnmigyŏng*, 1912), a Korean adaptation of *Blood-Soaked Straw Raincoat* (*Xue shou yi*, 1906) (which is the Chinese translation of the Japanese writer Murai Gensai's *Two Beauties* [*Ryōbijin*, 1897]), opens with a young girl beheading a man whom she believes murdered her father.[2] In *Flowers in the Mirror*, however, Kim Kyoje takes his earlier criticism against the place of women in traditional family and society to another level. No matter how fiercely they defy the social and gender norms, none of the female figures in Kim's earlier novels call into question the heterosexual foundation of the family institution itself. To understand what made it possible for Kim Kyoje to give such an incendiary portrayal of same-sex marriage in his last novel, one must consider the changing discourses of gender, sexuality, and feminism between the mid-1910s and the early 1920s.

"Sinyŏja" and Modern Women Writers

The period between the mid-1910s and the early 1920s witnessed the increasing visibility of women writers in the print media. Although women in Chosŏn Korea rarely had the opportunity to gain fluency in the elite language of literary Chinese and were often advised to be modest in their literary ambitions, a number of women wrote in a variety of genres— poetry, essays, conduct books, diaries, letters, funeral orations, recipe books, books on household management, and commentaries on Confucian

---

2. Kang Hyŏnjo suggests that Kim Kyoje's 1913 novel, *A Strange Union of Phoenixes* (*Nanbong kihap*), shows Kim taking a step back from his earlier advocacy of women's rights and egalitarian marriage because it portrays a heroic male figure's marriages with two women. One should remember, however, that this novel is set in King Sejong's reign during the Chosŏn period, whereas Kim's other, more "reformist" novels depict contemporary society. It would be more accurate to say that *A Strange Union of Phoenixes* was written in response to the increasing demand for traditional fiction in the publication market in the early 1910s. As women of the traditional world, the main female characters of the novel are indeed intelligent and independent. Kang Hyŏnjo, "Kim Kyoje pŏnyŏk pŏnan sosŏl," 197–225. See also Yi Chŏngwŏn, "Sinjak kusosŏl nanbong kihap," 195–223.

classics—mostly in the vernacular but also at times in literary Chinese. Not a few women contributed their essays and opinion pieces to modern newspapers and journals, including the all-vernacular daily newspaper *Cheguk sinmun* (*The Imperial Daily*, 1898–1910).[3] The number of pieces written by women was likely greater than the evidence indicates, considering that women were often reluctant to or shy about having their names printed in newspapers and journals.

Between the mid-1910s and the early 1920s, the number of women who wrote for the print market grew visibly, even though many still remained wary of publishing under their own names. Some journals openly invited women to submit their work by setting aside a space for amateur women writers. A Christian-affiliated Korean-language women's magazine that promoted middlebrow family-centered values, *Uri ŭi kajŏng* (*Our Home*, 1913–14), ran a want ad in its second volume that read, "This magazine welcomes writings, paintings, and songs by 'famous ladies and your esteemed female students' [*yumyŏnghasin punin nyŏhaksaeng chessi*]," stressing that each submission had to be accompanied by the writer's accurate address and name.[4] In volume 4, an opinion page for women appeared called "Ladies' Club" (Punin kurakbu). The space allotted to it was rather limited, and contributors to this section used pseudonyms that sound distinctively "domestic"—such as "an awakened lady" (*kaemyŏng puin*), "a lady from Seoul" (*kyŏngsŏng puin*), "a first wife" (*chŏngsil puin*), "a new lady" (*sae puin*), and so on. Nonetheless, these women writers were able to share their everyday experiences, opinions, and views regarding a range of issues: from a husband's drinking problem to women's liberation and education to the wonders of modern obstetrics. Some of them allow us a glimpse at the darker side of women's lives often more vividly than the main body of the magazine suggests.[5]

---

3. Yi Kyŏngha, "Cheguk sinmun yŏsŏng tokch'ugo," 67–98.

4. *Uri ŭi kajŏng* 2 (1913): 52. *Uri ŭi kajŏng* was founded and edited by the influential Japanese publisher Takeuchi Rokunosuke, who also published two other journals targeted at young elite Koreans between 1913 and 1919: *Sinmun'gye* (*New Culture*, 1913–17) and *Pando siron* (*Current Opinions on the Peninsula*, 1917–19).

5. *Uri ŭi kajŏng* 5 (April 1914), 45–48. An entry submitted by a "mother who loves her daughter" (*aenyŏja*), for example, laments on the lack of financial means to send her daughter to school. "An old-school lady" (*wango puin*) complains about her husband for not allowing her to go outside her house.

More overtly critical of gender inequality and the patriarchal institution of the family was *Sinyŏja* (*New Women*, 1920), a woman's magazine modeled after the Japanese literary journal *Seitō*.[6] This journal generally featured the writing of professional women, some of whom had already gained public recognition, such as Na Hyesŏk, a celebrated practitioner of Western-style painting with a college degree from the Private Women's School of Arts (Shiritsu josei bijutsu gakkō) in Tokyo; the educator and writer Pak Indŏk (or Inhuk Pahk, 1896–1980); a registered nurse at Severance Hospital, Chŏng Chongmyŏng (1896–?); the first female doctor and newspaper journalist, Hŏ Yŏngsuk; culinary expert Pang Sinyŏng (1890–1977); and the women's rights activist and chief editor of *Sinyŏja*, Kim Wŏnju (1896–1971).[7] Nevertheless, *Sinyŏja* made it clear that its aim was not merely to serve a small group of elite women but to speak for all women of Korea. At the end of volume 1, the editors invited readers to stop by the journal's office, while adding a note for those who might feel shy around men: "The [staff of the] magazine *Sinyŏja* is made up of all female editors except for the editorial advisor Mr. Yang Uch'on, who comes by infrequently."[8] The magazine did run a few works by male writers, which were marked out by the Chinese character *nam* (male/man) within a bracket.[9] In volume 2, editors urged readers to send "honest and inspiring accounts" concerning "dictatorial in-laws, [the] intransigent old-fashioned family, a lack of respect for women, violation of women's [right to] education, women's career paths."[10]

The publication of *Sinyŏja* as the first feminist journal was both enabled and disabled by the particular political and cultural milieu in the early 1920s. In the aftermath of the March First Movement, a series of

6. Kim Wŏnju, *Reflections of Zen Buddhist Nun*, 4. Also see Ji-Eun Lee, *Women Pre-Scripted*, 82–102. At that time in Japan it was a radical idea to put together a magazine with female contributors. Sarah Frederick observes that "[t]he very claim that *Seitō* would be written entirely by women . . . invited attention." Frederick, *Turning Pages*, 9.

7. Kim Wŏnju often used her pen name, "Ilyŏp," derived from the Chinese character of the first name of the renowned Japanese female writer Higuchi Ichiyō (1872–96).

8. *Sinyŏja* 1 (March 1920): 65.

9. Sŏ Chŏngja conjectures that some of the works published anonymously were probably written by a male writer of children's literature, Pang Chŏnghwan, who was known to help Kim Wŏnju with the running of the magazine. Sŏ Chŏngja, "Ilyŏp Kim Wŏnju," 33–73.

10. *Sinyŏja* 2 (April 1920): 64.

bloody uprisings against colonial rule that started on March 1, 1919, and lasted until the summer of that year, the Japanese governor-general, Saitō Makoto, revised his predecessors' dictatorial policies via "Cultural Rule" (*munhwa chŏngch'i*; Japanese: *bunka seiji*), which, according to Kyung Moon Hwang, "combined a discreet strengthening of bureaucratic and police forces with an outwardly more benign governing approach that encouraged Koreans to pursue social, economic, and political activities more freely."[11] With colonial authorities relaxing publication restrictions to a degree, the early 1920s witnessed the revitalization of vernacular publishing in Korea. Along with *Sinyŏja*, two vernacular newspapers, *Tonga ilbo* (*The Tonga Daily*, 1920–) and *Chosŏn ilbo* (*The Chosŏn Daily*, 1920–); a group of coterie journals—such as *Ch'angjo* (*Creation*, 1919–21), *P'yehŏ* (*Ruins*, 1920–21), *Munu* (*Friends of Literature*, 1920), *Paekjo* (*White Tides*, 1922), and *Changmich'on* (*Rose Village*, 1921); and a list of socialism-affiliated journals such as *Kaebyŏk* (*Opening of the World*, 1920–26), *Tongmyŏng* (*Eastern Light*, 1922–23), *Sinsaenghwal* (*New Life*, 1921–30), and *Light of Chosŏn* (*Chosŏn chi Kwang*, 1922–32) came into being. However, the more open climate did not mean that these periodicals were free from the burden of colonial censorship. Volume 4 of *Sinyŏja* was confiscated from sale and distribution on July 21, 1920 because censors deemed it had an article that could potentially corrupt public morals (*p'ungsok koeran*).[12] No more issues were published afterward, although it remains debatable whether political pressure should be entirely blamed for the magazine's termination.

Translating "A Doll's House" into Korean

Sinyŏja was short-lived, but its impact was not. One of its contributions was to help bring about the publication of a Korean translation of Henrik Ibsen's 1879 play, *A Doll's House* (*Inhyŏng ŭi ka*), which depicts the

11. Kyung Moon Hwang, *History of Korea*, 164. See also, Robinson, *Cultural Nationalism*, 3–8.
12. *Maeil Sinbo*, July 22, 1920. *Tonga Ilbo* reports the same incident as follows: *Sinyŏja* was "[banned] for sales and distribution because there was an article in danger of corrupt public morals." July 22, 1920.

female protagonist Nora's disillusionment with her role in marriage and ends with her departure from her husband's home to find her selfhood. Serialized in *Maeil sinbo* between January 24 and April 2, 1921, the play was initially co-translated by Yang Paekhwa—the pen name of Yang Kŏnsik, the author of the short story "Sad Contradictions" (Sŭlp'ŭn mosun, 1918), to which I turn in chapter 5—and Pak Kyegang. Both were affiliated with *Sinyŏja*. The former had published an essay in the journal's inaugural volume with the title "What kind of woman does a modern man [hyŏndae ŭi namja] want?"[13] The latter had published several translations of English poems, including "A Woman's Question" by the Victorian feminist poet Adelaide Anne Procter (1825–64). Before beginning the serialization, *Maeil sinbo* advertised *A Doll's House* as "the bible of the woman question" (*puin munje ŭi sŏngsŏ*). In a postscript to the first installment, the translators note that the project of translating *A Doll's House* was initiated by the editors of *Sinyŏja*, who had been working on staging this play, a project that ultimately foundered.[14] Three installments of the serialization were accompanied by Western-style illustrations by Na Hyesŏk, notably another frequent contributor to *Sinyŏja*.[15] Na also wrote lyrics to the music score of Kim Yŏnghwan's song "A Doll's House," which *Maeil sinbo* published the day after the completion of the serialization.[16] From April 6 to 9, 1921, an essay about Ibsen's *A Doll's House* was serialized in *Maeil sinbo*.

As is well-known, Ibsen's *A Doll's House* provoked controversy wherever it was circulated. The first Korean translation of the play was not an exception. It was published under a new title, *Nora*, in Yang Paekhwa as the sole translator, and the many commentaries included in the first book edition attest to its controversial nature. Na Hyesŏk's lyrics were

13.   Sŏ Chŏngja suggests that the person referred to as Mr. Yang Uch'on might be Yang Kŏnsik. Sŏ Chŏngja, "Ilyŏp Kim Wŏnju," 33–73.

14.   *Maeil sinbo*, January 25, 1921. The translators also show that they compared three different versions: R. Farquharson Sharp's English translation and two Japanese translations by Shimamura Hogetsu and Takayasu Kekko, respectively.

15.   A couple of weeks later Na held her first solo oil painting exhibition, which was cosponsored by *Maeil sinbo* and its Japanese stablemate *Kyŏngsŏng ilbo* (*The Kyŏngsŏng Daily*).

16.   For a more detailed analysis of the lyrics in *Maeil sinbo*, see Hyaeweol Choi, "Debating the Korean New Woman," 59–77.

revised, added to a new music score by Paek Uyong, and included in the book under the title "Nora." Four more essays were included: a foreword by the playwright Kim Chŏngjin (1886–1936) under his pen name, Unjŏngsaeng; Yi Kwangsu's essay on the woman question; the translator's note by Yang Kŏnsik; and an afterword by the editor of *Sinyŏja*, Kim Wŏnju.[17] Each essay engages with the play in a different way. Kim Chŏngjin's foreword mainly focuses on celebrating the Korean translation of the globally acclaimed play by "the father of modern drama." Written in part from Nora's first-person perspective, Na Hyesŏk's lyrics retell *A Doll's House* as a process of Nora's discovering herself as a human being: "I am a human being/before being a man's wife/before being a mother of children/above all I am a human being."[18] In the last stanza, the poetic voice of Nora encourages girls to follow her path. Similarly, Kim Wŏnju also emphasizes that the play will help awaken not only women but also men, expressing her wish that "a countless number of awakened Nora(s) will pour out in our women's society."[19] Supportive of Nora's decision, the translator Yang Kŏnsik holds the husband Torvald Helmer's empty love responsible for the breakup of the marriage.

The harshest critique of the controversial ending of the play comes from Yi Kwangsu. His essay in part takes the form of a letter addressed to Nora as if responding to the voice of Na Hyesŏk's first-person lyrics. Its title, "Nora-ya," adds to the name of the play's female protagonist the vocative case marker *ya*, which is used to address someone younger or lower in the social hierarchy than the speaker. The assumed hierarchy between addresser and addressee enhances the preachy tone of the essay. In the first two paragraphs addressed to the readers—not to Nora—Yi Kwangsu points to the highlight of *A Doll's House* as being Nora's awakening that "I am a human being [*saram*] as well!" in the same vein as Na Hyesŏk's lyrics.[20] His tone changes, however, when he starts "talking to" Nora. He reproaches her for "taking needles, wooden bowls [*hamjibak*], and babies away from the daughters of the world." Then he offers her his advice:

17. Ibsen, *Nora*, trans. Yang Paekhwa.
18. For an English translation of Na's earlier version of the lyrics, which was published in *Maeil sinbo*, see Kim Yung-Hee, "Creating New Paradigms," 13–14.
19. Ibsen, *Nora*, 178.
20. Ibid., 4.

"Nora-ya, you must also realize 'I am a girl [*kyejip*]!' and, furthermore 'I am a wife' and 'I am a mother.' Only then can you attain your individuality [*kaesŏng*]." His point is that women must stop trying to become like men and should embrace their domestic roles as the essential part of their individuality. Thus, he concludes: "Nora-ya! Cry out to the daughters of Chosŏn, shake them up, and take them out to the open field of the world. After that, return them to the women's quarter. Only turn that quarter into a palace, not a prison of slaves."[21]

In Search of Modern Love

The issue of how to define women's individuality, especially in relation to their domestic identities, was brought up not only in the proxy debates within the space of the translation *Nora* but also in various forms of controversies regarding how to redefine womanhood and modern domesticity. A number of works written by the first generation of modern women writers depict female figures' inner struggles in the process of choosing between pursuing one's path and adhering to traditional domestic identities. For example, the namesake female protagonist in Na Hyesŏk's short story "Kyŏnghŭi" (1918), a young girl attending a high school in Japan, has to make that choice when her father asks her to marry into an affluent family. Her rejection of the marriage proposal enrages her father and leads her to experience an intense soul-searching and self-discovery in a solitary room. In Kim Wŏnju's epistolary fiction "Awakening" (Chagak, 1926), a Nora-like figure named Sunsil writes to her friend to relate how she reached a painful decision to leave her husband and newborn son.[22]

And yet it would be too hasty to conclude that the female characters that decide to go their own way always succeed in living their lives as they choose. What they defy is not so much patriarchy itself as the old-fashioned conception of the family and the traditional marriage system,

21. Ibid., 7.
22. Kim Wŏnju, "Chagak," *Tonga Daily*, June 19–26, 1926; Kim Wŏnju, "Awakening," in *Questioning Minds*, 55–65.

which deprives them of their supposedly inborn right to choose their own partners.[23] In many short stories published in the early 1920s, women's pursuit of autonomy and freedom frequently takes the form of the desire for a modern marriage based on romantic companionship—the desire to become a modern wife. In "The Lost Life of a Young Widow" (Ch'ŏngsang ŭi saenghwal: hŭisaeng toen ilsaeng, 1920), the first-person narrator, an old widow, attests to the detrimental consequences of traditional marriage customs—especially the banning of remarriage by widows—by looking back on how painful it was for her to give up her desire to be with the object of her love—her sister-in-law's brother—owing to the oppressive Korean tradition. Supposing the individual pursuit of romantic love to be the essence of human life, she maintains that "giving up [on love] is mental suicide" (*tannyŏm ŭn chŏngsin chŏk chasal*).[24] Kim Myŏngsun's short story "I Love You" (Na nŭn sarang handa, 1926), centers on a married woman who ends her loveless marriage in order to be with the man she loves while calling her decision "the pursuit of freedom" through the voice of a minor character—the married woman's girlfriend. She firmly holds that "a loveless marriage is prostitution [*maeŭm*]."[25] In the closing scene of "Awakening," Sunsil finds hopes in future romantic love: "Now that I have escaped from a life of cruel slavery, I have the choice to be a full human being, leading a worthy and meaningful life. And I am going to look for a person who will take me as such."[26] Another short story by Kim Wŏnju, "Love" (Sarang, 1926), offers a snapshot of ideal conjugal love.[27] The male protagonist of the story, called by the letter "C," feels jealous when he finds out about his wife's past romantic relationship with his coworker, but after talking with his wife, he realizes that it does not matter as long as it is him that she loves at this moment. He apologizes to her for not trusting her. As if to emphasize that modern marriage is

---

23.   Haiyan Lee makes a similar observation about Chinese literature from the 1920s: "The numerous stories of 'free love' produced in the 1920s are often less about freedom of love or marriage per se, and much less about libertarian sexual practice, than about the severance of ties with family, tradition, and locality." Lee, *Revolution of the Heart*, 96.

24.   Kim Wŏnju, "Hŭisaeng toen ilsaeng," 12–35.

25.   T'an Sil (Kim Myŏngsun's pen name), "Na nŭn sarang handa."

26.   Kim Wŏnju, "Chagak," *Tonga ilbo*, June 26, 1926.

27.   Kim Wŏnju, "Sarang," 84–86.

based not only on solid companionship but also undying physical attraction, the story ends when "their burning lips were pressed together for a long time."

The assumption that women in these stories exercise their autonomy through romantic love and conjugal marriage based on companionship is, however, a precarious modern construct. The "free" choice of one's romantic partner often places these women in a vulnerable position. In short stories such as "The Death of Sunae" (Sunae ǔi chugǔm, 1926), "Sacrifice" (Hǔisaeng, 1929), and "To Mr. X" (X ssi ege, 1929), Kim Wǒnju shows the darker side of romantic love in portraying women whose relationships with men do not lead to conjugal unions.[28] The female protagonist of "The Death of Sunae" kills herself after being raped by a married man with whom she is in love. In "Sacrifice," the boyfriend of the main character, Yǒngsuk, refuses to marry her after she becomes pregnant with his baby. The first-person narrator, "I" (*na* in Korean), in "To Mr. X" is unable to stop loving a man who has no intention of marrying her.

Furthermore, the pursuit of romantic love can be an inadvertent step toward being subordinated within the modern patriarchy rather than helping women to claim their autonomy. According to Gayle Rubin, "[k]inship and marriage are always parts of total social systems, and are always tied to economic and political arrangements."[29] In a similar vein, Ueno Chizuko views the "romantic love revolution" in terms of the changing face of patriarchal power: "In order for a daughter under patriarchy to escape her 'father's control,' she needs a huge centrifugal force. Romantic love can be a source of passion that gives her the destructive energy she needs to escape her father's control, but it also results in her losing her 'father's protection.' . . . Modern patriarchy is full of plots to cut women off from their parents in order to enable their husbands to control them in their nuclear families."[30] According to Ueno, modern love was never free from the constraint of social class. Romantic love is a social device to help men and women internalize the new norm of marriage wherein they can "freely" choose their partner on the unspoken basis of class

---

28. Kim Wǒnju, "Sunae ǔi chugǔm," "Hǔisaeng," and "X ssi ege," 59–63.
29. Rubin, *Gayle Rubin Reader*, 63.
30. Chizuko Ueno, *Modern Family in Japan*, 74–79.

endogamy. She points out that "love . . . results in even stronger class endogamy than an arranged marriage."[31]

Radical Domesticity

In a context where women's interiority is often bound to romanticized notions of modern marriage and conjugal love, as in so many of the literary works written by the first generation of modern Korean women writers in the early 1920s, Kim Kyoje's domestic novel *Flowers in the Mirror* appears surprisingly radical.[32] The female characters "escape" from their old-fashioned families and marriage system, but, instead of internalizing the ideology of romantic love, they create an all-female domestic space together. Their lack of interiority distinguishes them from the female protagonists in the first generation of modern women writers' short stories.

Outspoken and openly rebellious against the old-fashioned marriage system, Ch'oe Sunjŏng in *Flowers in the Mirror*, might seem to resemble those protagonists. Unlike them, however, Ch'oe Sunjŏng neither deliberates upon her own motives nor looks back on her decision the way that Kyŏnghŭi does in Na Hyesŏk's "Kyŏnghŭi." Her defiant character comes to the surface through her actions and speech as well as by her choices in regard to her appearance.

The opening scene in the novel sheds light on Sunjŏng's recalcitrant nature through her hairstyle. The narrator introduces her as a "fifteen- or sixteen-year-old" schoolgirl with a "Western-style hairdo" (*yangje mŏri*), and as a "beauty" (*miin*) with a "perfect height and a delicate air." The narrator implicitly shows off his familiarity with the latest styles by pointing out a flaw in her hairdo: "If she were to have a Western-style hairdo, she should have had her hair puffed out in front instead of sweeping her hair back from the face."[33] Sunjŏng's fellow students (*tongmu haksaeng*) criticize her for having her hair styled in a way inappropriate for a schoolgirl. Sunjŏng simply turns a deaf ear to them. The narrator also recalls

31. Ibid., 79.
32. Kang Hyŏnjo aptly calls *Flowers in the Mirror* a parody of *sinsosŏl*. Kang, "Kim Kyoje pŏnyŏk pŏnan sosŏl," 218.
33. Kim Kyoje, *Kyŏng chung hwa*, 1.

what her teachers said early that day: "Schoolgirls must dress modestly by all means" and "Women dress up only to please men's eyes. Now that women have a considerable status in human society, why would they put up with being treated like the plaything of men?"[34]

This scene seems oddly disconnected from the rest of the story, as nowhere else is much attention given to women's hairstyles. Even though the teacher treats Sunjŏng like a delinquent only interested in getting men's attention, she is soon shown to be a serious student who relentlessly defends her right to a decent education against the objections of her mother and her in-laws. It is left unknown why Sunjŏng decided to wear her hair that way or how she feels about the criticisms of her classmates and teacher. The narrator never again sounds like a dandy with a delicate sense of the latest style. However, this scene might have made more intuitive sense to newspaper readers of the early 1920s, when women's hairdos and fashion were important topics for public discussion and debates.[35] Kim Wŏnju and Na Hyesŏk had virtual debates over the issue of the reform of women's clothing in the pages of *Tonga ilbo* in late September and early October of 1921.[36] Around six months prior to the publication of *Flowers in the Mirror*, a famous former *kisaeng* (female entertainer)-turned-schoolgirl, Kang Hyangnan, provoked public controversy by getting a short haircut at a Chinese-run barbershop and wearing a man's suit. On June 22, 1922, the gossip column of *Maeil sinbo*, "Telescope" (Malli kyŏng), delivered a harsh attack against her: "No matter how badly she wants to be a man, it won't be possible because of her physiological makeup. I suspect that she might have a mental problem."[37] An up-and-coming male writer, Yŏm Sangsŏp, describes her behavior as a thoughtless "self-display" that has nothing to do with women's liberation. He also points out that "Ibsen did not portray the icon of women's liberation Nora with short hair and wearing a man's suit."[38] Although Ch'oe Sunjŏng's hair is not scandalously short, but is done in a moderate and socially tolerated Western

34. Ibid., 1–2.
35. As for the shifting codes of style and fashion at the turn of the twentieth century, see Susie Ji Young Kim, "What (Not) to Wear."
36. Kim Wŏnju, "Puin ŭi pokchi kaeryang"; Na Hyesŏk, "Puin ŭibok kaeryang munje."
37. *Maeil sinbo*, June 22, 1922.
38. Yŏm, "Yŏja tanbal munje."

style for women, the teacher's lecturing of Sunjŏng about her hairdo resonates with Yŏm Sangsŏp's criticism of Kang Hyangnan. In other words, this scene seems to draw a parallel between Sunjŏng and the iconic women in the contemporary print media who transgressed a cultural boundary by wearing bold hairdos.

The discrepancy between the opening scene and the rest of the story seems less glaring if we take into account that Sunjŏng consistently appears as a transgressive figure. In the next scene she challenges the authority of her parents-in-law, especially their demand that she should quit school. It is not the first time she has caused a family dispute. The narrator recalls that earlier her widowed mother tried to stop her from going to school and had married her off to a conservative family. It was a traditional marriage with a fourteen-year-old boy, which was illegal under the modern legal system.[39] Therefore, their marriage has not been documented. Upon realizing that there is no way to keep Sunjŏng from going to school, the parents-in-law break up the marriage. Unlike Nora in Ibsen's play, Sunjŏng does not walk away from marriage of her own accord; rather she is forcefully expelled by the authority of her in-laws. However, she seems no less strong-willed than Nora, given how much authority parents-in-law had over their daughters-in-law in traditional Korean households.

Unlike Sunjŏng, Kŭmsŏn, the second wife of this boy, Yi Pŏmch'il, at first appears to be an old-fashioned passive woman. Whereas the narrative of Sunjŏng is mixed with gossip and debates about iconoclastic female figures in the early 1920s, Kŭmsŏn's story consists of a series of traditional motifs that frequently appear in early colonial domestic novels: abuse by a mother-in-law, the false accusation of an illicit relationship, abandonment, abduction, and an escape from rape. Kŭmsŏn's life begins turning around when she is adopted into a supposedly civilized Japanese family. One may argue that *Flowers in the Mirror* is a parody of Yi Injik's 1906 early colonial domestic novel *Tears of Blood*, the work that I focus on in chapter 1. Just as Ongnyŏn, the female protagonist in *Tears of Blood*, is

---

39. The Japanese general-government of Korea did not issue a license for marriage with parental consent unless the couple had reached the legal minimum age, seventeen for men and fifteen for women, beginning in 1915. See Yi Sŭngil, *Chosŏn ch'ŏngdokpu pŏpche.*

rescued by a childless army surgeon, Major Inoue, who brings her up in his home in Ōsaka as his adopted daughter, so is Kŭmsŏn rescued, by a childless Japanese international trader, Satō Sueji (whose name appears in the Korean reading of the kanji as Chwadŭng Malch'i), after throwing herself into the sea near a port city, Inch'ŏn, to escape from one of her abductors' attempt at rape. Satō adopts her and helps her go to school in Japan. The Japanese education turns Kŭmsŏn from a submissive wife to a strong-willed advocate of women's rights and an ardent opponent of patriarchy in a way similar to Ongnyŏn's change from a typical P'yŏngyang girl into the future wife of a reform-minded Korean man and a future leader of women in society, thanks to her education in Japan and the United States. While going through a series of life-changing incidents, neither Kŭmsŏn nor Sunjŏng contemplate the past; show fear, anxiety, or hesitation about the future; or delve into the question of "who I am" in a solitary setting. On the contrary, this question comes up in its most articulate form when they are making a pledge of lifelong sisterly love. It is Kŭmsŏn who calls their first meeting. After graduation, Sunjŏng is to give a series of lectures in Tokyo about women's education in the United States. From Sunjŏng's biography, which is published in a Japanese newspaper, Kŭmsŏn learns that Sunjŏng was once married to her ex-husband. At their meeting, Kŭmsŏn shares the story of her past with Sunjŏng and proposes to her: "Shall we pledge sisterly love and live together for the rest of our lives?" In the exchange that follows Kŭmsŏn's suggestion—a part of which I cited at the beginning of this chapter—the two women spell out what it means to form a lifelong partnership with each other:

SUNJŎNG: Now that we have a good amount of education, it is our important duty to claim women's rights to freedom. It is impossible to think of [going back to] the Yi family long after the breakup or to surrender our bodies to another family to be subjugated to a man. Let us take our vows. We shall grow old single and not be slaves of love. We would rather fulfill our greatest duty, to develop women's society, which has been left benighted over a thousand years. If you agree, I will pledge sisterly love with you. If we are not in agreement, I am sorry to say this, but I cannot accept your proposal.

KŬMSŎN: Even if you hadn't said so, I have been feeling the same way from the bottom of my heart. If you do not believe me, why don't we take a blood oath? I've accepted that marriage is for women the same as going to hell. I have sworn that I would rather die than marry again. I have made up my mind. Let's live together and die together. Let's share our glory and shame as well as our comfort and concerns with each other. As you said before, let us fulfill our duty to women's society.[40]

They vow to create a new space free of male dominance and to maintain it for the rest of their lives. This home is neither a "private" realm built upon male authority sanctioned by the state nor a space "closeted" from the public. Founded on the firm sense of the social duty of awakening more women to their right to freedom, it shows the possibility of forming an alternative home outside the norm of a male-centered heterosexual household.

Sunjŏng and Kŭmsŏn define the foundation of their relationship as *chamaeae*, "sisterly love" or "sisterhood." *Chamaeae* refers to relationships between sisters, or "homosocial bonding" among women, rather than to female same-sex love (*tongsŏngae*). The rest of the novel does not show clearly that their relationship might develop into an overtly erotic one with infatuation or obsessive passion. Nonetheless, I call their union "sapphic marriage," for several reasons. First of all, the scene of the two women's dialogue closely resembles the climactic scene from *Tears of Blood*, where Ku Wansŏ proposes to Ongnyŏn:

Mr. Ku asked one thing, that he and Ongnyŏn should continue studying hard for several more years until they had all the education they wanted, at which point they would return home and get married. Then Ongnyŏn could take upon herself the education of Korean women. When he showed his ambition, and when she heard what he proposed, she firmly made up her mind to educate Korean women, and agreed to marry Mr. Ku. . . . Ongnyŏn wanted to study hard and, after returning home, to broaden the knowledge of Korean women and help them to get *equal rights* with men, instead of being oppressed by men, and then to educate them so that women too would become useful people in the land and honored persons in society.[41]

40. Kim Kyoje, *Kyŏng chung hwa*, 34.
41. Yi Injik, "Tears of Blood," 213–14; Yi Injik, "Hyŏl ŭi nu," *Mansebo*, October 4, 1906 (emphasis added).

As I claim in chapter 1, this scene represents a break with traditional conjugal norms. As a strict family matter, marriage had traditionally been
presided over by the male heads of the two families, which were of the
same social status, regardless of the feelings or opinions of the future bride
and groom. An American-educated reform-minded young Korean man,
Ku Wansŏ, claims his right to choose his partner in the face of the traditional male patriarchy by proposing directly to Ongnyŏn when her father
is sitting right next to them. He does so to relocate individuality onto
the realm of the nation. Ku Wansŏ's terms of the marriage are that the
two of them should dedicate their lives to building a nation comprised
of citizens with equal rights.

The similarities between the two scenes are striking, most importantly in the sense that the private and the public remain inseparable in
both unions. Just as Ku Wansŏ brings Ongnyŏn to nation-building efforts with his marriage proposal, so Sunjŏng asks Kŭmsŏn to join her in
the women's movement before agreeing to pledge lifelong sisterhood with
her. Their union should be founded upon the cause of women's liberation, Sunjŏng insists. She won't commit to the relationship unless Kŭmsŏn
concurs. In response to Sunjŏng, Kŭmson swears never to marry again,
but ironically what she utters afterward sounds like a "wedding vow," a
very strong one: they will not only live together while sharing all that is
to come, they will die together. As if they were a newly wedded couple,
they move into a house that Kŭmsŏn's wealthy adoptive father, Satō Sueji,
has bought for them. They create a new home together while working as
teachers in a Christian girls' school. If Ku Wansŏ's marriage proposal
signals the introduction of egalitarian marriage cutting across the class-
based family hierarchy, the avowal of lifelong sisterly love between Sunjŏng
and Kŭmsŏn introduces a more radical form of gender equality.

As scholars of gender and queer studies such as Eve Kosofsky Sedgwick attest, the boundary between homosocial desire and homoerotic
desire often remains obscure when it comes to female intimacies.[42] The
term sapphism, which Susan Lanser uses to "encompass female same-sex
desires, behaviors, propensities, affinities," offers a useful conceptual tool
to explain the ambiguity of the relationship between Sunjŏng and

---

42. Sedgwick, *Between Men*.

Kŭmsŏn.[43] One may be tempted to write off the possibility that their relationship is ever "consummated" and to call it instead a "nonsexual cohabitation." And yet I must emphasize that a number of early colonial Korean domestic novels describe heterosexual marriages without obvious eroticism: the reformist discourse criticized traditional marriage for exposing young people to excessive sexual desire and, therefore, depriving them of the chance to become patriotic citizens. The ideal conjugal bonds, according to this line of thinking, should be civil unions furthering the advancement of the nation. That is to say, the absence of explicitly erotic content symbolically indicates the high civility of the relationship. To that extent, it would be more accurate to say that the marriage between Sunjŏng and Kŭmsŏn is no less sexual than the six-year-long relationship between Ku Wansŏ and Ongnyŏn.

Sapphism in Korean Fiction

The bond between Sunjŏng and Kŭmsŏn is not the first sapphic representation in Korean literature. In what has long been considered the first modern Korean novel, Yi Kwangsu's *The Heartless* (1917), one of the most explicit sexual encounters takes place between Yŏngch'ae and Wŏrhwa, two female entertainers who see each other as friends (*pŏt*) or siblings (*tonggi*):

> Yŏngch'ae had also begun to feel a longing for *the male sex*. Her face grew hot when she faced a strange man, and when she lay down alone at night, she wished that there was someone who would hold her. Once, when Yŏngch'ae and Wŏrhwa came back from a party late at night and had gone to bed together in the same bed, Yŏngch'ae put her arms around Wŏrhwa in her sleep, and kissed her on the mouth. . . . Yŏngch'ae buried her face in Wŏrhwa's breasts, and though ashamed, she bit her white breasts.[44]

Yŏngch'ae and Wŏrhwa experience this female homoerotic encounter as nothing but a way to relieve the former's desire for men by proxy. Neither

43. Lanser, "Sapphic Picaresque," 252.
44. Yi, *Yi Kwang-Su*, 148; and *Parojabŭn Mujŏng*, 213 (emphasis added).

of them raises any doubt about the heterosexuality of their desire. Yŏngch'ae constantly dreams of heterosexual love with the male protagonist, Hyŏngsik, regardless of her physical and emotional intimacies with Wŏrhwa. Similarly, Wŏrhwa looks for the man of her dreams—someone awakened to lofty ideals—and kills herself when she realizes that her love cannot be fulfilled. Later, Yŏngch'ae remembers Wŏrhwa as her sister (*hyŏngnim*) and friend.

Friendship between women takes on a more openly subversive tone in an earlier example of sapphic marriage, a nineteenth-century vernacular novel by an anonymous writer, *The Tale of Pang Hallim* (*Pang Hallim chŏn*).[45] The story is set not in Korea but in China, during the time of the Ming dynasty (1368–1644), as is often the case with premodern Korean fiction. The protagonist Pang Kwanju is biologically female: she was born as the only daughter of an aged couple. Yet everything else about her indicates that she is a natural-born male hero. Her birth was greeted by "splendid light" and "mysterious scents." There is no trace of femininity in her physical appearance once she turns three. Without any qualms, her parents raise her as a boy, keeping her biological sex hidden even from their relatives and servants. No one other than her parents and wet nurse knows about her secret. Her exceptional talents please her parents immensely. At a young age, she masters the Confucian classics and attains a superb level of skill in poetry writing. After losing both parents at the age of eight, she runs her household as a male head. She passes the civil service examination at twelve and is assigned to the position of *hallim*, a royal archivist.

Kwanju's first encounter with her later "wife," Yŏng Hyebing, is a typical love-at-first-sight story. The meeting is arranged by Hyebing's father, Prime Minister Yŏng. He invites Kwanju to his house to propose that she marry his youngest daughter. Since Kwanju has no parents to interview a potential bride on her behalf, the minister lets her take a look at his daughter: "She appeared incredibly elegant. There was nothing unnatural about her looks or her manners, but as soon as he looked at her, the *hallim*'s

45. See Chang Sigwang, *Chosŏn sidae tongsŏng hon*; *Pang Hanim chŏn*, for an unpublished handwritten manuscript. There are two more versions of the story: *Naksŏng chŏn* (The Tale of the Fallen Star) and *Sangwan kibong* (A Strange Union of Two Beauties). C.f. Cho, *Kojŏn sosŏl ibon mongnok*. For a short comparison between *Flowers in the Mirror* and *The Tale of Pang Hallim*, see Kwŏn Podŭrae, *Sinsosŏl, ŏnŏ chŏngch'i*, 65–67.

gemlike face was wreathed in warm smile. With awe, affection, and admiration, she said in her mind 'I won't be able to find a woman like her anywhere else in the world.' "[46]

The attraction is mutual. Yŏng Hyebing describes Kwanju as "beautiful" (*yŏnyŏn*) and "sparkling" (*soerak*) like "dewy flowers." With her exceptional insight, Hyebing almost immediately penetrates Kwanju's secret: "Such a delicate and quiet voice cannot be a man's." It is probably because she has always wished to spend her life with a heroic woman as her close friend. She has been critical of the unequal social system: "Women are prisoners. She has power over nothing. If you are not a boy, you would do better to live outside human norms [*illyun*]." It is painful for her to imagine herself "pencil[ing] her eyebrows to fawn over a man as his beloved wife." On the second night after the wedding, Kwanju "comes out" to Hyebing, mostly because the latter urges her to do so. The shared secret between the two makes their bond stronger.

An alternative way of living requires a new vocabulary. Kwanju and Hyebing try to figure out a word to define their relationship. If they are not husband and wife, what are they? Kwanju suggests they should call themselves *hyŏngje* (siblings, brothers or sisters) to avoid confusion. Hyebing objects to that idea for the reason that it would invite suspicion from her parents: "We will just follow the protocol of husband and wife" (*pubu ŭi ye rŭl ch'alhil taŭm ira*), she says.[47] Their relationship slips between nonsexual friendship and sexual conjugal love. As Kwanju's wife, Hyebing holds a memorial service for Kwanju's ancestors, while Kwanju serves the king as his loyal servant. Later they even become the parents of a baby boy, Naksŏng (literally, "Fallen Star"), who is given to Kwanju by heaven in the form of the incarnation of a mysterious fallen star. On the other hand, they often define their relationship as *chiŭm* (知音), *chigi* (知己) ("soul mates," "best friends"), *p'yŏngsaeng chigi* (平生知己) ("friends forever"), or *saseng chigi* (死生知己) ("friends who ride together and die together").[48] Oftentimes they playfully call each other by their respective *cha*-names, given after an initiation ceremony, usually considered too

46. Sigwang, *Chosŏn sidae tongsŏng hon*, 121, 122.
47. Ibid., 136.
48. The original manuscript is entirely written in the vernacular Korean. The Chinese characters are added by Chang Sigwang in the annotated modern edition for clarification. Chang Sigwang, *Chosŏn sidae tongsŏng hon*, 117, 125, 127, 144, 148, and 149.

casual to be used between husband and wife—as if they were innocent childhood friends.[49] Like other elite-class couples in premodern love stories, they exchange love poems when Kwanju has to be away from home for an extended period of time. In these poems, they always refer to each other as *chiüm*, *chigi*, and *chigi pungu*, turning these words into homoerotic code words.[50]

Not surprisingly, Kwanju's "closeted" life is filled with self-conflicts. She constantly struggles with shame and guilt: she has never learned how to live as a woman, but to live her life the only way she knows how, she cannot help but deceive others, even the king, to whom she has devoted her life. She feels conflicted even more after she marries Hyebing, because she believes that, without Kwanju, Hyebing would have lived a life according to "the human norms." But she fights back when her wet nurse—the only person who knows her secret other than her deceased parents and Hyebing—calls their marriage "queer behavior" (*kohihan kōjo*) and urges Kwanju and Hyebing to find men and to live normal lives.[51]

The ending clearly tries to contain the subversive force of the story by restoring the authority of human norms. One should remember that, in her public life, Pang Kwanju faithfully adheres to the Confucian principle of loyalty to the emperor: she brings prosperity and peace to a chaotic province and suppresses an uprising of barbarians. Her family prospers, thanks to her wisdom and benevolence: her son marries a young lady from a noble family, passes the civil service examination, and rises to a top position at the tender age of seventeen. However, Kwanju's fortune is too good to last for a long time. When she is thirty-nine years old, she is visited by a Taoist master who foretells that she will die before reaching forty years old as punishment for her transgressive behavior against the human norm. Prior to her death, she reveals her secret to the emperor and to Hyebing's parents in tears, asking for their forgiveness. Hyebing dies on the same day. As it later turns out, their births were punishment for what they had done in their previous lives. On the first anniversary of their

---

49. Ibid., 167. Hyebing calls Kwanju Munbaek hyŏng (*hyŏng* is a term commonly used by a man to refer to his biological older brother, or a male friend or colleague who is somewhat but not much older than him), and Kwanju calls Hyebing by her *cha*-name, Myoju.

50. Ibid., 148–49.

51. Ibid., 123.

death, they appear to their dutiful son Naksŏng in a dream and tell him their story: they were celestial beings called Mungok and Sanga. As a married couple, they loved each other too much, to the degree that they neglected their duties and spent all their time with each other. As punishment, the husband, Mungok, was reborn as a daughter in the Pang family, the wife, Sanga, as a daughter in the Yŏng family. Thus, Mungok and Sanga's heterosexual love story not only replaces Kwanju and Hyebing's story of sapphic marriage but also restores the authority of the Confucian principle undermined by the latter. The same-sex love between Kwanju and Hyebing is a temporal deviation from the normative form of love. Hyebing's harsh criticism of the patriarchy turns out to be a means to reunite with her destined husband, who was reborn as a woman.

If Kwanju and Hyebing constantly battle with guilt and shame about their closeted relationship under the unassailable authority of the Confucian patriarchy in *The Tale of Pang Hallim*, Sunjŏng and Kŭmsŏn do not show much remorse about creating an all-female alternative family in *Flowers in the Mirror*. Although Sunjŏng occupies a slightly higher position than Kŭmsŏn at work, there exists no performative gender division between them. Neither wears male attire or assumes the "male" role in the relationship. Nonetheless, it would be too quick to assume that the sapphic marriage of Sunjŏng and Kŭmsŏn is immune to patriarchal attempts at containment. One can argue that they may seem to have autonomy because the old-fashioned patriarchy they contest is already on the verge of extinction. Ch'oe Sunjŏng's father dies before her first marriage. Under the old-fashioned rule of Pŏmch'il's father, Yi Chinsa, the Yi family remains completely unprepared for the modern world, which runs on the basis of the modern civil codes and capitalist economy. The Yi family goes down, symbolically, because of a lawsuit. When Kŭmsŏn goes missing, her father presses charges against Yi Chinsa for the alleged death of his daughter. After losing most of his property to compensate Kŭmsŏn's father for his losses, Yi Chinsa sets out on a lonesome life of wandering. His family is left in poverty.

The sapphic marriage of Sunjŏng and Kŭmsŏn becomes more vulnerable to the power of patriarchy once their mutual ex-husband, Pŏmch'il, becomes an eligible modern bachelor and the capable head of a modern family. The story quickly moves toward one of the typical endings of early colonial Korean domestic novels: a happy reunion of scattered family members. Pŏmch'il's transformation from a spoiled child of a *yangban* family to a wealthy lawyer shows what is necessary to succeed in capitalist society: labor, education, and a money-lending business. In the beginning, Pŏmch'il seeks help from a former beneficiary of his father, but realizes that, in a modern society, benevolence and mutual aid are no longer reliable means for survival. With no one to rely on but himself, he decides to turn his life around: he works as a day laborer and attends night school while making extra money by loan sharking on the side. It takes only three years for him to become ready to go to law school, both financially and in terms of academic qualifications.

One may argue that the family reunion has already begun in a furtive way toward the midpoint of the novel when the two women save Pŏmch'il's vicious mother, Madam Han, and his little sister, Kapsun, from living hand-to-mouth without a home. Against the odds they do so, not realizing they are their ex-in-laws. The narrator also admits this needs an explanation: "Since Sunjŏng was thrown out of her in-laws' house only three days after the wedding, it would be plausible to say that she forgot her mother-in-law's face. One might ask why Kŭmsŏn could not recognize her after living in her in-laws' house nearly for a year, no matter how many years have passed since then."[52] The hardships Madam Han has gone through have changed her appearance completely so that "her husband, Yi Chinsa, would not be able to recognize her," so the narrator adds. Madam Han fails to recognize Kŭmsŏn because of her Western hairdo as well as her much "livelier and healthier looks" than before. For the following seven years, while Madam Han is working for Sunjŏng and Kŭmsŏn as their live-in maid, she keeps her past a secret: she is too embarrassed to let other people see a *yangban* woman like her making a living as a domestic worker. Sunjŏng and Kŭmsŏn find no reason to share the minute details of their peculiar histories with their live-in maid. In retrospect, we can say that the mutual misrecognition helps Madam Han and her young daughter live through the uncertain time of the transition from the demise of the premodern patriarchy to the rise of its modern counterpart under the protection of the former members of their family.

52. Kim Kyoje, *Kyŏng chung hwa*, 48.

Not surprisingly, the traditional hierarchy between daughters-in-law and mother-in-law is no longer valid in the domestic space created by the sapphic marriage. Sunjŏng and Kŭmson treat Madame Han well not because they were her daughters-in-law but because they feel sympathy for her. By sharing the space with Sunjŏng and Kŭmsŏn, the old-fashioned women of the Yi family not only come to open their eyes to the value of women's education but also learn a couple of basic rules about living in the capitalist economy. Sunjŏng and Kŭmsŏn persuade Madame Han to send Kapsun to school. They compensate Madame Han for her domestic labor with a monthly salary—a type of recompense rarely given to domestic workers at the time. Madame Han increases her savings through the modern banking system.

The alternative all-female family does face the threat of dissolution when Pŏmch'il is reunited with his family, first with his mother and sister and then with his father. The father still adheres to the traditional way as before, but he can no longer exert influence over the rest of the family now that it has a new male head capable of keeping it thriving in capitalist society. As an eligible bachelor, Pŏmch'il wants to marry Sunjŏng or Kŭmsŏn, but neither of them is interested in remarrying him. Pŏmch'il declares that he would rather spend the rest of his life as a "celibatarian" (*much'ŏjuŭi*) unless he can marry one of them.[53] As he is the sole male heir of the Yi family, his celibacy would endanger the continuation of the family line. Thus, the two families—Pŏmch'il's patrilineal family and the alternative family of Sunjŏng and Kŭmsŏn—are put in a relationship of rivalry. One must perish in order for the other to survive. The story ends without showing the result of the competition between the two families. The narrator, who has been recounting the story from an omniscient point of view, suddenly starts playing the innocent, saying that he heard this story by word of mouth.

This ambiguous ending distinguishes *Flowers in the Mirror* from the short stories written by the first generation of new women writers in the early 1920s as well as from the subversive sapphic representations in Yi Kwangsu's *The Heartless* and *The Tale of Pang Hallim*. Unlike the others, *Flowers in the Mirror* portrays a female same-sex couple that refuses to succumb to the normality of family and marriage, to either Confucian

53. Ibid., 70.

norm or its modern equivalent. Female same-sex desire appears as a temporary aberration of heterosexuality in *The Heartless,* as does sapphic marriage in *The Tale of Pang Hallim.* The figures of educated young women portrayed by Na Hyesŏk and Kim Wŏnju criticize the old-fashioned patriarchal family but implicitly endorse the new form of patriarchy by romanticizing modern conjugal marriage.

Then what makes Sunjŏng and Kŭmsŏn resist the lure of a modern self-made man? I would like to suggest that it has to do with the fact that the selfhoods of the two women remain inseparable from their domestic and public identities. The main characters of this work—the two women and their ex-husband—become individuals as each struggles to exercise her or his right to pursue education, wealth, and happiness. However, their individuality is unfolded in a way that redraws gender differences. Whereas Pŏmch'il follows the typical path of a self-made man, Sunjŏng and Kŭmsŏn become "modern" by forming family(-like) ties, first with Mrs. Hulbert and Satō Sueji, respectively, and then with each other, and more importantly by creating an alternative domestic space that lives up to the ideal of equality and solidarity. To accept Pŏmch'il's marriage proposal, they would first have to cancel out the very act through which they have become modern individuals—their pledge of life-long sisterly love and of a devotion to women's society. *Flowers in the Mirror* thus casts a radical light on the figures of domestic women by reclaiming home as a site enabling women's autonomy, solidarity, and same-sex desire (*chamaeae*), instead of seeing it as the arena of traditional patriarchal oppression or as a romanticized pathway to modern patriarchy. In doing so, it urges us to call into question the canonical assumption that self-regulating interiority should be the only precondition of modern individuality and, furthermore, to explore alternative, interpersonal forms of individuality.

CHAPTER FIVE

Sensitive Young Men
and the Private Desire for Progress

In the opening scene of Hyŏn Sangyun's short story "Persecution" (P'ippak, 1917), a first-person narrator complains about his illness.

> As of late, I have become ill perhaps. But no cause exists for the illness. Fresh air blows unhindered, bright sunlight shines unobstructed, birds chirp, flowers smile, the spring runs clear, and the mountains are beautiful— hence not a single cause for an illness. . . . Nonetheless, an illness it is. Food has lost its sweetness, and sleep is no longer restful. My face has become pale and my body angular. My blood feels thin and my muscles are tense—even when I am with good friends, no laughter flows from me, and when others give me praise, I feel no joy. . . . But exactly what illness this is, I myself have no way of knowing. What torture me are the darting looks coming from this way and that. The looks seem to say, "Hey you lowlife, get yourself together!"

At first the narrator does not even seem certain that he is sick. Although he comes to attribute his pains to the gaze of other people, nothing is clear-cut in the story, which is written from a mentally unstable man's point of view. Thus readers are confronted by the challenge of parsing a work the diegesis of which is in the hands of an unreliable narrator.

This first-person narrator is one example of what I call "sensitive young men," the young male characters that populated a number of short stories in the Korean literature of the mid-1910s, such as Chu Yohan's "Village Home" (Maŭljip, 1917); Yang Kŏnsik's "Sad Contradictions" (Sŭlp'ŭn mosun, 1918); Chin Hangmun's "Cry" (Purŭjijim, 1917); and Yi Kwangsu's "A Boy's Sorrow" (Sonyŏn ŭi piae, 1917), "Wandering" (Panghwang, 1918), and "Yun Kwangho" (1918), to name a few. Typically marked by negative emotions—including distress, sadness, fear, despair, and guilt—the figures of sensitive young men try to come to grips with their physical and mental illnesses, self-abasement, unrequited love, crushing poverty, a lover's death or betrayal, and other inexplicable agonies. Due to their extended depiction of inner thoughts, these short stories about sensitive young men are, along with Yi Kwangsu's novel *The Heartless*, often taken as the first works in Korean literature to portray the modern individual.[1] The canonical narrative supposes that, by describing men who explore their interiority, these short stories made a clear break from the early colonial domestic novel as well as from premodern literary legacies.

I aim in this chapter to offer an alternative narrative by underscoring that the figures of sensitive young men are early colonial translations of the individual, which are, not unlike those of domestic women, rooted in the aspirations for the nation's progress as well as in the power of colonialism. To render the proximity between domestic women and sensitive young men visible, I focus first on Chang Ŭngjin's "Confession under the Moon" (Wŏrha ŭi chabaekm, 1907), a short story that appeared while the early colonial domestic novel was still flourishing—notably, a decade prior to the publication of the two short stories of sensitive young men that I analyze in the latter part of this chapter: Hyŏn Sangyun's "Persecution" and Yang Kŏnsik's "Sad Contradictions." "Confession under the Moon" recounts an old *yangban* man's solitary and emotional last moments before he commits suicide. While written in the form of a confession, which Karatani Kojin points to as one of the cultural forces behind the discovery of interiority in modern Japanese literature, it does not portray a private man detached from society.[2] On the contrary, the old man's confession of his past sins works as a testimony to the demise of old Korea—akin to the accounts of domestic women, which act as narratives of both their own families and of the nation. "Persecution" and "Sad Contradictions"

---

1. Pak Sukcha, *Han'guk munhak kwa kaeinsŏng.* See also Shin, "Interior Landscapes," 248–87.
2. Karatani, *Origins of Modern Japanese Literature,* 77.

may seem at first to portray figures cut off from the outside world, especially given that both stories revolve around solitary first-person narrators. My reading of these two stories, however, emphasizes that these male figures' psychological struggles are not so much driven by their resolve to find their own unique paths or by their estrangement from society as by their desire to further the progress of the nation as well as by their internalization of colonial surveillance.[3] It is not my intention to show that sensitive young men do or do not meet some narrow definition of what constitutes the modern individual, but to show how, in James Clifford's words, "the individual is culturally constituted" in early colonial Korean literature.[4]

Public Confession and Individuality: Chang Ŭngjin's "Confession under the Moon"

No matter how ironic it may seem, early colonial Korean translations of terms for the individual—*kaein, paeksŏng, min, inmin,* and so on—were more often contextualized within a collective frame, whether society or the state, rather than representing the idea of one's uniqueness or autonomy. The reform-minded newspaper writers of this time tended to stress individuals' responsibility to the state over their own pursuit of freedom, supposing a strong bond between individuals and the community.[5] The recurrent emphasis on individuals' social duty over personal freedom certainly stemmed from the urgent need to muster the nation's citizens as a collective force to resist Japan's colonization of Korea, but it was also rooted in global debates on individualism.

---

3. Recall Stephen Greenblatt's definition of individuality: "Each person, however bound by the surrounding codes governing behavior, however fashioned internally by the spoken and unspoken laws of feeling, perception, and action, is unique and is entitled to the uniqueness." Greenblatt, "Fiction and Friction," 32.

4. Clifford, "On Ethnographic Self-Fashioning," 140–62.

5. For example, "Kukka sasang non" (On nationalism), *Hwangsŏng sinmun,* February 16, 1905; "Na wa sahoe ŭi kwangye" (The relationship between me and society), *Taehan maeil sinbo,* March 6, 1908; and "Kŭnbonjŏk kaeryang" (Fundamental reform), *Hwangsŏng sinmun,* March 12, 1908, to name but a few.

The front-page editorial of the July 29, 1909 issue of *Taehan maeil sinbo*, entitled "An Abridged Translation of 'On the Struggle for Rights'" (Kwŏlli kyŏngjaeng ron yŏkyo), is a case in point. In the form of a call to arms, it admonishes readers that "each individual [*kae kaein*]'s indifference to his own rights will bring on the fall of the nation." On the premise that the power of the state lies in the agency of its citizens as individuals, the editorial urges readers to exercise their legal rights so as to strengthen the nation. Here the individual is defined not only as the possessor of legal rights but also, to the extent that such legal rights are sanctioned by state authority, as an integral part of the nation-state. At one point, the editorial asserts: "People are nothing without their rights."

The postscript to the editorial indicates that it is a short summary of the German legal philosopher Rudolf von Jhering's widely translated book, *Der Kampf ums Recht* (*The Struggle for Law*, 1872), which explained the relationship between individuals and society from the perspective of social utilitarianism. One can find a similar avowal of the hierarchal relationship between the nation-state and the individual in the Chinese reformist writer Liang Qichao's manifesto *Xinmin shuo* (*On the New People*, 1902), a whole chapter of which is devoted to the essential points of Jhering's *Der Kampf ums Recht*.[6] Lydia Liu explains how Liang understood the individual as follows: "Liang Qichao allowed the nation-state to take absolute precedence over the individual and tried to maintain a careful distinction between the freedom of a people and individual freedom while opposing the former to the latter."[7]

The notion of the individual advanced by the editorial sheds light on the main character of a 1907 short story by Chang Ŭngjin (1890–1950), "Confession under the Moon."[8] Written in a hybrid style that mixes the vernacular Han'gŭl with Chinese characters, it depicts the last moments in the life of an old bureaucrat of Chosŏn Korea. The story opens with the third-person narrator describing the tranquility of a moonlit summer night in an archaic and ornate style: "After a gust of rain and southwesterly wind, the relentlessly sizzling sun—which was sapping the vitality

---

6. Liang Qichao, *Yin bing shi cong zhu*, 51–66; Angle, "Should We All Be More English?"

7. Liu, "Discourse of Individualism," 96.

8. Paegak Ch'unbu (Chang Ŭngjin's pen name), "Wŏrha ŭi chabaek," 43–47.

of the whole of creation as if the earth were put on a burning brazier—is withdrawing its rays one by one and going down behind the Western mountain." Then follows the remorseful utterance of a man in a theatrical tone: "Oh, my world was full of tears! Oh, I am the most unforgivable villain on earth [*ch'ŏnji kan e yongsŏ ch'i mottan akkan*]!" In a similarly grandiose fashion, the narrator offers a close-up of the old man:

> Clasping his chest with both his hands, he is choking up with tears. His warm heart-rending tears are streaming down his cheeks, which are wrinkled and emaciated with hardship. He dares not to look up at the clear sky with his sunken and misty eyes. Wailing alone on a precipice under the moon with his face turned toward the Western Sea, this old man—who feels trapped by lifelong agonies [*insaeng muhan ŭi pŏnnoi rŭl pigam hanŭn*]—confesses his lachrymose history [*ruyŏksa*].[9]

The narrator's depiction of the old man's appearance is combined with an omniscient act of mind reading. The narrator states that "his sunken and fishy eyes dare not face the blue sky (*ch'ŏngch'ŏn*)" as if he knows that the reason why the old man is not looking up at the sky is his shame and apprehension.[10] The narrator also interprets the old man's gaunt and wrinkly face as evidence of how much "hardship" he has experienced. Just before the old man begins relating his story, the narrator tells the reader exactly what is going through the old man's mind: he "feels trapped by lifelong agonies." Once the old man's confession begins, however, the third-person narrator disappears from the story and does not return until the very last scene. Without the mediation of the narrator, one can read the entire confession as a first-person narrative. In other words, this part of the story may seem similar to what Karatani terms "the literary form of confession."

Following the pattern of this genre, the old man's story reveals the dark side of his past and his strong sense of shame and remorse: having been born into a prestigious *yangban* family, the old man grew up taking everything for granted. After rising to a position of prestige and authority on the basis of his family's reputation, he ingratiates himself with the powerful, while regularly extorting money from the powerless. Even after

9. Ibid., 43.
10. Ibid., 44.

losing his twelve-year-old son to the rebels who rose up against his tyrannical rule, he cannot stop indulging in alcohol, women, reckless spending, and opium, and even takes a Western concubine (*yangch'ŏp*). When he finally comes to his senses, his virtuous wife has already killed herself, along with their three-year-old son, and he finds himself penniless, with no place to go. The old man closes his confession with a self-denigrating supplication to God that he be thrown into eternal hellfire. The returning narrator hears something plunging into the sea before finding that the old man is no longer standing on the precipice. The story ends with the narrator's heartless question: "Is it good fortune or bad? (*haeng inji pulhaeng inji*)?"

One cannot overlook Christian influences on this story. A number of Christian terms and phrases from the Bible appear in the old man's confession: "omniscient and omnipotent God" (*chŏnji chŏnnŭng hasin hananim*), "the God who made the world" (*man yu ŭi chuin toesinŭn hananim*), "heaven" (*ch'ŏnguk*), "holy water" (*sŏngnyŏng ŭi mul*), and "holy spirits" (*sŏngnyŏng*). It is not known, however, whether the author, Chang, converted to Christianity. His two short, memoir-like essays, published in 1927 and 1929, respectively, do not mention anything about Christianity while chronicling the major events in his life. These include his public speech at the People's Assembly (Manmin kongdong hoe) as a student representative of the first government-sponsored English school (Kwallip yŏngŏ hakkyo) at the age of nineteen; his years in Japan as a financially struggling student; his year in Los Angeles, where he worked as a day laborer; the process by which he succeeded in entering and graduating from the prestigious Tokyo Normal School (Tōkyō kōtō shihan gakko); his job at the Taesŏng School (Taesŏng hakkyo) in Korea; and his imprisonment for allegedly plotting to assassinate the first Japanese governor-general of Korea, Terauchi Masatake, a couple of years after the annexation.[11]

Still, it is not at all unreasonable to assume that a well-educated Korean man like Chang would be knowledgeable about the basic doctrines of Christianity. Since the publication in 1882 of the first Korean translation of the Gospels of Luke and John, the result of the collaboration of two Scottish Presbyterian missionaries in Manchuria, John Ross and John McIntyre, and their Korean tutors, Sŏ Sanglyun and Yi Ŭngch'an, the

---

11. Chang Ŭngjin, "Isip nyŏn chŏn hangguk hakekye iyagi," 16–17; Chang Ŭngjin, "Na ŭi chŏlmottŭn sijŏl cheil t'ongkoae hadŏn il," 60–62.

other Gospels, books of the Bible, tracts, pamphlets, and other forms of Protestant literature had become available in Korean, classical Chinese, or the mixed style.[12] They were distributed throughout the country by colporteurs (*kwŏnsŏ*), especially between 1889 and 1906.[13] According to one estimate, about 950 private schools were established by Christian missionaries, whereas another puts the figure at 796; however, both sources agree that Methodists and Presbyterians built the majority of them. Furthermore, regardless of the exact figure, private schools outnumbered schools run by the state.[14] Two out of every seven private schools founded by Koreans between 1895 and 1909 were Christian institutions. Chang taught at one, Taesŏng School in P'yŏngyang, soon after graduating from Tokyo Normal School.

Clearly, Chang was familiar enough with the Christian tradition to draw upon its rhetoric of confession, which had broad implications for the early Korean translation of the individual. Michel Foucault's observation about confession in *The History of Sexuality* offers a useful starting point: the Christian system of confession transformed sex into a "truth" that waits to be concealed or revealed in the form of an "individual secret."[15] In the context of modern Japan, Karatani argues that "the confessional literary form . . . produced an inner life," derived from the so-called Christian spiritual revolution that supposes a split between the body and the mind and puts one's mind under constant surveillance. Karatani describes the establishment of modern selfhood in Japan as a process of inversion: such interiority did not exist prior to the introduction of the Christian system of confession in the Meiji period, yet present-day Japanese have become completely oblivious to the constructed nature of interiority and imagine their modern selfhood as an innate part of themselves, inherently independent from the objective external world.[16]

But does Chang's confessional literary form represent the genesis of this same inner life in Korea? In "Confession under the Moon," the old man acknowledges his past mistakes and at one point even briefly mentions his transgressive sexual life, namely, his relationship with a West-

12.   Ross, "Corean New Testament," 491–97.
13.   *Christian Encyclopedia* (*Kidokkyo taebaekkwa sajŏn*), 782.
14.   Son Insu, *Han'guk kaehwa kyoyuk yŏngu*, 79.
15.   Foucault, *History of Sexuality*, 59–66.
16.   Karatani, *Origins of Modern Japanese Literature*, 76–96.

ern concubine. And yet, compared to the novel that Karatani offers as an example of the confessional literary form, Tayama Katai's *The Quilt* (*Futon*, 1907), Chang's short story presents a confession that is distinctively public.[17] The old man does not confess anything that was a secret, whereas the protagonist in *The Quilt*, Takenaka Tokio, a married middle-aged man with three children, conceals his desire for his young female student, Yoshiko. Tokio's desire for the nineteen-year-old girl and his wild jealousy of her lover are veiled from the other characters of the story, but most of what the old man confesses in Chang Ŭngjin's short story—the exploitation of the powerless, the abusive suppression of uprisings, the consecutive deaths of his two sons, his own prodigal life, his wife's suicide, and even his possibly scandalous sexual life with a Western concubine—are already openly known to his family and others.[18]

More important, instead of supposing a rift between himself and the world outside, the old man frames his wrongdoings as crimes against the nation and his fellow human beings: "I am a traitor to the nation [*kukka*], a public enemy of humanity, a betrayer of the universe, and the most unforgivable man on earth." The public nature of his confession is amplified by the fact that, in describing the old man's act of confession, Chang uses the word *chabaek*, which refers to a suspect's admission in a legal context that he or she has committed a crime.[19] At the same time the old man ascribes his corrupt behavior to the depravity of traditional Korean customs: "I exploited my family name just the way my ancestors did. I was infected [*kamyŏm toeya*] by the vicious mores that brought about the decline of the peninsula." As a relic of the old society, he is culpable for "not knowing the nation above and the people [*paeksŏng*] below"— namely, the new order of the national community arising in place of the old Korea. The old man's last prayer, which paraphrases a passage from the Gospel of Matthew, depicts him as one of many Koreans caught up in a corrupted tradition: "Oh, this peninsular state [*pandoguk*] has tens

17. Tayama, *The Quilt and Other Stories*, 35–96.

18. J. Keith Vincent's reading of *The Quilt* shows that this process of inversion is at the same time the one through which heterosexual desire is naturalized and normalized. See Vincent, *Two-Timing Modernity*, 18–19.

19. Such usage of the term *chabaek* is commonly found in various texts from Chosŏn Korea, including the annals of the kings, *Veritable Records of the Chosŏn Dynasty* (*Chosŏn wangjo sillok*), as well as in early colonial Korean print media.

of thousands of pitiful folks [*chongjok*] who have lost their homes and go begging for food and shelter all over the fields and mountains. Lord God! Have mercy on these wretched folks! Provide drink and food for the hungry. Provide clothing and shelter for the naked."[20]

Just as "An Abridged Translation of 'On the Struggle for Rights'" stresses an interdependent relationship between individuals and the state, so "Confession under the Moon" draws a parallel between the old man's fate and the demise of Chosŏn Korea. It is in this vein that we can understand the enigmatic ending of the story. A nationalist sentiment is apparent in the passage above, especially where the old man prays for the salvation of other lost souls on the peninsula. Quite peculiarly, however, the old man does not seek his own redemption, but before committing suicide he asks God to throw him into hellfire. Furthermore, the narrator, who remains a passive witness to the old man's solitary confession without the omniscience of a traditional storyteller, does not show much sympathy toward the old man, even after listening to his moving story, nor does he try to stop the old man from killing himself. Then the narrator's question follows, "Is it good fortune or bad?"

This detached and unsympathetic reaction to the protagonist's decision to take his own life becomes somewhat comprehensible when we recognize that the narrator is expressing the reformist conviction that the old social values represented by the old man are no longer valid. Consequently, the old man's choice to kill himself and his wish to be punished in hell should be understood as his last attempt to do the right thing for the nation. As a symbol of the old Korea, he must vanish not only from this world but also from the celestial world. Thus, the individual man's death marks the end of a chapter of national history. Insofar as his personal tragedy brings closure to the nation's shameful past, it also signals a hopeful beginning of the new nation. There thus seems to be no fundamental discrepancy between the two points of view of "Confession under the Moon"—the partially omniscient third-person narrator and the old man confessing his past. Yet I am hesitant to conclude that the old man's individuality is completely integrated into the public narrative of

---

20. Paegak Ch'unbu, "Wŏlha ŭi chabaek," 47. Mt. 25:35. "For I was hungry, and you gave me something to eat; I was thirsty, and you gave me something to drink; I was a stranger, and you invited me in."

the nation's reform, for the narrator does not answer the final question—whether the old man's death is good fortune or bad. Just as the figures of domestic women that I examined in the previous chapters act as the standard-bearers of reform and progress but are not without reservations, so the undeniably reform-minded narrator of "Confession under the Moon" displays uncertainty by leaving his last question unanswered. Such uncertainty takes on a much more amplified form in the figures of sensitive young men.

Illness and Interiority: Hyŏn Sangyun's "Persecution"

As described at the beginning of this chapter, the opening passage of the short story "Persecution" takes the reader into the head of a young man who does not feel certain about anything: "As of late, I have become ill perhaps. But no cause exists for the illness."[21] To the end of the story he remains uncertain. This neurotic doubt separates "Persecution" from Korean literature up to this point, whether traditional prose fiction, the early colonial domestic novel, and even "Confession under the Moon." Premodern prose fiction typically begins by locating main characters in a temporal, spatial, and social map—where and in what time period they live; who their parents are; how prestigious their families are; how talented, good-looking, virtuous, or eccentric they are; and so forth. Although this formulaic opening had faded away by the early colonial domestic novel, the all-knowing narrator in works of this genre often blurts out the main characters' family genealogy, major turning points in their lives, or an assessment of their moral caliber at one point or another. "Confession under the Moon" moves further away from the traditional literary convention by having its main character talk about his past for the most part, instead of the narrator. And yet the narrator does not hide that he already knows who the old man really is. Before the old man's confession begins, the narrator comments that the old man "feels trapped by lifelong agonies"; what he is about to say is "lachrymose history."

21. Hyŏn Sangyun, "P'ipak," 86.

Entirely written in the present tense and in the first person, "Persecution" gives the reader a sense of immediacy and closeness. Nonetheless, neither the first-person narration nor the present tense allows the reader to gain a well-rounded understanding of the main character. Although details are provided on the numerous symptoms and changing feelings that the narrator is experiencing, nothing is stated explicitly about his background, but rather the reader has to read between the lines to understand who he is. One can probably make out that the first-person narrator is a well-educated man from his use of terms derived from medical, agricultural, and natural sciences. His conversation with local farmers suggests that he is a member of a landowning family who attended school in a distant city and has recently returned to his hometown, Chŏngju.[22] He is already married and, like the majority of young Korean men of his age in the 1910s, lives with his wife in the same house as his parents and siblings. Given that, in the latter part of the story, one of his neighbors offers him advice on what type of job he needs to pursue, we can also guess that he does not have a regular job. His life seems comfortable, at least on a material level, as does that of his extended family—his parents, siblings, and wife. His friends also tell him that his life has no conspicuous lack. Still, he is not well.

The first-person narrator does not feel certain about the cause of his illness, either. "If it is an illness, it is not *tuberculosis*, which makes you clutch your chest and vomit blood; nor is it *malaria*, which makes you grab

---

22. Chŏngju, a small northern provincial town, was Hyŏn Sangyun's (1893–?) hometown. Born to a traditional *yangban* family, he married Paek Sukyang at the young age of twelve. This traditional and much criticized child marriage, however, turned his life around. His father-in-law, Paek Ihaeng, who worked as the first principal of Osan School, a private school established by Yi Sŭnghun, an entrepreneur-turned-reformist, convinced him to enroll in a modern elementary school (Puho Yukyoung sohakyo). Later he moved to P'yŏngyang to attend Taesŏng School, a private school established and run by Yun Ch'iho and An Changho, the leading figures of the reformist movement at the time. When Taesŏng School was closed down in 1911 because these two leaders of the school were arrested for their alleged attempt to assassinate the governor-general, Terauchi Masatake, Hyon Sangyun transferred to Posŏng School in Seoul. Hyŏn Sangyun notes that "Persecution" was originally written during the time he was staying in his hometown after graduating from Posŏng School in 1913, although this story did not came out until 1917, when he was studying history and sociology at Waseda University in Tokyo. See Yun Sasun, ed., *Kidang Hyŏn Sangyun*.

your head and moan; nor *neurasthenia*, which congests your brain and causes headaches and dizziness; nor a *gastric dilation*, which makes you belch and your stomach growl. Yet I am drained of all my energy and feel unbearably weary, so, an illness it is nonetheless."[23] The list of his symptoms is quite long: loss of appetite, a sore throat, chest pains, anxiety, weight loss, sleep deprivation, fatigue, headaches, lack of interest in social relationships, and excessive perspiration. Pedantically reciting the diseases that he suspects he might have—tuberculosis, malaria, neurasthenia, or gastric dilation—he also reveals his familiarity with modern medical science. His access to this knowledge does not help him find an objective explanation for his symptoms. He concludes that he might not have any of these diseases, attributing the sources of his pains to "the darting looks coming from this way and that."[24]

One cannot fail to notice that these "looks" may be the protagonist's own subjective projections. The "I," designated as the Korean first-person singular pronoun *na*, feels that not only neighbors, strangers, and policemen but also farm animals, stars, and pillars are staring at him. *Na* often hears them criticizing him. Although some of them do try to cheer him up, it is the critical voices that keep following him, even when he no longer feels their gazes. Does the gaze belong to the people or *na*? The gaze might be entirely created within the mind of *na*, but the reader cannot be completely sure of that, either. What can we learn, then, from a story told from the perspective of a mentally unstable man? Why do we need to listen to him when it is obvious that he is not a reliable narrator?

What the gaze does in this story over and over again is in fact bear out the irreducible gap between *na* and those staring at him. The following episode gives us a closer look at those whom *na* feels staring at him. One evening, solely out of boredom, *na* attends a gathering of farmers of his village. He immediately senses that they are staring and laughing at him. Afterward they confirm his suspicion by mocking and criticizing him. One farmer, identified as "Oedol's dad," bluntly criticizes *na* for living off of his family's wealth: "I heard that you were an excellent student. Tell us how to make money without working." Another farmer, "Elder Brother Sugil," reminds Oedol's dad that they should respect *na* because he will

23. Ibid., 86 (emphasis added).
24. Ibid., 86.

eventually inherit the land that they are cultivating as tenants, which only makes *na* once again uncomfortable and anxious.[25] The literary critic Kim Poksun interprets *na*'s oversensitive reaction in this scene as derived from his class consciousness—his shame at being a privileged landowner's son—and thereby places "Persecution" in the genealogy of proletarian literature, which did not come to prominence in Korea until the 1920s and 1930s.[26]

However, other episodes suggest that less-privileged characters may not necessarily see *na* through the lens of class disparity. In a later scene, *na* has two encounters with strangers: one with a drunken man, who offers that "it is said that only few get to live past seventy. So while you are still alive, why not eat well and have a good time? Ha! Ha!" The other is with a group of farmers who are heading home after working all day in the field. Neither the drunkard nor the farmers are viewed as victims or critics of the unjust social system. The drunken man appears simply self-content. The farmers' masculine and robust bodies bear no signs of exhaustion or of having been broken down by hard labor. If anything, *na* looks at them with a faint sense of envy: "Their faces are sunburned red, and their hands are chapped by the autumn wind."[27] In his head, *na* pictures one of the farmers going home to be greeted by his family and enjoying a delicious dinner with them, as if believing that the farmer must have a perfect, idyllic life. As always, he is quick to sense the contemptuous gaze of the drunkard and the farmers: "Hey, you lowlife! We eat by the sweat of our brow. We know no shame or pain. You immature and childish fool! What have you got to say? I don't give a damn about rights, duty, ethics, morals, equality, freedom, or whatever."[28] This time it is clear that the voices are within *na*'s head—as it is simply implausible that the two unrelated groups of people could utter these words in unison. From *na*'s perspective, there thus seems to be no difference between the drunkard, the farmers, and his neighbors.

While *na* is always anxious and nervous when subject to other people's gazes, he reacts much more strongly to the gaze of those representing the

25.   Ibid., 89.
26.   Kim Poksun, *1910 nyŏndae han'guk munhak*, 89–90, 103.
27.   Hyŏn Sangyun, "P'ippak," 90.
28.   Ibid.

colonial apparatus. For example, *na* nearly has a nervous breakdown when he encounters a deputy policeman (*pojowŏn*), even though in the Japanese government-general's police system, this was one of the lowest-ranking positions and was mostly assigned to Koreans. In another instance, *na* feels stifled when he is advised by a village elder (*chonwi nim*) to work for the Land Survey Bureau, a subdivision of the Japanese government-general: "'Hey, listen to me as I am telling you the truth. Since you are so learned, you could easily find work as a civil servant. That's the best. Over in the next village, Paek sŏndal's son got a job as a clerk at the Land Survey Bureau and his elders were so happy.[29] And why not—he came to visit the other day and how impressive he seemed indeed! How grand to see him with that golden chain and the long sword. That is what you should do.'"[30] *Na* says: "For some reason his words weigh heavily on me. My breathing feels smothered and my chest tight."[31] Kim Poksun argues that *na* suffers here because the village elder's advice threatens his resolution not to collaborate with the Japanese.[32] Yet her reading does not explain why *na* feels anxious about the gazes of those who neither represent nor bring up colonial power. Given the diversity of the gazes that make him feel restless, the critic Chŏng Chua's ascription of *na*'s symptoms to his insecurity about not meeting the expectations for educated young men (*ch'ŏngnyŏn*) also seems insufficient.[33]

What is more consistently prevalent in all the encounters with others' gazes is *na*'s feeling of separation from others. Whomever he meets, the result is always the same: they end up staring at him with contempt. Other gazes function as mirrors in which *na* sees his selfhood. One might even say that he finds himself *beneath* the eyes of others—his neighbors, strangers, and colonial policemen. There is nothing strange about a person who asks "who he is" through interactions with others. However, what is peculiar about the first-person narrator in "Persecution" is that he always views himself as inferior to those around him, no matter how little power they actually have over him.

29. *Sŏndal* is a title for a man who fails to gain a government position after passing a civil or military service examination in Chosŏn Korea.

30. Ibid., 89.

31. Ibid.

32. Kim Poksun, *1910 nyŏndae han'guk munhak*, 92.

33. Ch'ŏng Chua, *Sŏbuk munhak kwa rok'ŏllit'i*, 139–40.

Na's symptoms are similar to those of the disease called neurasthenia (or nervous exhaustion). Popularized by an American neurologist, George Beard, in the late nineteenth century, neurasthenia referred to a psychosomatic disorder with symptoms of fatigue, headache, and anxiety. Beard attributed the cause of this illness to "modern civilization," especially the tendency to specialization.[34] In his 1881 book, *American Nervousness, Its Causes and Consequences*, he writes that neurasthenia results from "the exclusive concentration of mind and muscle to one mode of action," for example, punctuality marked by the common use of watches and clocks, noises from the city, the rapidity of business transactions that the telegraph made possible, and long-distance travel enabled by the expansion of railways.[35]

According to the scholar of Japanese literature Christopher Hill, this term, translated as *shinkei suijaku*, entered the Japanese medical lexicon in the late 1870s and, around the Russo-Japanese War in 1904 and 1905, gained cultural significance beyond the medical community. Referring to it as "the disease of civilization" (*bunmei no yamai*) or nervous disease (*shinkei byō*), commentators often brought up neurasthenia as a pathological sign of the broad social changes that had resulted from modern civilization—"the changes in the economy, education, and daily life that followed the Meiji Restoration of 1868."[36] It was believed that intellectuals were especially prone to this disease. For this reason, there was less social stigma attached to neurasthenia than other mental illnesses. Meiji writers such as Nastume Sōseki and Shimazaki Tōson incorporated this disease as a trope in their literary works to reflect on the various unwelcome effects of civilization and to criticize the superficial state-led program of progress.

The Korean translation of neurasthenia, *sin'gyŏng soeyak*, does appear in "Persecution" amid a list of the names of the diseases that *na* goes through to try to find the cause of his symptoms. Although he rules out the possibility that he might have it, what *na* is actually experiencing is not dissimilar from Beard's description of neurasthenia. He constantly

34. Beard, *American Nervousness*, 96.
35. Ibid., 96–102.
36. Hill, "Exhausted by Their Battles," 241.

both complains about "headaches, fatigues, and anxiety" and remarks on his knowledge of modern science:

> I read newspapers. Occasionally, I also read magazines and books. I am not entirely unaware of the ways of this neurotic world that shifts with each sunrise and again at sunset, and I also avail myself of laughter, tears, sentiment, and blood through poetry and fiction. Thanks to my early schooling, I know why it rains or snows when the air temperature increases, and how the air temperature rises when it snows or rains.[37] I am informed enough in farming to know that sandy soil is right for growing watermelons, and that eggplants shouldn't be raised in rotation with other plants.[38]

The narrator describes himself as being acquainted with the modern world, which is in constant flux. Not to be left behind, he regularly reads newspapers and periodicals. *Na* also shows his familiarity with the modern arts, agricultural science, and meteorology—another sign of his being in step with modern civilization. This passage contrasts starkly with a later episode, in which *na* listens to a group of hard-working farmers, one of whom says rather proudly, "I don't know anything about right, duty, ethics, moral, equality, freedom, or whatever."[39] The self-characterization that follows this also serves to distinguish him from some of the people whose gazes, he believes, make him unwell. The first-person narrator's illness, in other words, draws a line between him and others in terms of the opposition between the civilized and the uncivilized.

Considering that the early colonial domestic novel tends to describe "the uncivilized" as relics of a bygone era or of a failing nation, one might assume Hyŏn Sangyun is trying to show modern civilization's darker side through a figure suffering from the ills of progress, neurasthenia in particular. If so, one will find it perplexing to read Hyŏn Sangyun's two essays about his experiences in Tokyo and Seoul, respectively, because these—both published in a cultural and literary magazine targeted at

37.   The protagonist is not, in fact, correct: this should be "why it rains or snows when the air humidity increases, and how the air temperature rises when it snows or rains." It is not clear whether this factual mistake was intended by the author.

38.   Hyŏn Sangyun, "P'ippak," 87.

39.   Ibid., 90.

young elites, *Ch'ŏngch'un* (*Youth*)—present him as an unabashed advocate of modern civilization and capitalist progress. The first, "A Study-Abroad Student's Life in Tokyo" (Tonggyŏng yuhaksaeng saenghwal) was written about a year after he arrived in Tokyo to pursue his degree at Waseda University in Japan in 1915. The second, "My Impressions of Kyŏngsŏng" (Kyongsŏng sogam; Kyŏngsŏng is an old name for Seoul), came out in the same journal three years after the first essay. "A Study-Abroad Student's Life in Tokyo" is a testimony to Hyŏn Sangyun's unreserved excitement about his life in Tokyo.[40] He had always wished to visit Tokyo, he says, and when his wish finally came true, he was too overwhelmed not to write about his experience. The essay gives a detailed account of his daily routine, including what it looks like in the morning at the boardinghouse where he lives with other Japanese and Chinese students, how Japanese food tastes compared to Korean food, how thrilled he is to walk shoulder-to-shoulder with a crowd of students in Tokyo and to hear the profound ideas regarding religion, arts, politics, and philosophy expressed by his much-admired old professors, and how he spends time after school reading Western classics by the likes of Turgenev, Emerson, Wordsworth, and Bergson. Full of hope about his future, he is happy to find himself among hard-working Korean students who share with him their hopes for the future. He closes the essay by expressing his deep admiration for the self-sufficient and hard-working Japanese people. In Japan, no one lives freely without working, even if they have more than enough wealth, he emphasizes. They have to use their own arms and legs to make a living. They invest in their children's education, no matter how poor they are.

The optimistic undertone of "A Study-Abroad Student's Life in Tokyo" seems all the more striking when compared to the sense of dissatisfaction running through "My Impressions of Kyŏngsŏng."[41] In this essay, which he wrote after spending nearly three years in Tokyo, Hyŏn Sangyun talks about how disappointed he is with the current state of development in the capital city of Korea during a recent visit. His critical gaze finds that Seoul lacks what he was expecting from a modern urban space—the

40. Hyŏn Sangyun, "Tonggyŏng yuhaksaeng saenghwal," 110–17.
41. Hyŏn Sangyun, "Kyongsŏng sogam," 124–29.

mood of competition, the spirit of hard work, the regulated work sched-
ule, and respect for scholars and scholarly attainment. He harshly
criticizes the rich and idle young folks, who spend their days amusing
themselves in the city, and conceited high school students for strutting
around wearing the newest makeup and scented oils. He ends his essay
with a lamentation on the lack of good role models in Seoul. His negative depiction of Seoul does not reflect disillusionment with modern civilization, however. His complaint is with the slow pace of its advance in
his home country. His time in Tokyo has provided him with a vision of
what Seoul should look but does not. We are thus confronted by the question: Why do "Persecution" and Hyŏn's essays differ so sharply concerning the desirability of progress?

To answer this, I would like to call attention to the peculiar way in
which neurasthenia was received—or more precisely, "translated"—by
young Korean elites of the 1910s. The term *sin'gyŏng soeyak* appeared spo-
radically in newspapers and journals as early as the 1900s without stir-
ring much public anxiety; that would change in the late 1920s and the
1930s.[42] Na Hyesŏk's feminist essay "Miscellaneous Thoughts—Dear
Elder Sister K" (Chapkam—K ŏnni ege yŏham) gives us a glimpse of how
young Korean elites in Japan (i.e., those pursuing high school or college
degrees in the metropole) understood the nature of neurasthenia in the
1910s.[43] A member of the first generation of feminist writers and the first
female artist to paint in a Western style, Na Hyesŏk published this manifesto under the alias C.W.—the initials of her pen name, Chŏng Wŏl.
The essay was published in *Hak chi kwang* (*Lux Scientiae*), the organ of
the Fraternal Society of Korean Students in Japan, while Hyŏn Sangyun
was working as editor and only a month before his "Persecution" came
out in *Ch'ŏngch'un*. The essay is in epistolary form and is addressed to a
young woman with whom the author has a close sisterly relationship. Referred to as "elder sister K," this woman had been studying in Japan before
moving to a remote Korean village for treatment of her severe symptoms
of *sin'gyŏng soeyak*. After saying how shocked she is to hear about K's

---

42. On the discourse of neurasthenia in Korea between the late 1920s and the mid-
1930s, see Hanscom, *Real Modern*, 66.
43. Na Hyesŏk (C.W.), "Chapkam—K ŏnni ege yŏham."

infirmity, the author writes: "I am relieved to know that your illness, unlike ordinary people's, is invaluable, as it will become a powerful source for creativity in the future."[44] Na Hyesŏk's understanding of neurasthenia is not only positive but also goes as far as characterizing sufferers as extraordinary and more deeply immersed in superior modern culture.

Na Hyesŏk's particular view on the relationship between neurasthenia and the progress of civilization offers insight into the illness that Hyŏn Sangyun's protagonist in "Persecution" experiences. The neurasthenic symptoms of the main character—who stresses his familiarity with Western science and modern culture—suggests that *na* "internalizes" the alienating effects of modern civilization. He is not an outsider or an apprentice with regard to modern civilization insofar as he owns it in the form of illness. And yet he is not a typical neurasthenic man who has a rude awakening vis-à-vis the harmful effects of modern civilization and moves to the countryside to find solace. On the contrary, his symptoms become more pronounced when he comes back to his hometown—a small northern town, where he finds an irrevocable chasm between himself and those who seem to live contentedly untroubled by the presence of the colonial apparatus. What defines him is, therefore, neither the place where he was born and grew up nor his level of modern education but his illness, which seems exacerbated by idyllic rural environments. He no longer feels at home in his hometown, not because he has discovered his autonomous self, but because he has internalized the values of modern civilization— the very force that occasioned colonization in Korea.

The Irritated Flâneur in Yang Kŏnsik's "Sad Contradictions"

Yang Kŏnsik's "Sad Contradictions" reminds us of Hyŏn Sangyun's "Persecution" in many ways.[45] Like the latter, "Sad Contradictions" features

44. Ibid., 66.
45. Like Hyŏn Sangyun, Yang Kŏnsik (1889–1944) did not join a coterie group in the 1920s. Better known as an expert on Chinese literature, he translated Chinese literary works from a range of eras into Korean, from the thirteenth-century play *Xixiangji*

a first-person narrator, *na*, a young man who is sufficiently well-versed in Western literature to have read Dostoevsky's novels and to have a portrait of the Russian socialist novelist Maxim Gorky hanging on his wall.[46] Akin to the *na* of "Persecution," he suffers from physical discomfort, emotional turmoil, and auditory hallucinations. Both stories revolve around a peripatetic narrator: "Sad Contradictions" is set in the capital city of Seoul, and the story follows the footsteps of the narrator one cold day in February. He wakes up with a dull feeling in his head and spends all morning smoking in his room before boredom drives him out of the house. He then strolls aimlessly around the city all day long, getting on and off streetcars. The reader witnesses his "feelings"—frustration, anxiety, insecurity, and despair—but is told very little about his social status and family background. Often overcome by a sense of helplessness and fear, the sensitive protagonist in "Sad Contradictions" fails at making emotional connections with others and finding his place in the hustle and bustle of the big city—just as Hyŏn Sangyun's *na* carries with him a sense of isolation when walking around his hometown.

As in "Persecution," the *na* of "Sad Contradictions" is in an anxious, self-critical state. After walking aimlessly for a while in the morning, he hops on a streetcar bound for Kwanghŭi Gate with no destination in mind. Looking at the other passengers, who all seem busy, he concludes that he might be the only one with too much time on his hands. Out of embarrassment, he impulsively gets off the streetcar and transfers to another, this one bound for the Great East Gate (Tong taemun), with the idea that he will visit friends who live in that area. Once it occurs to him that he will have to walk a long way to get to a particular friend's house from the streetcar station, he gives up on the idea of visiting and suddenly gets off the streetcar a few stops before the Great East Gate. At this point he assumes that he is the target of the disapproving gaze not only

---

(*The Story of the Western Wing*) to Lu Xun's short story "Toufa de gushi" (The Story of Hair, 1920) to Guo Morou's play *Sange pannide nixing* (*Three Rebellious Women*, 1926), in the 1920s and 1930s. As I mention in chapter 4, he translated Henrik Ibsen's *A Doll's House* with Pak Kyegang and serialized it in *Maeil sinbo* in 1921. Devoted to Buddhist reform, he also published many didactic Buddhist stories and essays in various Buddhist journals. See Nam Yunsu, Pak Chaeyŏn, and Kim Yŏngbok, *Yang Paekhwa Munjip*.

46. Yang Kŏnsik, "Sŭlp'ŭn mosun," 71–76.

of strangers but also of lifeless objects around him: "As soon as I take a few steps, the streetcar rushes off with its bells ringing, leaving me in the dust. I am disturbed because it feels as though the speeding streetcar and the noisy sound of its bells are mocking my stupidity, saying, 'Look at that man. He is the picture of failure!' My irritation only grows and I can no longer stand to feel so disgruntled about everything that I see and hear."[47]

Compared to the *na* in "Persecution," the first-person narrator of "Sad Contradictions" is more often an onlooker than the object of someone else's gaze. His gaze is different from, for example, what feminist film critic Laura Mulvey calls the voyeuristic "male gaze," through which classic Hollywood cinema portrays female bodies as fetishized sexual objects.[48] Instead of giving phallocentric "order and meaning to the world" through "the image of castrated women," the protagonist of "Sad Contradiction" not only stares at others but, no less frequently, directs his critical gaze inward at himself: "With thoughts of drinking, my stomach starts growling. But I have never gone to a bar alone before. All at once, I find myself reluctant to go. Feeling more irritated than ever, I walk on resignedly in silence. How could I be so pathetic? That is when it occurs to me that a weakling like myself has no right to walk unashamedly among others in this vibrant world in broad daylight."[49]

I should stress, however, that as self-effacing as he is, Yang Kŏnsik's *na* still remains the owner of the gaze, not the object of someone else's gaze. One may detect in him a trace of the flâneur, that iconic modern figure who originated in nineteenth-century French urban culture: a voyeuristic stroller, man of leisure, and introspective city dweller who takes part in city life but at the same time remains detached as an autonomous individual from the perfunctory aspects of the city.[50] Focusing on a peripatetic spectator's day in the downtown of the old capital in the earliest stage of its metamorphosis, "Sad Contradictions" could be read as one of the earliest flâneur pieces in Korea, preceding by nearly two decades the better-known fictional manifestation of the flâneur in Pak T'aewŏn's 1934

47. Ibid., 72.
48. Mulvey, "Visual Pleasure and Narrative Cinema," 6–18.
49. Yang Kŏnsik, "Sŭlp'ŭn mosun," 73.
50. Simmel, *Sociology of Georg Simmel*, 409–24; Baudelaire, *Painter of Modern Life*, 1–42.

novella, "One Day in the Life of Kubo, the Novelist" (Sosŏlga kubo ssi ŭi ilil, 1934).[51]

And yet Yang Kŏnsik's flâneur finds nothing glamorous or exciting about Seoul. He recurrently succumbs to an unbearable feeling of irritation while observing people in the city. Assuming an air of superiority, he passes judgment on strangers he encounters on the streets. In a bustling commercial district, for example, he bumps into an old and overweight (presumably) senior court lady (*sanggung*) wearing an oddly colored silk outfit and thick makeup.[52] Utterly disgusted, *na* makes the absurd conjecture that "a woman looking like that is sure to have a secret lover, most likely a young man half her age, while assuming the most dignified air in public." The assumption that she should be hiding a male concubine at home is groundless. Why is she so repulsive to him? Is it that he perceives it as shameless to display such extravagance in public? Is it because he believes her showy outfit and makeup are inappropriate for her age? Or does it come from his misogynistic discomfort with unmarried professional women like court ladies? Once she moves out of his sight, the object of his irritation changes to "a little boy carrying extremely heavy loads on an overloaded carrier as big as himself" and then to a rickshaw man pulling an imported British cigarette, K'alp'yo (literally, "knife-logo"), out of his pocket.

This scene is often cited as evidence that Yang Kŏnsik was developing a critical consciousness of class inequality in anticipation of the emergence of the socialist movement in Korea in the early 1920s.[53] The rickshaw man and the little boy stand for have-nots; *na*'s hostile attitude toward the court lady mirrors Yang Kŏnsik's disapproval of the profligacy flaunted by the rich. The figure of the rickshaw man frequently appears as a helpless

51. Pak T'aewŏn, "Sosŏlga kubo ssi ŭi ilil."

52. *Sanggung*, senior court ladies, were in charge of various housekeeping and personal assistance tasks in the court during the Chosŏn dynasty.

53. See Kim Poksun, *1910 nyŏndae han'guk munhak*, 139; An Hamgwang, *Chosŏn munhaksa*, vol. 9, 43–46. Notably, An Hangwang, a North Korean critic, was the first one who called attention to "Sad Contradiction." Since then, this story has repeatedly been mentioned in North Korean literary histories as a representative work from the 1910s. See *Chosŏn minjujuŭi inmin konghwaguk Kwahakwŏn*, Chosŏn munhak t'ongsa, 13–14; Pak Chongho, Ch'oe T'akho, and Ryu Man, *Chosŏn munhaksa*, 89. South Korean literary scholars did not turn their attention to this work until the late 1980s.

victim of class-divided society in Korean fiction of the 1920s and 1930s, such as in Yi Iksang's "Will to Life" (Saeng ŭl kuhanŭn mam, 1922), Hyŏn Chin'gŏn's "A Lucky Day" (Unsu chohŭn nal, 1924), and Chu Yosŏp's "A Rickshaw Man" (Ilyŏkkŏ kkun, 1925).[54] However, *na*'s fleeting portrait of the rickshaw man in "Sad Contradictions" does not clearly link him with *na*'s criticism of wealth disparity. Is *na* annoyed because he believes the rickshaw man unjustly suffers from poor working conditions, or because the rickshaw man smokes an expensive imported cigarette beyond his means?

Na's observation later in the story about ill-treated day laborers also makes the previous assumption about his sympathy toward working-class people questionable. He witnesses a crowd of people gathering around a police station to watch a group of day laborers being interrogated and beaten by a deputy policeman. The laborers had rampaged through a high-end bar after they were denied entry based on their shabby appearances. The deputy policeman punishes them not just for destroying others' property, but also for wasting their time at bars instead of working hard to earn more money and better their station in life. Na's reaction to this commotion is clearly distinguished from that of someone with class consciousness. Instead of decrying the everyday discrimination against lower-class workers, *na* cynically points out the absurdity of the deputy policeman imagining himself to be superior to the day workers. So he ponders: "Needless to say, people are lacking in ambition and self-awareness, and both the day laborer and the deputy policeman, equally lacking in ambition and self-awareness, have settled for their positions in life. I cannot see a big difference between the two. But the deputy policeman's uniform and sword give him the right and authority to punish the day laborer. This is an egregious contradiction."[55] This passage recalls Hyŏn Sangyun's essay on Seoul, in which he bemoans the lack of motivation on the part of the city's residents to adopt the modern sense of time and work ethic. Similarly, Yang Kŏnsik's young elite narrator decries not the inhumane consequences of modern civilization but people's disinterest in striving for progress. *Na*

54.   Yi Iksang (under the pen name Sŏnghae), "Saeng ŭl kuhanŭn mam," 153–63; Ping Hŏ (Hyŏn Chingŏn's pen name), "Unsu chohŭn nal"; Chu Yosŏp, "Iryŏkkŏ kkun," 8–19.

55.   Yang Kŏnsik, "Sŭlp'ŭn mosun," 74.

scornfully calls it a "contradiction" (*mosun*) that the deputy policeman arrogantly assumes he has the right to lecture the day laborers, for the reason that the former appears to him just as unfit for the transition to modern life as they are. Yang Kŏnsik's *na* is much more introspective and self-reflective than is Hyŏn Sangyun in his "My Impression on Kyŏngsŏng." As soon as *na* passes judgment on others, he turns his critical gaze toward himself and laments that he is as flawed as the policeman and laborers. Marked by abstract language and vague metaphors, his confession of his own shortcomings describes a process of finding that what he believed early in life was a delusion and stresses his deep sorrow over his inability to lead a congruent life:

> It is also true, however, that life's pressures have produced contradictions within myself. Standing in the midst of this wilderness called everyday life, I could see how at every moment my dreams have been destroyed. My innocent self, once full of ideal dreams, was thrown against the wall of cold, hard reality, only to end up broken and in wretched ruins. The man who knew not how to deceive nor flatter nor yield to force is but a creation of dreams of yesterday. Watching myself walking like this now, I realize that I have remorselessly cloaked myself in falsehood and have been stamped with all the signs of a weak man held in the clutches of the easy means to life's ends. Such a life is sad and dirty. I am truly sorrowful that my innate and genuine nature is being gradually chipped away and becoming self-contradictory. This thought brings back the earlier feelings of anxiety and worries, leaving me to wander in a nightmarish state.[56]

This scene makes it clear that, whether triggered by the observation of others or his own introspection, *na*'s strong affective responses—shame, anxiety, anger, disgust, irritation, and sorrow—are derived from a single cause: the failure to live up to the ideal of modern civilization. He calls the discrepancy between the ideal and reality a "contradiction." Whereas in "Persecution" the gaze helps *na* define his interiority by setting up a barrier between *na* and others, the first-person narrator of "Sad Contradictions" switches the direction of his gaze between inward and outward to identify the personal contradictions not only of others but also his

56. Ibid.

own. They are all contradictory figures as long as they are aware of the desirability of progress but are unable or unwilling to undertake the task of realizing it.

Nonetheless, it would be inaccurate to take *na*'s self-disparaging as a simple sign of self-criticism, because the very act of identifying his own flaws differentiates him from and perhaps even renders him slightly superior to those around him. Unlike others, he is at least aware that there is something lacking in the lives of Koreans. The concluding episode of the short story drives this point home. Before heading home, *na* runs into his friend Yŏnghwan and learns from him that no one has heard from their mutual friend Paekhwa since he ran away from home without a penny in his pocket three days previously. The significance of this minor character is shown through the idiosyncratic choice of his name—Paekhwa (白化, literally, "becoming white") is homonymous with the author's supposedly Buddhist-inspired pen name (白華), not a common name in Korean.[57] *Na* shows an unusual amount of sympathy for Paekhwa, something he never expresses for those he encounters in the street or even for his mother, who briefly appears at the beginning and end of the story. When he hears what has happened to Paekhwa, his heart sinks. "Feeling unhinged and burning from a mental fever," he comes home to find Paekhwa's suicide note waiting for him. Run into the body of the text at the end of "Sad Contradictions," the note allows readers to experience Paekhwa's raw feelings without the narrator's mediation. Full of despair and anger, it details why he has decided to kill himself, despite being a relatively young man in good health. His father has thrust the responsibility of being the family's breadwinner onto Paekhwa but has also tried to force him to quit attending the night school that he has been attending for the last seven or eight years. Paekhwa describes his father, who adheres to outmoded moral codes such as filial piety (*hyo*), as "ignorant" and "negligent of [his] parental

---

57. As is often the case with Korean writers, Yang Kŏnsik tended to leave the sources of his pen names unspecified, but it is likely that Paekhwa (白華) might have come from the Buddhist phrase 小白華, "one of the four divine flowers, the mandāra-flower." See Soothill and Hodous, *Dictionary of Chinese Buddhist Terms*. Yang took part in the Buddhist reform movement, and he published this story under the name of Paekhwa in a Buddhist periodical, *Chosŏn pulgyo kye* (*The Buddhist World of Chosŏn*), in April 1916. The first edition of "Sad Contradictions" lists the author as Kugyŏ (菊如), another pen name under which Yang wrote.

duties." His extreme act of ending his life not only manifests his strong disapproval of the old system, which his father's parasitical life epitomizes, but also echoes *na*'s frustration with people who are "lacking in ambition and self-awareness."

In the closing scene of the story, *na* no longer appears feeble and passive. At the end of the letter, Paekhwa requests that *na* rescue Paekhwa's sister, Tongsun, from his greedy father's attempt to give her to a rich aristocrat as a concubine: Tongsun resists her father "like a lotus in the mud." The story ends with a one-line report on what happens afterward: "Three or four days later, I visit Paekhwa's house accompanied by Yŏnghwan"— he is probably trying to carry out his dead friend's will. Whether or not he is successful remains an open-ended question; however, the last scene does make it clear that *na* is no longer an irritated but impotent city stroller. One can even register *na*'s sign of maturity in his having become a man of action who decides to save a girl from her "uncivilized" father's tyranny. Both the flâneur and the man of action aspire to bring about reform and progress—the latter significantly decides to act according to the ideals of reform instead of complaining about the lack of progress. The last scene sets *na* apart from the other "contradictory" characters whom he had met on the street that day.

Private Desire as the Wellspring of Civilization

Both "Persecution" and "Sad Contradictions" depict their protagonists' negative emotions in minute detail while leaving their family backgrounds, social statuses, and moral calibers—that is, the basic frames of reference through which literary figures were defined in traditional fiction—vague and unclear. Their negative emotions—such as shame, guilt, sadness, fear, anxiety, self-doubt—allow the reader to have access to the inner self of the first-person narrator, which is what primarily defines who he is. The feelings are not purely psychological but bound to the body of the narrator, whether they take the form of physical pain or are mediated by the corporeal acts of "looking" and "walking." As a result, the physical body serves as the unmistakable partition between one's inner self and others. The protagonists' negative emotions arise from their encounters with other minor characters, but they rarely share these feelings with anyone else—including their friends or family. The first-person narrator of "Persecution" struggles to figure out the cause of his numerous symptoms on his own. In "Sad Contradictions" *na* talks about his emotional detachment from his family before he begins strolling the city: "The rest of my family and I have completely different tastes. This is a quite annoying fact." While sharing concerns about Paekhwa with their mutual friend, Yŏnghwan, *na* does not let Yŏnghwan see how deeply he is shaken up by the news of his suicide, nor does he tell the latter about the dream he had woken up from that morning—in which Paekhwa was telling him, in tears, that he is dying.

While the tendency toward individuation is clearly characteristic of the figures of sensitive men, it would be a mistake to say that sensitive young men simply prioritize their own feelings over what matters to the community. As I have shown through my analysis of "Persecution" and "Sad Contradictions," their negative emotions are rooted in the desire for modern civilization and social progress, being implicitly propelled by the colonialist idea that Korea is lagging behind in terms of its development. Far from trying to find their unique selfhood apart from social constraints, these characters hold aspirations for social progress in the form of private feeling. These figures of sensitive men have thoroughly internalized the desire for progress so that they feel irritated and anxious even with subtle indications of underdevelopment or stalled progress in rural or urban spaces in Korea. The same desire explains not only why the protagonist of "Sad Contradiction" always feels inadequate and ashamed of himself but also why he seeks to distinguish himself from those living a self-satisfied life. Only by directing a condescending gaze at "less-advanced" folks can he convert his inferiority complex into an equally problematic sense of superiority.

Significantly, these negative emotions are not directed toward the colonizers nor result from a raw feeling of defeat or anticolonialist resentment against the Japanese. However, this is not to suggest that colonialism had no role in the genesis of the sensitive men. On the contrary, these figures' internalization of the ideology of progress invites us to ask whether this iteration of the individual was influenced by the Japanese colonial government's propagation of development and progress. As a matter of fact, the issue of progress appears in the official documents of annexation, such as the "Imperial Japanese Rescript Attached to the Proclamation and the Treaty Annexation," which maintains that "all Koreans, being under our sway, will enjoy growing prosperity and welfare, and with assured repose and security will come a marked expansion in industry and trade."[58] For this reason, Bruce Cumings calls the Japanese government-general in Korea "a 'developmental' colonial regime," describing it as a "state capitalist" who "act[ed] as entrepreneur, financier, and manager." The Japanese colonizers' industrializing effort in Korea was modeled after the state-led industrialization in Meiji Japan, but as Cumings stresses, the former was inevitably more distorted than the latter because it was intended to maximize benefits for the metropole, resulting in the extreme exploitation of lower-class Koreans.[59]

Kyung Moon Hwang's recent revisionist account, however, cautions us against attributing the drive toward progress in early twentieth-century Korea entirely to colonialist influence. According to him, "the Great Korean Empire," which "the state formally proclaimed in 1897 upon the restoration of the Joseon [Chosŏn] monarch's authority," used increased revenue to fund what could be deemed "proto-developmentalist" projects, including the construction, on a massive scale, of an industrial infrastructure, of which some elements were the telegraph system, the postal service, the streetcars in Seoul, and the initial portion of a railway system (which was later taken over and completed by the Japanese), up until it became Japan's protectorate in 1905. The mass mobilization of state-led industrialization from 1897 to 1904 did not lack "nationalist legitimacy," which Hwang identifies as a "common force" behind developmental states around the world. Hwang also points out that the colonial regime maintained a rather ambivalent attitude toward industrial development in Korea—the question kept coming up among Japanese high officials as to whether Korea was more useful to Japan as a major supplier of agricultural products—until the late 1930s, when it became clear that Korea's industrialization was indispensable to imperial expansion.[60]

On the basis of this insight, we can articulate more fully the political ideology underlying the desire for progress of the male protagonists in

---

58. "Imperial Japanese Rescript," 283–84.
59. Cumings, *Korea's Place in the Sun*, 148–54; see also Eckert, *Offspring of Empire*.
60. Kyung Moon Hwang, *Rationalizing Korea*, 123.

"Persecution" and "Sad Contradictions." Given the Japanese government-general's tactical use of the ideology of progress to justify its rule of Korea, it might be difficult to completely absolve those subscribing to that ideology from the charge of being either intentional or unintentional accomplices of the colonial regime. Nonetheless, the desire for progress was at times driven by the hope for the future independence of the nation. According to the historian Pak Ch'ansŭng, during the 1910s a group of young members of the Korean elite subscribed to the belief that individual Koreans' "cultivation of competency" (*sillyŏk yangsŏng*) would lead to the recovery of the lost national sovereignty. Vladimir Tikhonov suggests that the "gradualist philosophy of strength," which was systematized by An Ch'angho (1878–1938), "may be characterized as the comprehensive, coherent, and self-conscious ideology of bourgeois modernisation and nation-building."[61]

Among the vocal advocates of a gradual increase of capability as the practical path toward independence was the author of "Persecution," Hyŏn Sangyun. His idea of individuality draws on social Darwinism: in his 1917 essay "Self-Expression and Civilization" (Chagi p'yojang kwa munmyŏng), for instance, he claims that cultivating individuality would speed the advancement of civilization: "We can say that the individual sentiment of self-expression is the cause [*wŏnin*] and wellspring [*wŏnch'ŏn*] of civilization. Therefore, one does not have to turn to philosophical thought [*ron*] to understand that a society made up of numerous individuals [*kaein*] with the strong sentiment of self-expression will take the lead of those lacking in them."[62] Hyŏn goes on to urge readers to flout traditional decorum and learn how to make their singular and unique qualities known to others in order to advance their civilization. In his mind, each individual's growth is not divided from that of the society to which he or she belongs.

Hyŏn Sangyun's notion of individuality as "the wellspring of civilization" helps us explain how the inner self is understood in "Persecution" and "Sad Contradictions." What makes the main characters of these stories so sensitive is not so much their desire for autonomy and self-governing

61. Pak Ch'ansŭng, *Han'guk kŭndae chŏngch'i*, 109–65; Tikhonov, *Social Darwinism and Nationalism*, 80–81.
62. So Sŏng (Hyŏn Sangyun's pen name), "Chagi p'yoch'ang kwa munmyŏng," 30.

power as their realization of the lack of progress in Korean society. In these stories the protagonists' search for their unique singularity is inherently linked to the question of civilization. Their characteristic negative emotions derive from their awareness that their own individuality will never attain its fullest expression unless the society to which they belong is populated with a critical mass awakened to the sense of individual selfhood. Therefore, it is misleading to view the shift from domestic women to sensitive men as marking the simple arrival of the supposedly universal form of modern individuality in Korea—no matter how much closer the stories about men may appear to some European examples than the narratives featuring women. The figures of the sensitive man do take the inward turn, but what they discover inside is not their innermost feelings, existing in isolation from external social forces, but rather the desire for the nation to achieve a higher degree of civilization—as do the female protagonists of early colonial domestic novels as well as the old man in Chang Ŭngjin's "Confession under the Moon."

If sensitive men seem more isolated than domestic women, it is because the unmediated and visible link between individuals and society that constitutes the identities of the figures of domestic women is no longer easily available to them. The early colonial domestic novel often describes a single character's awakening to new ideas as propelling the nation toward the better future. The figures of domestic women have therefore only to depart from the old ways and embrace the norms of advanced civilization in order to aid the nation in its quest for reform, whether this means creating the modern conjugal family, rejecting superstitions, going to a modern school either in a foreign country or in Korea, or dedicating their lives to education. For sensitive young men, on the other hand, the paths toward self-awakening and social progress are far from self-evident. Their aspirations for progress are simultaneously furthered and hindered by a sense of uncertainty and negative emotions—an inferiority complex, paranoia, anxiety, and fear. We can place the old *yangban* man in "Confession under the Moon" between the two figures, as his solitary death signifies the demise of the old corrupted Chosŏn.

The significance of the shift from domestic women to sensitive young men is thus multilayered. With the rise of sensitive young men, the individual becomes more closely associated with male elites than females. For these male figures, individuality is realized through a process conducted mainly through solitary mental exercises rather than as the pursuit of human rights collectively defined and defended or as the collective endeavor to free the community from traditional constraints. They favor private desires and feelings over a domestic or public space as the main site where they find a deep connection to civilizational advancement. In other words, the egalitarian and communal dimension that the figures of domestic women enact through their efforts to reform the family, and implicitly also the nation, is no longer available to those of sensitive young men.

CODA

In *From Domestic Women to Sensitive Young Men* I have explored the evolution of Korean fiction in the early colonial period, as an aleatory practice of translating the notion of the individual into Korean rather than as a teleological process of learning to simulate the "authentic" form of the European individual. In doing so, I have suggested that a group of female figures in a genre commonly considered less than modern engaged in the translation of individuality in a surprisingly imaginative and dynamic fashion prior to the advent of what has been deemed the archetypal figure exemplifying individuality in Korea—the deep-thinking male intellectual. By claiming that the first literary iterations of the Korean individual were prototypically female figures, this book calls into question the canonical assumption that male writers' portrayals of women in early colonial Korean literature, no matter how diverse and iconoclastic they might be, eventually become passive and objectified products of men and male nationalism. My emphasis, instead, has been that, while enacting their individuality through their relationship to the nation as well as to family, the figures of domestic women do not silently perform a set of prescribed roles but unsettle and even radicalize them.

The question of individuality is inevitably one of gender; both questions are intertwined at the core of literary modernity in Korea. My inquiries about the relationship between individuality and gender in early colonial Korean literature depart from those identifying an unambiguous difference between women's writings and men's. Instead, I have suggested in this book that the fact that these female images were created by male writers—whose political visions often seem dubious—should not keep us from appreciating the aesthetic significance of these literary figures, nor should we assume that pristine female images, untouched by nationalism or colonialism, eventually became available through the works of female writers.[1] To intervene in the gender-neutral concept of "the discovery of interiority," I have emphasized that the figures of domestic women are translations of individuality that are as valid as those of the sensitive young men. Instead of looking at the shift from domestic women to sensitive young men in the mid-1910s as a movement toward the "universal" form of individuality transferable across cultural, temporal, and gender boundaries, I have tied it in with specific moments in Korean history when young male elites came to understand modern "private" desires as a means not merely to contribute to the colonized nation's progress but also to secure their cultural hegemony.

This revisionist point of view allows an alternative reading of Yi Kwangsu's *The Heartless*. *The Heartless* is a story not simply about a young man who discovers a universal form of individuality but about how the nation's lack of progress keeps him from becoming a modern individual. As is the case with the figures of sensitive men in short stories from the late 1910s, the question of civilization is part and parcel of his individuality. The male protagonist of the novel, Ri Hyŏngsik, becomes aware of his individuality only through a halting process that involves not only forward but also backward steps. Hyŏngsik's first experience of self-awakening has three phases. The first takes place when Hyŏngsik looks at a portrait of Christ in Elder Kim's house and is moved to ask what it means to be a human being. He experiences the second phase of awakening that same day, when he sees his two female pupils, Sŏnhyŏng and Sunae, not simply as "girls" but as sources of "the mysterious meaning of life and the universe." The third stage of his awakening occurs later that day, when he suddenly realizes all his surroundings are filled with unknown meanings, while walking in the neighborhood he routinely passes by. After experiencing these three phases of awakening, however, Hyŏngsik's mind drifts back into the supposedly traditional and dutiful thought that has

1. I would like to thank Janet Poole for helping me clarify my points in this chapter.

been troubling him on and off—how to rescue Yŏngch'ae, the daughter of his former benefactor, who is in danger of being violated by a beastly man. His mind thus constantly glides back and forth between a sense of obligation and the pursuit of his desire, which is rendered as the tension between concern for Yŏnch'ae and attraction to Sŏnhyŏng. He remains restless and indecisive until the end of the novel. When he runs into Yŏngch'ae in the train that he takes with Sŏnhyŏng, now his fiancée, on his way to go to the United States, he feels so ashamed of himself that he almost calls off his engagement to Sŏnhyŏng and proposes to Yŏngch'ae.

The Heartless thus does not culminate in Hyŏngsik's once-and-for-all discovery of modern selfhood—rather it chronicles his stumbling attempts to become a modern man. The faltering aspect of his quest for selfhood manifests most vividly through his relationships with other characters. Over the course of the novel he develops romantic feelings for several characters—including his male student Hŭigyŏng as well as the two main female characters, Sŏnhyŏng and Yŏngch'ae. The reader frequently sees him under the unruly power of desire, not unlike the self-destructive force that drives Bunkichi (Mungil, in Korean) in Yi Kwangsu's short story "Is This Love?" (Aika, 1909) and the namesake figure in his "Yun Kwangho" (1918) to suicide.[2] After becoming engaged to Sŏnhyŏng, Hyŏngsik is overcome with emotion to the point that "if Sŏnhyŏng left him, he would kill her as well as himself with a knife."[3] His devotion to his students knows no bounds: "He would have severed his own artery if his blood were needed to cure an ill student."[4]

Hyŏngsik's relationships do not seem so much to help him grow or find his new selfhood as to reveal what impedes him from doing so. All of his relationships take distinctively precarious forms, which is attributed to lack of progress not merely on Hyŏngsik's part but also on that of Korea. In marrying Yŏngch'ae, Hyŏngsik runs the risk of the loss of his self-claimed status as "a pioneer with the most advanced thinking in Korea," since her feelings for him are no more than those of a traditional

2. Yi Pogyŏng (Yi Kwangsu's pen name), "Aika," 35–41; Janet Poole "Is This Love?" (unpublished manuscript). Also see John Treat's translation of the story, "Maybe Love"; Ch'unwŏn (Yi Kwangsu's pen name), "Yun Kwangho," 68–81.

3. Yi Kwangsu, *Yi Kwang-Su*, 286, *Parojabŭn Mujŏng*, 566.

4. Yi Kwangsu, *Yi Kwang-Su*, 225, *Parojabŭn Mujŏng*, 410.

chaste wife to her husband.[5] The relationship between Hyŏngsik and Sŏnhyŏng seems hardly more advanced. It is initiated by Sŏnhyŏng's parents, whom Hyŏngsik views as nothing but clumsy and superficial imitators of Western style. Officiated by a pastor who has little knowledge about Western marital practices, the engagement ceremony between Sŏnhyŏng and Hyŏngsik is a farcical copy of a Western custom. Both bride and groom are too embarrassed to respond to the pastor's request to say out loud that they agree to be married in front of other people. Hyŏngsik believes marriage should be based on romantic love between two people not because he has experienced romantic love but because "foreign books" he has read say so. Sŏnhyŏng's Western-style education and upbringing notwithstanding, she feels completely at a loss when Hyŏngsik suggests that they should annul their engagement if they do not love each other. She tells him that she loves him only because "she fe[els] frightened when she look[s] at Hyŏngsik's miserable face."[6] We can observe a similar instability in his relationship with his students at the all-boy Kyŏngsong School. His love for his students is crushed when his students walk out on him over the allegation that he has been visiting *kisaeng* houses, but, to be precise, his students had already begun drifting away from him well before the unfortunate incident happened—when they started to see Hyŏngsik as "at their level or beneath them."[7]

What holds Hyŏngsik back from continuing to grow is, in other words, Korea's belatedness with regard to "progress." Hyŏngsik's longing for the supposedly advanced feeling of romantic love will never be satisfied because those with whom he initiates intimate relationships have not yet attained the necessary level of spiritual development to understand why they need to experience it. His own inadequate knowledge sets a clear limit on what he can do to move Korea forward. That is to say, his private desire and personal growth—the things that make up his individuality—are inseparably conjoined with the question of civilizational progress. To that extent, we can call him an early colonial Korean translation of the individual, "a sensitive man." As in the case with the first-person male protagonists of Hyŏng Sangyun's "Persecution" and

5. Yi Kwangsu, *Yi Kwang-Su*, 229, *Parojabŭn Mujŏng*, 423.
6. Yi Kwangsu, *Yi Kwang-Su*, 290, *Parojabŭn Mujŏng*, 575.
7. Yi Kwangsu, *Yi Kwang-Su*, 229, *Parojabŭn Mujŏng*, 421.

Yang Kŏnsik's "Sad Contradictions," Hyŏngsik's search for modern self-hood does not free him from the problems of the national community but, on the contrary, awakens him to the need for the advancement of civilization in Korea.

This reading helps shed light on the controversial climactic scene in *The Heartless*, where Hyŏngsik appears to discard his restless attitude and starts to act like a mature leader of the nation. On a train that he boards with Sŏnhyong on the way to attending college in the United States, he runs into Yŏngch'ae. She, for her part, is going to Japan to study music, along with Pyŏnguka, a reform-minded female student at a music school in Japan who prevented Yŏngch'ae from killing herself and has helped her awaken to her value as a human being. The unexpected encounter puts the three main characters—Yŏngch'ae, Hyŏngik, and Sŏnhyŏng—into emotional chaos. When Yŏngch'ae learns that Hyŏngsik is engaged to another woman, she chokes up with anger and despair, regretting that she did not kill herself earlier. Completely overpowered by guilt and shame, Hyŏngsik, albeit briefly, considers breaking up with Sŏnhyŏng and canceling his travel to the United States with her. His struggle with his pent-up feelings for another young woman causes Sŏnhyŏng to be seized by jealousy in a way that she has never experienced before.

Shortly thereafter Hyŏngsik takes what happens to him in the train as an opportunity for self-reflection and emotional growth. Pondering how easily his feelings for Sŏnhyŏng could be pushed aside, he realizes that, despite his prior assurances of his superiority to his fellow countrymen, he is "still very immature in terms of spiritual and emotional development."[8] Once he gets off the train, however, his growth does appear to accelerate at a great speed: flooding in the southeastern region unexpectedly strands the train in a small city called Samnangjin. For the first time Hyŏngsik's growth takes the form of solidarity instead of isolated self-reflection. Together with the three other women he witnesses the miserable condition of the people who have just lost their homes, causing him to look beyond his self-interest and to share his concern with the others about the well-being of the community. The four of them work together to help a visibly pregnant flood victim find relief from excruciating pain and get medical help. Led by the music student, Pyŏnguk, they later organize an impromptu

8. Yi Kwangsu, *Yi Kwang-Su*, 323, *Parojabŭn Mujŏng*, 658.

concert to raise money for the victims. In the speech he makes to the other three after the concert, Hyŏngsik sounds like nothing less than an iron-willed reformist nationalist:

> "We must teach and guide them through education and actual practice. However, who will do this?" Hyŏng-sik closed his mouth. The three young women felt shivers run over their skin. "Who will do this?" Hyŏng-sik asked again more emphatically. . . . "Yes. We must do it. This is why we are going overseas to study. Who is giving us the money to take the train, and money for tuition? Korea. Why? So that we can acquire strength, knowledge, and civilization, and bring them back with us. So that we can establish a solid foundation for the people's livelihood, based on modern civilization. Isn't that why?"[9]

Hyŏngsik raises these women's national consciousness by stressing that the capabilities they will acquire through their education will be needed in Korea: Korea is what enables them to move forward. Here Hyŏngsik replaces his earlier question of "who am I" with the statement of what "we" should do. The scene ends with all of them moved to tears: they become one through their shared love of the nation.

In an essay published in 1935, the novelist Kim Tongin (1900–51) points out the discrepancy between Ri Hyŏngsik's indecisive character and his strong reformist attitude in the Samnangjin scene. He scornfully comments: "I doubt a spineless person like Ri Hyŏngsik would hold this feeling longer than a day."[10] Since then, a number of scholars have returned to this point either to call attention to the incongruity of the ending of the novel or to offer an explanation for the abrupt shift in this scene. The South Korean critic Kim Hyŏnju, for example, tries to make sense of this discrepancy by explaining the last scene of *The Heartless* as the moment when the main characters from dissimilar backgrounds coalesce into the homogeneous community of *minjok* (the nation/ people) through the medium of sympathy.[11] Modifying the Japanese literary critic Karatani Kojin's theory that modern Japanese literature results from the alien-

9. Yi Kwangsu, *Yi Kwang-Su*, 341–42, *Parojabŭn Mujŏng*, 707.
10. Kim Tongin, *Ch'unwŏn yon'gu*, 48.
11. Kim Hyŏnju, "1910 nyŏndae 'kaein,'" 285.

ation of human beings from one another through the simultaneous discovery of interiority and landscape, Michael Shin interprets the scene in Samnangjin as a moment in which Ri Hyŏngsik's earlier "discovery of *chŏng* [feeling]" or "interiority" enables him not only to discern, for the first time, the landscape of *minjok* but also to help "others to visualize the future of *minjok*."[12]

If we look at Ri Hyŏngsik as an iteration of the individual of early colonial Korean prose fiction, however, what happens to him in Samnangjin does not seem completely unexpected. Just like other works of early colonial Korean literature, *The Heartless* does not separate the question of individuality from that of civilization, or of one's emotional maturity, or lack thereof, from the degree of Korea's progress. This scene does not portray Hyŏngsik as a fully formed modern man but rather as a person yet again striving to find his true modern selfhood, for his growth will not be completed until Korea attains the highest level of "civilization."

Individuality remains inseparable from gender and sexuality no less in *The Heartless* than in other early colonial Korean literary works. Hyŏngsik's growth is mediated, on the one hand, through his longing for "civilized" romantic heterosexual relationships with women and, on the other, through his male homosocial bonding with his students. Before his arrival in Samnangjin, and indeed even before, according to the diegetic temporality of the novel, starting to tutor Sŏnhyŏng, Hyŏngsik writes in his diary that he experiences the ecstatic feeling of solidarity with the students of all-male Kyŏngsŏng School, all four hundred of them: " 'You are my parents, siblings [*hyŏngje yo chamae yo*], wife, friend, son,' he once wrote in his diary. 'You alone take up all of my love, and all my mind. I will work for you, and love you until my blood runs dry, my fresh is all spent, and my bones break.' These words expressed Hyŏngsik's genuine emotions."[13] Hyŏngsik's affection for his students is both genuine and profound, being fueled by his lonely upbringing as an orphan. One may say that his male homosocial bonding with the students seems more resolute and

12. Shin, "Interior Landscapes," 283–84. Travis Workman explains the connection between the nation and the individual in Yi Kwangsu's *The Heartless* as one of the examples that Yi assimilated with "the culturalist notion of the human being as a genus formed through the reconstruction of everyday cultural practice and bios that enacted it." See Workman, *Imperial Genus*, 64.

13. Yi Kwangsu, *Yi Kwang-Su*, 225, *Parojabŭn Mujŏng*, 410.

stronger than his heterosexual relationships with either Sŏnhyŏng or Yŏngch'ae. Whereas his relationships with these two women are filled with questions, hesitation, and self-doubt, he leaves no room for uncertainty when it comes to his love for his students. He "felt toward a few students like Hŭi-gyŏng, moreover, the kind of very passionate love that a man feels for a woman."[14] Hyŏngsik's emotion for his male students at times verges on homoeroticism. Far from vilifying his homosexual emotion as a sin (from a religious perspective) or as an abnormal behavior (from a pathological point of view), *The Heartless* views it as a superior form of feeling enabled by a spiritual bonding among people with "civilized" education. His relationships with Sŏnhyŏng and Yŏnch'ae remain fragile because their limited access to civilized education prevents him from achieving a superior form of bonding with either. On the other hand, the once-gratifying relationship between Hyŏngsik and his students begins to disintegrate when his students start thinking that they have nothing more to learn from him. It is not until the end of the novel that Hyŏngsik becomes fully aware of his limitations: "[He] thought that he was the only Korean educator who understood modern civilization and could see Korea's future." The narrator points out how ignorant Hyŏngsik is regarding his own aptitude by ascribing Hyŏngsik's failure in organizing the Kyŏngsŏng Education Association squarely to his paucity of practical knowledge and communication skills.

Thus, Ri Hyŏngsik's personal limitations delay the progress of the community as much as his personal growth is hampered by Korea's backwardness. During their intense discussion at the inn in Samnangjin, the four main characters express their desire to devote themselves to the nation's progress through education while jointly experiencing an emotional elevation. Their spiritual maturity and collective progress are both understood in teleological terms. Hence the Samnangjin scene does not present the last stage of their journeys—in it the main characters only move one step closer to the future of Korea's civilization. The tight coupling of the question of individuality and that of civilization which the figures of the individual in early colonial Korean literature are grappling with explains why Hyŏngsik and Sŏnhyŏng have yet to realize an ideal form of heterosexual companionship based allegedly on both spiritual and phys-

14. Yi Kwangsu, *Yi Kwang-Su*, 225, *Parojabŭn Mujŏng*, 410.

ical bonding. It is as if the completion of their development as individuals were deferred to an indefinite future when Korea is finally civilized and perhaps ready for self-rule. No matter how hard Ri Hyŏngsik strives to overcome his immaturity, his development will inevitably be arrested one way or another insofar as his nation is lagging behind. Hyŏngsik's search for modern selfhood, then—like that of the figure of the domestic woman—is deeply bound up with the colonial condition, instead of setting him free from it.

Bibliography

Anderson, Benedict. *Imagined Communities: Reflections on the Origin and Spread of Nationalism*. London: Verso, 1991.

Angle, Stephen C. "Should We All Be More English? Rudolf Jhering, Liang Qichao, and Rights." *Journal of the History of Ideas* 61, no. 2 (April 2000): 241–61.

An, Hamgwang. *Chosŏn munhaksa*. Vol. 9. P'yŏngyang: Kodŭng kyoyuk tosŏ ch'ulp'ansa, 1956.

Armstrong, Nancy. *Desire and Domestic Fiction: A Political History of the Novel*. Oxford: Oxford University Press, 1987.

———. *How Novels Think: The Limits of Individualism from 1719–1900*. New York: Columbia University Press, 2006.

Balibar, Etienne. "'Possessive Individualism' Reversed: From Locke to Derrida." *Constellations* 9, no. 3 (September 2002): 299–317.

———. *We, the People of Europe? Reflections on Transnational Citizenship*. Princeton, NJ: Princeton University Press, 2004.

Barlow, Tani, ed. *Formation of Colonial Modernity in East Asia*. Durham, NC: Duke University Press, 1997.

Barraclough, Ruth. *Factory Girl Literature: Sexuality, Violence, and Representation in Industrializing Korea*. Berkeley: University of California Press, 2012.

Baudelaire, Charles. *The Painter of Modern Life and Other Essays*. Edited and translated by Jonathan Mayne. New York: Da Capo Press, 1964.

Beard, George. *American Nervousness, Its Causes and Consequences*. New York: G. P. Putnam's Sons, 1881.

Bhabha, Homi. *The Location of Culture*. New York: Routledge, 2007.

Brown, Gillian. *Domestic Individualism: Imagining Self in Nineteenth-Century America*. Berkeley: University of California Press, 1990.

Chandra, Vipan. "An Outline Study of Ilchinhoe (Advancement Society) of Korea." *Occasional Papers on Korea* 2 (March 1974): 43–72.

Chang, Chiyŏn. *Nyŏja tokpon.* Seoul: Kwanghak sŏpo, 1908. Reprinted in *Han'gukhak munhŏn yŏn'guso.* Vol. 8. Edited and compiled by *Han'guk kaehwagi kyogwasŏ ch'ongsŏ.* Seoul: Asea, 1977.

Chang, Hyohyŏn, Yun Chaemin, Ch'oe Yongch'ŏl, and Chi Yŏnsuk. *Kyogambon Hanmun sosŏl.* Seoul: Korea University Press, 2007.

Chang, Kang-I Sun, and Stephen Owen, eds. *The Cambridge History of Chinese Literature.* Vol. 2, *From 1375.* Cambridge: Cambridge University Press, 2010.

Chang, Nohyŏn. "Sinsosŏl chakka Pak Yŏngun ŭi kyemong hwaltong kwa tongnip undong." *Kukche ŏmun* 61 (2014): 129–55.

Chang, Sigwang, ed. *Chosŏn sidae tongsŏng hon iyagi: Pang Hallim chŏn.* P'aju: Han'guk haksul chŏngbo, 2006.

Chang, Tŏksu [Sŏl San, pseudo.]. "Kaein kwa sahoe." *Hak chi kwang* 13 (1917): 11–19.

Chang, Ŭngjin. "Isip nyŏn chŏn hangguk hakkye iyagi." *Pyŏlgŏngon* 5 (March 1927): 16–17.

———. "Na ŭi chŏlmottŭn sijŏl cheil t'ongk'oae hadŏn il." *Pyŏlgŏngon* 21 (June 1929): 60–62.

———[Paegak Ch'unbu, pseud.]. "Wŏlha ŭi chabaek." *T'aegŭk hakbo* (September 1907): 43–47.

Chatterjee, Partha. *The Nation and Its Fragments: Colonial and Postcolonial Histories.* Princeton, NJ: Princeton University Press, 1993.

Cho, Hŭiung. *Kojŏn sosŏl ibon mongnok.* Seoul: Chipmundang, 1999.

Ch'oe, Chongsun. *Yi Injik sosŏl yŏn'gu.* Seoul: Kukhak charyowŏn, 2005.

Ch'oe, Kisuk. "Pulmyŏl ŭi chonjaeron, 'han' ŭi saengmyŏngryŏk kwa 'kwisin' ŭi ŭmsŏnghak." *Yŏlsang kojŏn yŏn'gu* 16 (December 2002): 313–55.

Ch'oe Wŏnsik. *Han'guk kŭndae sosŏlsa ron.* Seoul: Ch'angjak kwa pip'yŏng, 1986.

———. *Han'guk kyemong chuŭi munhaksaron.* Seoul: Somyŏng, 2002.

———. "Hwasŏngdon chŏn yŏn'gu." *Minjok munhaksa yŏn'gu* 18 (2001): 273–99.

Choi, Hyaeweol. "Debating the Korean New Woman: Imagining Henrik Ibsen's 'Nora' in Colonial Era Korea." *Asian Studies Review* (March 2012): 59–77.

———. *Gender and Mission Encounter in Korea: New Women, Old Ways.* Berkeley: University of California Press, 2009.

———, comp. and trans. *New Women in Colonial Korea: A Sourcebook.* London: Routledge, 2013.

———. "'Wise Mother, Good Wife': A Transcultural Discursive Construct in Modern Korea." *Journal of Korean Studies* 14 (Fall 2009): 1–33.

Choi, Kyeong-Hee. "Another Layer of Pro-Japanese Literature: Ch'oe Chŏnghŭi's The Wild Chrysanthemum." *Poetica* 52 (1999): 61–87.

———. *Beneath the Vermilion Ink: Japanese Colonial Censorship and the Making of Modern Korean Literature.* Ithaca, NY: Cornell University Press, forthcoming.

Chŏn, Kirak, ed. "Changhwa Hongnyŏn chŏn." In *Kajae kong sillok* (1865). Reprinted with Song Chaesŏng and Chŏn Yonggap, eds., 1968. http://www.nl.go.kr.

Chŏn, Kwangyong. "Sinsosŏl yŏn'gu: Moranbong." *Sasanggye* 33 (April 1956): 233–50.

Chŏn, Sŏngt'ak. "Changhwa wa hongnyŏn chŏn ŭi il yŏn'gu: Pak Insu chak hanmunbon ŭl chungsim ŭro." *Kugŏ kyoyuk* 13 (1967): 1–21.

Chŏng, Chinsŏk. "Kŭndae minjokchuŭi hyŏngsŏng kwa kaehwagi ch'ulp'an." *Han'guk ŏllon chŏngbo hakbo* (Spring 2008): 7–38.

Chŏng, Chiyŏng. "Changhwa Hongnyŏn chŏn: Chosŏn hugi chaehon kajok kusŏngwŏn ŭi wich'i." *Yŏksa pipy'ŏng* 61 (November 2002): 422–41.

———. "Munhak sok ŭi sahoesa: Pyŏn Kangsoe chŏn." *Yŏksa pip'yŏng* (November 2003): 352–70.

Ch'ŏng Chua. *Sŏbuk munhak kwa rok'ŏllit'i.* Seoul: Somyŏng, 2014.

Chŏng, Ch'urhŏn. "P'yogi muncha chŏnhwan e ttarŭn 16-17 segi sosŏl mihak ŭi pyŏni yangsang." In *Much'ŏjin munhaksa ŭi pokwŏn: 16 segi sosŏlsa,* edited by *Minjok munhak yŏn'guso kojŏnsosŏlsa yŏn'guban,* 168–98. Seoul: Somyŏng, 2007.

Chŏng, Kŭnsik. "Singminji chŏk kŏmyŏl ŭi yŏksajŏk kiwŏn." *Sahoe wa yŏksa* 64 (November 2003): 5–46.

Chŏng, Pyŏnghŏn. "Yŏsŏng yŏngung sosŏl ŭi sŏsa kujo wa pyŏni yangsang." *Han'guk ŏnŏ munhak* 36 (1996): 389–416.

Chŏngwŏl (C.W.). See Na Hyesŏk.

Ch'ŏngch'un (1914–1918).

Chōsenfu sōtoku keimu sōkanbu, ed. *Keimu geppō* 16 (1911), 278.

Chōsenfu sōtoku keimu sōkanbu, ed., *Keimu ihō* 32 (1913), 590.

Chu, Yŏngha, Ok Yŏngjŏng, Chŏn Kyŏngmok, Yun Chinyŏng, and Yi Chŏnwŏn. *Chosŏn sidae ch'aek ŭi munhwasa.* Seoul: Hyumŏnisŭtŭ, 2008.

Chu, Yosŏp. "Ilyŏkkŏ kkun." *Kaebyŏk* 58 (April 1925): 8–19.

Ch'unwŏn. See Yi Kwangsu.

Chung, Chong-wha, ed. *Korean Classical Literature: An Anthology.* London: Kegan Paul, 1989.

"Chyanghwa Hongnyŏn chyŏn." In *Han'guk pangak pon sosŏl chŏnjip.* Vol. 1. Seoul: Nurimedia, 2001.

Clifford, James. "On Ethnographic Self-Fashioning: Conrad and Malinowski." In *Reconstructing Individualism,* edited by Thomas C. Heller, Morton Sosna, and David E. Wellbery, 140–62. Stanford, CA: Stanford University Press, 1986.

Confucius. *Confucian Analects, The Great Learning & The Doctrine of the Mean.* Vol. 1. Translated by James Legge. New York: Dover Publications, 1971.

Cornyetz, Nina, and J. Keith Vincent, eds. *Perversion and Modern Japan: Psychoanalysis, Literature, Culture.* New York: Routledge, 2010.

Cumings, Bruce. *Korea's Place in the Sun.* New York: W.W. Norton and Company, 2005.

Deuchler, Martina. *The Confucian Transformation of Korea: A Study of Society and Ideology.* Cambridge, MA: Council on East Asian Studies, Harvard University, 1992.

———. "Propagating Female Virtues in Chosŏn Korea." In *Women and Confucian Culture in Premodern China,* edited by Dorothy Ko, JaHyun Kim Haboush, and Joan R. Piggott. Berkeley: University of California Press, 2003.

Douglas, Ann. *The Feminization of American Culture.* New York: Knopf, 1977.

Du, Fangqin, and Susan Man. "Competing Claims on Womanly Virtue in Late Imperial China." In *Women and Confucian Culture in Premodern China, Korea, and Japan*, edited by Dorothy Ko, JaHyun Kim Haboush, and Joan R. Piggot. Berkeley: University of California Press, 2003.

Dudden, Alexis. *Japan's Colonization of Korea: Discourse and Power*. Honolulu: University of Hawai'i Press, 2005.

Dutta, Sutapa. "Identifying Mother India in Bankimchandra Chatterjee's Novels." *Women's History Magazine* 74 (2014): 4–10.

Eckert, Carter. *Offspring of Empire: The Koch'ang Kims and the Colonial Origins of Korean Capitalism 1896–1945*. Seattle: University of Washington Press 1991.

Eley, Geoff, and Ronald Grigor Suny, eds. *Becoming National*. Oxford: Oxford University Press, 1996.

Foucault, Michel. *The History of Sexuality*. New York: Vintage Books, 1990.

Fraiman, Susan. *Unbecoming Women: British Women Writers and the Novel of Development*. New York: Columbia University Press, 1993.

Frederick, Sarah. *Turning Pages: Reading and Writing Women's Magazines in Interwar Japan*. Honolulu: University of Hawai'i Press, 2006.

Friedman, Alisa. *Tokyo in Transit: Japanese Culture on the Rails and Road*. Stanford, CA: Stanford University Press, 2010.

Gilbert, Sandra M., and Susan Gubar. *The Mad Woman in the Attic: The Woman Writer and the Nineteenth-Century Literary Imagination*. New Haven, CT: Yale University Press, 2000.

Gordon, Andrew. *A Modern History of Japan: From Tokukawa Times to the Present*. London: Oxford University Press, 2003.

———. *Labor and Imperial Democracy* in Prewar Japan. Berkeley: University of California Press, 1992.

Greenblatt, Stephen. "Fiction and Friction." In *Reconstructing Individualism*, edited by Thomas C. Heller et al., 30–52. Stanford, CA: Stanford University Press, 1986.

Haboush, JaHyun Kim, and Martina Deuchler, eds. *Culture and the State in Late Choson Korea*. Cambridge, MA: Harvard University Asia Center, 1999.

Hak chi kwang (1914–1930).

Ham, T'aeyŏng. "Hyŏl ŭi nu ich'a kaejak yon'gu." *Taedong munhwa yŏn'gu* 57 (January 2007): 203–32.

Han, Jung-Sun. *Yoshino Sakuzō and a New Liberal Order in East Asia, 1905–1937*. Cambridge, MA: Harvard University Asia Center, 2012.

Han, Kihyŏng. "Ch'ogi Yŏm Sangsŏp ŭi anak'ijŭm suyong kwa t'alsingminjijŏk t'aedo." *Hanminjok ŏmunhak* 43 (December 2003): 73–105.

———. *Han'guk kŭndae sosŏlsa ŭi sigak*. Seoul: Somyŏng, 1999.

Han'guk kaehwagi munhak ch'ongsŏ: Sinsosŏl pŏnan sosŏl. Seoul: Asea munhwasa, 1978.

Han'guk panggak pon sosŏl chŏnjip. Vol. 1. Seoul: Nurimedia, 2001.

Han'guk yŏsŏng kwan'gye charyojip: hanmal yŏsŏngji. Seoul: Ihwa yŏja taehakkyo ch'ulp'anbu, 1981.

Hanscom, Christopher. *The Real Modern: Literary Modernism and the Crisis of Representation in Colonial Korea.* Cambridge, MA: Harvard University Asia Center, 2013.

Hatano, Setsuko. *Ilbon yuhaksaeng chakka yŏn'gu.* Trans. Ch'oe Chuhan. Seoul: Somyŏng, 2011.

———. *Kankoku kindai sakka tachi no nihon ryūgaku.* Tokyo: Hyakuteisha, 2013.

Heller, Thomas C., Morton Sosna, and David E. Wellbery, eds. *Reconstructing Individualism.* Stanford, CA: Stanford University Press, 1986.

Hill, Christopher. "Exhausted by Their Battles with the World." In *Perversion and Modern Japan: Psychoanalysis, Literature, Culture,* edited by Nina Cornyetz and J. Keith Vincent. New York: Routledge, 2010.

Hong, Yanghŭi. "Singminji hojŏk chedo wa kajok chedo ŭi pyŏnyong." *Sahoehak yŏn'gu* 79 (September 2005): 167–205.

Hotei, Toshihiko. "Futatsu no Chōsen yaku 'Keikoku bidan' ni tsuite." In *Kindai Chōsen bungaku ni okeru nihon to no kanren yōsō,* edited by Ōmura Musuo and Hotei Toshihiko, 3–66. Tokyo: Ryokuinshobō, 1998.

Howland, Douglas R. *Translating the West: Language and Political Reason in Nineteenth-Century Japan.* Honolulu: University of Hawai'i Press, 2002.

Hwang, Jongyon. "The Heartless (Yi Kwangsu, Korea, 1917)." In *The Novel,* edited by Franco Moretti. Princeton, N.J.: Princeton University, 2006.

———. "The Story of the Novel in Korea: A Modern Episode." *Korea Journal* (Autumn, 2005): 209–29.

Hwang, Kyung Moon. "Citizenship, Social Equality, and Government Reform: Changes in the Household Registration System in Korea, 1894–1910." *Modern Asian Studies* 38 (2004): 355–87.

———. *A History of Korea.* New York: Palgrave Macmillan, 2010.

———. *Rationalizing Korea: The Rise of the Modern State, 1894–1945.* Oakland: University of California Press, 2016.

Hwangsŏng sinmun (Capital Gazzete), 1898–1910.

Hyŏn, Chingŏn [Ping Hŏ, pseud.]. "Unsu chohŭn nal." *Kaebyŏk* 48 (June 1924): 139–50.

Hyŏn, Sangyun [So Sŏng, pseud.]. "Chagi p'yojang kwa munmyŏng." *Hak chi kwang* 14 (November 1917): 26–32.

———. *Chosŏn Yuhaksa.* Seoul: Minjung sŏgwan, 1949.

———. "Kangnyŏk chuŭi wa chosŏn ch'ŏngnyŏn." *Hak chi kwang* 6 (July 1915): 43–49.

———. "Kyongsŏng sogam." *Ch'ŏngchun* 12 (November 1918): 124–29.

———. "Persecution." Translated by Yoon Sun Yang and Sandra Lee. Unpublished manuscript.

———. "P'ippak." *Ch'ŏngch'un* 8 (1917): 86–90.

———. "Tonggyŏng yuhaksaeng saenghwal." *Ch'ŏngch'un* 2 (December 1915): 110–17.

Ibsen, Henrik. *Nora.* Translated by Yang Paekhwa. Seoul: Yŏngch'ang sŏgwan, 1922.

Im, Hwa. *Im Hwa sin munhaksa.* Edited by Im Kyuch'an and Han Chinil. Seoul: Han'gil, 1993.

Im, Hyŏngt'aek. *Han'guk munhaksa ŭi sigak*. Seoul: Ch'angjak kwa pip'yŏngsa, 1984.

"Imperial Japanese Rescript Attached to the Proclamation and Treaty of Annexation." *American Journal of International Law* 4 (4) Supplement: Official Documents (Oct., 1910): 283–84.

Ito, Ken K. *An Age of Melodrama: Family, Gender, and Social Hierarchy in the Turn-of-the-Century Japanese Novel*. Palo Alto, CA: Stanford University Press, 2008.

Jameson, Fredric. *The Ideologies of Theory Essays 197–1986*. Vol. 2, *The Syntax of History*. Minneapolis: University of Minnesota Press, 1988.

——. *The Political Unconscious: Narrative as a Socially Symbolic Act*. Ithaca, NY: Cornell University Press, 1981.

——. "Progress versus Utopia; or, Can We Imagine the Future?" *Science Fiction Studies* 9, no. 2 (July 1982): 147–58.

Kang, Hwasŏk. *Puyu toksŭp*. Seoul: Hwangsŏng sinmunsa, 1908. Reprinted in *Han'guk kaehwagi kyogwasŏ ch'ongsŏ* 8. Edited and compiled by *Han'gukhak munhŏn yŏn'guso*. Seoul: Asea, 1977.

Kang, Hyŏnjo. "Kim Kyoje pŏnyŏk pŏnan sosŏl ŭi taebon yŏn'gu." *Hyŏndae sosŏl yŏn'gu* (2011): 197–225.

Kang, Myŏnggwan. *Yŏllyŏ ŭi t'ansaeng: kabujangje wa Chosŏn yŏsŏng ŭi chanhokhan yŏksa*. Paju: Tolbyegae, 2009.

Kaplan, Amy. *The Anarchy of Empire in the Making of U.S. Culture*. Cambridge, MA: Harvard University Press, 2005.

Karatani, Kojin. *Origins of Modern Japanese Literature*. Translated by Brett de Bary. Durham, NC: Duke University Press, 1993.

Kidokkyo taebaekkwa sajŏn. Vol. 8. Seoul: Kidokkyo munsa, 1980–1985.

Killick, Andrew. *In Search of Korean Traditional Opera*. Honolulu: University of Hawai'i Press, 2010.

Kim, Chaeyŏng. "Kŭndae kyemonggi sosŏl kaenyŏm ŭi pyŏnhwa: tugaji oeraejŏk wŏnch'ŏn." *Hyŏndae munhak ŭi yŏn'gu* 22 (2004): 7–46.

Kim, Hyŏnju. "1910 nyŏndae 'kaein' 'minjok' ŭi kusŏng kwa kamjŏng ŭi chŏngch'ihak." *Hyŏndae munhak ŭi yŏn'gu* 22 (2004): 260–94.

Kim, Iryŏp. See Kim Wŏnju.

Kim, Jee-Woon. *A Tale of Two Sisters (Changhwa hongnyŏn)*. 2003. DVD. Directed by Jee-Woon Kim. Tartan Video, 2005.

Kim, Kyoje. *Ch'iaksan*. Vol. 2. Seoul: Tongyang sŏwŏn, 1911.

——. *Kyŏng chung hwa*. Seoul: Pomun kwan, 1923. Reprinted in *Sinsosŏl chŏnjip* 4:75–148. Seoul: Kyemyŏng munhwasa, 1987.

Kim, Myŏngsun [T'ansil, pseud.]. "Na nŭn sarang handa." *Tonga ilbo*, August 17–September 3, 1926.

Kim, Poksun. *1910 nyŏndae han'guk munhak kwa kŭndae sŏng*. Seoul: Somyŏng. 1999.

Kim, P'yŏnju. See Kim Wŏnju.

Kim, Sun Joo, and Jungwon Kim, eds. and trans. *Wrongful Deaths: Selected Inquest Records from Nineteenth-Century Korea*. Seattle: University of Washington Press, 2014.

Kim, Susie Ji Young. "What (Not) to Wear: Refashioning Civilization in Print Media in Turn-of-the-Century Korea." *positions: east asia cultures critique* 15, no. 3 (Winter 2007): 609–36.

Kim, Tongin. *Ch'unwŏn yon'gu*. Seoul: Sin'gumunhwasa, 1956.

Kim, Wŏnju [Kim P'yŏnju, Kim Iryŏp, pseud.]. "Awakening." In Yung Hee Kim ed. and trans., *Questioning Minds: Short Stories by Modern Korean Women Writers*. Honolulu: University of Hawai'i, 2010, 55–65.

―――. "Chagak," *Tonga ilbo*, June 19–26, 1926.

―――. "Hŭisaeng." *Chosŏn ilbo*, January 1–5, 1929.

―――. "Hŭisaeng toen ilsaeng: ch'ŏngsang ŭi saenghwal." *Sinyŏja* 4 (1920).

―――. "Puin ŭi pokchi kaeryang e taehan ŭigyŏn." *Tonga ilbo*, September 10–12, 14, 1921.

―――. *Reflections of a Zen Buddhist Nun: Essays by Zen Master Kim Iryop*. Translated by Jin Young Park. Honolulu: University of Hawai'i Press, 2014.

―――. "Sarang." *Chosŏn mundan* (April 1926).

―――. "Sunae ŭi chugŭm." *Tonga ilbo*, January 31–February 8, 1926.

―――. "X ssi ege." *Pulgyo*, 1929.

Kim, Yŏngmin. *Han'guk kŭndae sosŏlsa*. Seoul: Sol, 1997.

―――. *Han'guk ŭi kŭndae sinmun kwa kŭndae sosŏl*. Seoul: Somyŏng, 2006.

Kim, Yung-Hee. "Creating New Paradigms of Womanhood in Modern Korean Literature: Na Hyesŏk's 'Kyŏnghŭi.'" *Korean Studies* 26, no. 1 (2002): 1–60.

―――, ed. and trans. *Questioning Minds: Short Stories by Modern Korean Women Writers*. Honolulu: University of Hawai'i Press, 2010.

Ko, Dorothy, JaHyun Kim Haboush, and Joan R. Piggott, eds. *Women and Confucian Culture in Premodern China*. Berkeley: University of California Press, 2003.

Kornicki, Peter F. "Disraeli and the Meiji Novel." *Harvard Journal of Asiatic Studies* 44, no. 1 (1984): 29–55.

Ku, Inhwan, ed. *Hong keywŏl chŏn*. Seoul: Sinwon munhwasa, 2004.

Kukyŏ. See Yang Kŏnsik.

Kwŏn, Podŭrae. *Sinsosŏl, ŏnŏ wa chŏngch'i*. Seoul: Somyŏng, 2014.

―――. "Tongp'o ŭi susahak kwa 'yŏksa' ŭi kamgak: 1900–1904 nyŏn tongp'o kaenyŏm ŭi ch'ui." *Han'guk munhak nonch'ong* 41 (December 2005): 267–87.

―――. "Tongp'o ŭi yŏksa chŏk kyŏnghŏm kwa chŏngch'i sŏng: Tongnip sinmun kisa punsŏk ŭl chungsim ŭro." In *Kŭndae kyemonggi chisik kaenyŏm ŭi suyong kwa kŭ pyŏnyong*, edited by Ihwa yŏdae han'guk munhwa yŏn'guwŏn, 97–125. Seoul: Somyŏng, 2004.

Kwŏn, Yonggi. "Tongnip sinmun e nat'anan 'tongp'o' ŭi kŏmt'o." *Han'guk sasang sahak* 12 (1999): 239–60.

Lanser, Susan. "Sapphic Picaresque, Sexual Difference and the Challenges of Homo-Adventuring." *Textual Practice* 15, no. 2 (2001): 251–68.

Lee, Chulwoo. "Modernity, Legality, and Power in Korea under Japanese Rule." In *Colonial Modernity in Korea*, edited by Gi-Wook Shin and Michael Robinson, 21–51. Cambridge, MA: Harvard University Asia Center, 1999.

Lee, Haiyan. *Revolution of the Heart: A Genealogy of Love in China, 1900–1950*. Stanford, CA: Stanford University Press, 2007.

Lee, Ji-Eun. *Women Pre-Scripted: Forging Modern Roles through Korean Print.* Honolulu: University of Hawai'i Press, 2015.

Lee, Jin-kyung. "Autonomous Aesthetics and Autonomous Subjectivity: Construction of Modern Literature as a Site of Social Reforms and Modern Nation-Building in Colonial Korea, 1915–1925." Ph.D. diss., University of California, Los Angeles, 2000.

Lévi-Strauss, Claude. *Structural Anthropology.* Translated by C. Jacobson and B. G. Schoepf. New York: Basic Books, 1963.

Levy, Indra. *Sirens of the Western Shore: Westernesque Women and Translation in Modern Japanese Literature.* New York: Columbia University Press, 2010.

Liang, Qichao. *Yin bing shi cong zhu.* Vol. 1. Shanghai: Shang wu yin shu guan, 1916, 51–66, https://babel.hathitrust.org/cgi/pt?id=wu.89016080442;view=1up;seq =16.

Liu, Lydia H. "The Discourse of Individualism." In *Formation of Colonial Modernity in East Asia,* edited by Tani Barlow, 83–112. Durham, NC: Duke University Press, 1997.

———. *Translingual Practice: Literature, National Culture, and Translated Modernity: China, 1900–1937.* Stanford, CA: Stanford University Press, 1995.

Mansebo (Three Thousand Generations), 1906–1907.

Maeil sinbo (The Daily), 1910–1945.

Moon, Yumi. *Populist Collaborators: The Ilchinhoe and the Japanese Colonization of Korea: 1895–1910.* Ithaca, NY: Cornell University Press, 2013.

Moretti, Franco, ed. *The Novel.* Princeton, NJ: Princeton University Press, 2006.

———. *The Way of the World: The Bildungsroman in European Culture.* London: Verso, 2000.

Mulvey, Laura. "Visual Pleasure and Narrative Cinema." *Screen* 16 (3) (Autumn 1975): 6–18.

Musuo, Ōmura, and Hotei Toshihiko, eds. *Kindai Chōsen bungaku ni okeru nihon to no kanren yōsō.* Tokyo: Ryokuinshobō, 1998.

Muta, Kazue. "Meijiki sōgō zasshini miru kazokuzō—katei no tōjō to sono paradokkusu." *Shakaigaku hyōron* 41, no. 1 (June 1990): 12–25.

Myers, Ramon H., and Mark R. Peattie, eds. *The Japanese Colonial Empire, 1895–1945.* Princeton, NJ: Princeton University Press, 1984.

Namgung, Chun. *Sanch'ŏn ch'omok.* Seoul: Yuil sŏgwan, 1912.

Na, Hyesŏk [C. W., initials of Chŏng Wŏl, pseud.]. "Chapkam—K ŏnni ege yŏham." *Hak chi kwang* 13 (1917): 65–68.

———. "Puin ŭibok kaeryang munje: Kim Wŏnju hyŏng ŭi ŭigyŏn e taehayŏ." *Tonga ilbo,* September 28–30, October 1, 1921.

Nam, Yunsu, Pak Chaeyŏn, and Kim Yŏngbok, eds. *Yang Paekhwa Munjip.* Vol. 1. Ch'unch'ŏn: Kangwŏn University Press, 1995.

National Institute of Korean History. "Chosŏn Wangjo Sillok: The Annals of the Joseon Dynasty." http://sillok.history.go.kr.

New American Standard Bible. La Habra, CA: Foundation Press Publications, 1971.

No, Sangnae, and Sin Misam. "Yi Injik sosŏl e nat'anan yŏsŏng kwan yŏn'gu." *Hanminjok ŏmunhak* 50 (June 2007): 467–94.

No, Yŏnsuk. "Ilbon chŏngch'i sosŏl ŭi suyong kwa sinsosŏl ŭi tach'ŭnghwa—Ku Yŏnhak ŭi Sŏlchungmae hwa Suehiro Tetchō ŭi Setchūbai rŭl chungsim ŭro." *Inmun nonch'ong* 59 (2008): 1–40.

———. "20 seji ch'o hanjungil chŏngch'i sŏsa wa kŭndae ŭi chŏngch'ijŏk sangsang." *Han'guk hyŏndae munhak yŏn'gu* 33 (2011): 35–64.

Oh, Young Kyun. *Engraving Virtue: The Printing History of a Premodern Korean Moral Primer.* Leiden: Brill, 2013.

Ōtani, Morishige. *Chosŏn hugi tokcha yŏn'gu.* Seoul: Kodae minjok munhwa yŏn'guwŏn, 1985.

Pae, Chŏngsang. *Yi Haejo munhak yŏn'gu.* Seoul: Somyŏng, 2015.

Paegak Ch'unbu. See Chang Ŭngjin.

Paek, Taejin. "Sinnyŏn pyŏktu e insaeng chuŭip'a munhakcha ŭi paech'ulham ŭl kidaeham." *Sinmun'gye* 34 (January 1916): 13–16.

Pak, Ch'ansŭng. *Han'guk kŭndae chŏngch'i sasang yŏn'gu: minjok chuŭi up'a ŭi sillyŏk yangsŏng undong non.* Seoul: Yŏksa pip'yŏngsa, 1992.

Pak, Chinyŏng. *Pŏnyŏk kwa pŏnan ŭi sidae.* Seoul: Somyŏng, 2011.

Pak, Chongho, Ch'oe T'akho, and Ryu Man. *Chosŏn munhaksa: 19 segi mal-1925.* P'yŏngyang: Kwahak, Paekkwa Sajŏn Ch'ulp'ansa, 1980.

Pak, Chuwŏn. "Kŭndaejŏk kaein sahoe kaenyŏm ŭi hyŏngsŏng kwa pyŏnhwa—han'guk chayujuŭi ŭi t'ŭksŏng e taehayŏ." *Yŏksa pip'yŏng* (May 2004): 207–38.

Pak, Hŭibyŏng, ed. *Han'guk chŏn'gi sosŏl ŭi mihak.* Seoul: Tongbegae, 1997.

———. *Han'guk hanmun sosŏl kyohap kuhae.* Seoul: Somyŏng, 2005.

Pak, Hŭibyŏng, and Chŏng Kilsu, eds. and trans. *Sarang ŭi chu'gŭm.* Seoul: Tolbaegye, 2007.

Pak, Hyesuk. "Yŏsŏng yŏngung sosŏl kwa p'yŏngdŭng, ch'ai, chŏngch'esŏng munje." *Minjok munhaksa yŏn'gu* 31 (2006): 156–93.

Pak, Ilyong. *Chosŏn sidae ŭi aejŏng sosŏl.* Seoul: Chipmundang, 1993.

Pak, Sukcha. *Han'guk munhak kwa kaeinsŏng.* Seoul: Somyŏng, 2008.

Pak, Sunch'ŏl and Kim Yŏng. "Han'guk ŭi munhwa: Chung han yang'guk ŭi chŏngjŏl kwannyŏm kwa yangsang koch'al: Myŏng Ch'ŏng kwa Chosŏn ŭl chungsim ŭro." *Han'guk sasang kwa munhwa* 46 (2009): 377–411.

Pak, T'aewŏn. "Sosŏlga Kubo ssi ŭi iril." *Chosŏn chungang ilbo*, August 1–September 19, 1934.

Pang Hanim chŏn. Unpublished handwritten manuscript.

Park, Sunyoung. *The Proletarian Wave: Literature and Leftist Culture in Colonial Korea, 1910–1945.* Cambridge, MA: Harvard University Asia Center, 2015.

Pinghŏ. See Hyŏn Chingŏn.

Poole, Janet. "Is This Love?" Unpublished manuscript.

———. *When the Future Disappears: The Modernist Imagination in Late Colonial Korea.* New York: Columbia University Press, 2014.

Pyŏlgye ch'aet'am. Hwangsŏn Sinmun. February 20–25, 1910.

Ragsdale, Kathryn. "Marriage, the Newspaper Business, and the Nation-State: Ideology in the Late Meiji Serialized Katei Shōsetsu." *Journal of Japanese Studies* 24 (1998): 229–55.

Robinson, Michael E. "Colonial Publication Policy and the Korean National Movement." In *The Japanese Colonial Empire, 1895–1945*, edited by Ramon H. Myers and Mark R. Peattie. Princeton, NJ: Princeton University Press, 1984.

———. *Cultural Nationalism in Colonial Korea, 1920–1925*. Seattle: University of Washington Press, 2014.

Romero, Lora. *Home Fronts: Domesticity and Its Critics in the Antebellum United States.* Durham, NC: Duke University Press, 1997.

Ross, John. "Corean New Testament." *Chinese Recorder and Missionary Journal* 14(6) (1883): 491–97.

Rubin, Gayle S. *A Gayle Rubin Reader: Deviations.* Durham, NC: Duke University Press, 2011.

Sakaki, Atsuko. "Kajin no Kigū: The Meiji Political Novel and the Boundaries of Literature." *Monumenta Nipponica* 55, no. 1 (Spring 2000): 83–108.

Sarkar, Sumit, and Tanika Sarkar. *Women and Social Reform in Modern India: A Reader.* Bloomington: Indiana University Press, 2008.

Schmid, Andre. *Korea between Empires.* New York: Columbia University Press, 2002.

Scott, Joan Wallach. *Only Paradoxes to Offer: French Feminists and the Rights of Man.* Cambridge, MA: Harvard University Press, 1996.

Sedgwick, Eve Kosofsky. *Between Men: English Literature and Male Homosocial Desire.* New York: Columbia University Press, 1985.

Serikawa Tetsuyo. "Hanil kaehwagi uhwa sosŏl ŭi pigyo yŏn'gu–Illygonggyŏk kŭmsu kukhoe wa kŭmsu hoeŭi rok ŭl chungsim ŭro." *Ilbon hakbo* (Japan Bulletin) 5 (1977): 163–79.

Shin, Gi-wook, and Michael Robinson, eds. *Colonial Modernity in Korea.* Cambridge, MA: Harvard University Asia Center, 1999.

Shin, Michael D. "Interior Landscapes: Yi Kwangsu's 'The Heartless' and the Origins of Modern Korean Literature." In *Colonial Modernity in Korea*, edited by Shin, Gi-wook and Michael Robinson, 248–87. Cambridge, MA: Harvard University Asia Center, 1999.

Simmel, Georg. *The Sociology of Georg Simmel.* Translated by Kurt Wolff. New York: Free Press, 1950.

Sin, Chaehyo. *Pyŏn Kangsoe ka.* Edited by Kim Ch'angjin. Seoul: Chimanji, 2009.

Sin, Ch'unja. *Kaehwagi sosŏl yŏn'gu.* Seoul: Inmundang, 1990.

Sin, Myŏngho. *Kunggwŏl ŭi kkot kungnyŏ.* Seoul: Sigongsa, 2005.

Sinha, Mrinalina. "Gender in the Critique of Colonialism and Nationalism: Locating the 'Indian Woman.'" In *Women and Social Reform in Modern India: A Reader*, edited by Sumit Sarkar and Tanika Sarkar, 452–72. Bloomington: Indiana University Press, 2008.

———. "Gender and Nation." In *Women's History in Global Perspective*, edited by Bonnie G. Smith, 229–74. Urbana: University of Illinois Press, 2004.

Sinsosŏl chonjip. Seoul: Kyemyŏng munhwasa, 1987.

Sinyŏja (1920).

Smith, Anthony D. "The Origins of Nations." In *Becoming National*, edited by Geoff Eley and Ronald Grigor Suny. Oxford: Oxford University Press, 1996.

Smith, Bonnie G., ed. *Women's History in Global Perspective*. Urbana: University of Illinois Press, 2004.

Sŏ, Chaegil. "*Kŭmsu hoeŭirok* ŭi chŏbon *Kŭmsu hoeŭi illyu konggyŏk* e kwanhan il koch'al." *Han'guk kŭndae munhak yŏn'gu* 26 (October 2012): 67–93.

Sŏ, Chŏngja. "Ilyŏp Kim Wŏnju, Sinyŏja, kŭ ŭi sasang tasi ilki." *Na Hyesŏk yŏn'gu* (June 1913): 33–73.

Sŏ, Hyeŭn. "'Changhwa Hongnyŏn chŏn'—ibon kyeyŏl ŭi sŏnggyŏk kwa tokcha ŭisik." *Ŏmunhak* 97 (September 2008): 387–418.

So, Sŏng. See Hyŏn Sangyun.

Sŏlsan. See Chang Tŏksu.

Sommer, Matthew H. "The Uses of Chastity: Sex, Law, and the Property of Widows in Qing China." *Late Imperial China* 17, no. 2 (1996): 78–80.

Son, Insu. *Han'guk kaehwa kyoyuk yŏn'gu*.Seoul: Ilchisa, 1980.

Sŏnghae. See Yi Iksang.

Sŏng, Hyŏnja. "Sinsosŏl e mich'in manch'ŏng sosŏl ŭi yŏnghyang." *Chungguk sosŏl yŏn'gu hoebo* 16 (November 1993): 89–93.

Sonyŏn Hanbando (1906–1907).

Soothill, William Edward, and Lewis Hodous. *A Dictionary of Chinese Buddhist Terms: With Sanskrit and English Equivalents and a Sanskrit-Pali Index*. Taipei: Ch'eng Wen Publishing, 1976. Digitalized edition, http://mahajana.net/texts/kopia_lokalna /soothill-hodous.html#index-div1-div185697848.

Speare, Morris Edmund. *The Political Novel: Its Development in England and in America*. New York: Russell and Russell, 1966.

Spivak, Gayatri Chakravorty. "Three Women's Texts and a Critique of Imperialism." *Critical Inquiry* 12 (1985): 243–61.

Sumunsaeng. See Yi Haejo.

T'ansil. See Kim Myŏngsun.

Taehan maeil sinbo (1904–1910).

Tajiri, Hiroyuki. *Yi Injik yŏn'gu*. Seoul: Saemi, 2006.

Tate, Claudia. *Domestic Allegories of Political Desire: The Black Heroine's Text at the Turn of the Century*. New York: Oxford University Press, 1992.

Tayama, Katai. *The Quilt and Other Stories*. Translated by Kenneth G. Henshall. New York: Columbia University Press, 1981.

Taylor, Charles. *Sources of the Self: The Making of the Modern Identity*. Cambridge, MA: Harvard University Press, 1989.

Tian, Ming (Chŏn Myŏng). "Aeguk kyemonggi chungyŏkpon chŏngch'i sosŏl ŭi han'guk chŏk pyŏnyong yangsang—Hyŏn Kongnyŏm ŭi *Hoech'ŏn kidam* kwa *Kyŏngguk midam* ŭl chungsim ŭro." Master's thesis, Inha University, 2012.

Tikhonov, Vladimir. "Masculinizing the Nation: Gender Ideologies in Traditional Korea and in the 1890s–1900s Korean Enlightenment Discourse." *Journal of Asian Studies* 66, no. 4 (November 2007): 1029–65.

————. *Social Darwinism and Nationalism in Korea: The Beginnings (1880s–1910s): "Survival" as an Ideology of Korean Modernity*. Boston: Brill Academic Publishers, 2010.

Tompkins, Jane. *Sentimental Designs: The Cultural Work of American Fiction, 1790–1860*. Oxford: Oxford University Press, 1986.

Tong'a Ilbo (1920–).

Tongnip sinmun (1896–1899).

Toshitani, Nobuyoshi. "Kazokuhō no jikken." In *Kazoku no shakaishi*, edited by Ueno Chizuko, Nagai Hisao, and Miyama Noboru, 99–118. Tokyo: Iwanami shoten, 1991.

Treat, John. "Maybe Love" (Aika, 1909), *Azalea: Journal of Korean Literature & Culture* 4 (2011): 322–27.

U, Rimgŏl (C: Niu Linjie). *Han'guk kaehwagi munhak kwa Yang Kech'o*. Seoul: Pagijong, 2002.

Udang. See Yun Hŭigo.

Ueda, Atsuko. *Concealment of Politics, Politics of Concealment: The Production of "Literature" in Meiji Japan*. Stanford, CA: Stanford University Press, 2007.

Ueno, Chizuko. *Kindai kazoku no seiritsu to shūen*. Tokyo: Iwanami shoten, 1994.

————. *The Modern Family in Japan: Its Rise and Fall*. Melbourne: Trans Pacific Press, 2009.

Ueno, Chizuko, Nagai Hisao, and Miyama Noboru, eds. *Kazoku no shakaishi*. Tokyo: Iwanami shoten, 1991.

Unyŏngjŏn. Translated by Kan Hoyun. Seoul: Ihoe munhwasa, 2003.

Unyŏng-jŏn: A Love Affair at the Royal Palace of Chosŏn Korea. Translated and annotated by Michael Pettid. Berkeley: Center for Korean Studies, Institute of East Asian Studies, University of California, 2009.

Uri ŭi kadyŏng (1913–1914).

Vincent, J. Keith. *Two-Timing Modernity: Homosocial Narratives in Modern Japanese Fiction*. Cambridge, MA: Harvard University Asia Center, 2012.

Walraven, Boudewijn. "Popular Religion in a Confucianized Society." In *Culture and the State in Late Choson Korea*, edited by JaHyun Kim Haboush and Martina Deuchler, 160–98. Cambridge, MA: Harvard University Asia Center, 1999.

Watt, Ian. *The Rise of the Novel*. Berkeley: University of California Press, 2001.

Wang, David Der-wei. *Fin-de-Siècle Splendor: Repressed Modernities of Late Qing Fiction, 1849–1911*. Stanford, CA: Stanford University Press, 1997.

Wells, Kenneth M. "Background to the March First Movement: Koreans in Japanese, 1905–1919." *Korean Studies* 13 (1989): 5–21.

Wexler, Laura. *Tender Violence: Domestic Visions in an Age of U.S. Imperialism*. Chapel Hill: University of North Carolina Press, 2000.

Williams, Raymond. *Keywords: A Vocabulary of Culture and Society*. New York: Oxford, 1983.

Willcock, Hiroko. "Meiji Japan and the Late Qing Political Novel." *Journal of Oriental Studies* 33, no. 1 (1995): 1–28.

Woo, Hyo Kyung. "Korean Englishes, Uneven Asias, and Global Circulation, 1895–1945." Ph.D. diss., University of Pittsburgh, 2016.

Workman, Travis. *Imperial Genus: The Formation and Limits of the Human in Modern Korea and Japan.* Oakland: University of California Press, 2015.

Yanabu, Akira. *Hon'yakugo seiritsu jijō.* Tokyo: Iwanami Shinsho, 1982.

Yanagida, Izumi. *Seiji shōsetsu kenkyū, jo.* Vol. 8 of *Meiji bungaku kenkyū.* Tokyo: Shunjuisha, 1967.

Yang, Kŏnsik. "Sad Contradictions." Translated by Yoon Sun Yang and Sandra Lee. Unpublished manuscript.

———[Kukyŏ, pseud.]. "Sŭlp'ŭn mosun." *Pando siron* 10 (February 1918): 71–76.

———. "Yŏ nŭn Ch'unwŏn ŭi sosŏl ŭl hwanyŏng hanora." *Maeil sinbo*, December, 29, 1916.

Yang, Yoon Sun. "Nation in the Backyard: Yi Injik and the Rise of Korean New Fiction, 1906–1913." Ph.D. diss., University of Chicago, 2009.

Yeh, Catherine. *The Chinese Political Novel.* Cambridge, MA: Harvard University Asia Center, 2015.

Yi, Chongmin. "1910 nyŏndae kyŏngsŏng chumin ŭi choe wa pŏl." *Sŏul hak yŏn'gu* 17: 95–130.

Yi, Chŏngwŏn. "Sinjak kusosŏl nanbong kihap yŏn'gu." *Han'guk munhak iron kwa pip'yŏng* 62 (March 2014): 195–223.

Yi, Haejo. *Hwa ŭi hyŏl.* Seoul: Pogŭp sŏgwan, 1912.

———. [Sumunsaeng, pseud.]. *Pak chŏng hwa. Taehan Minbo*, March 10–May 31, 1910.

———. *Sanch'ŏn ch'omok.* Edited by Nam Kungjun. Seoul: Yuil sŏgwan, 1912.

Yi, Hyeryŏng. *Han'guk kŭndae sosŏl kwa seksyuŏllit'i ŭi sŏsa.* Seoul: Somyŏng, 2007.

Yi, Hyesun. *Chosŏn cho hugi yŏsŏng chisŏngsa.* P'aju: Tolbegae, 2004.

Yi, Hyesun and Kim Kyŏngmi. *Han'guk ŭi yŏllŏjŏn.* Seoul: Wŏlin, 2002.

Yi, Hyosŏk. "Tosi wa yuryŏng." *Chosŏn chi kwang* 79 (July 1928): 106–21.

Yi, Iksang [Sŏnghae, pseud.]. "Saeng ŭl kuhanŭn mam." *Sin saenghwal* (September 1922): 153–63.

Yi, Injik. *Ch'iak san.* Vol. 1. Seoul: Yuilsŏgwan, 1908.

———. "Hyŏl ŭi nu." *Mansebo*, July 20–October 10, 1906.

———. "Hyŏl ŭi nu ha p'yŏn." *Cheguk sinmun*, May 17–June 1, 1907.

———. "Kafu no yume." *Miyako shinbun*, January 28–29, 1902.

———. *Moktanbong.* Seoul: Tongyang sŏwŏn, 1912.

———. "Moranbong." *Maeil Sinbo*, February 7, 1913–June 3, 1913.

———. "Tears of Blood." In Chung Chong-wha, ed., *Korean Classical Literature: An Anthology.* London: Kegan Paul International, 1989, 159–221.

———. *Ŭnsegye.* Seoul: Tongmunsa, 1908.

Yi, Kiyŏng. "Kananhan saramdŭl." *Kaebyŏk* 59 (May 1924): 59–85.

Yi, Kwangsu [Yi Po'gyŏng, pseud.]. "Aika." *Shirogane gakubō* 19 (December 1909): 35–41. Reprinted in *Kindai Chōsen bungaku nihongo sakuhinshū: sōsaku (1).* Edited by Ōmura Matsuo and Hotei Toshihiro, 13–19. Tokyo: Ryokuinshobō, 2004.

———. "Munhak iran hao." *Maeil sinbo*, November 10–23, 1916.

———. "Puhwal ŭi sŏ kwang." *Ch'ŏngch'un* 12 (March, 1918): 18–37.

———. *Parojabŭn Mujŏng*. Annotated by Kim Ch'ŏl. Paju: Munhak Tongnye, 2003.

———. *Yi Kwang-Su and Modern Korean Literature, Mujŏng*. Translated by Ann Sunghi Lee. Ithaca, NY: East Asia Program, Cornell University, 2005.

———[Ch'unwŏn, pseud.]. "Yun Kwangho." *Ch'ŏngch'un* 13 (April 1918): 68–81.

Yi, Kyŏngha. "Cheguk sinmun yŏsŏng tokcha t'ugo e nat'anan kŭndae tamnon." *Han'guk kojŏn yŏsŏng munhak yŏn'gu* 8 (2004): 67–98.

Yi, Po'gyŏng. See Yi Kwangsu.

Yi, Sangsu, ed. and trans., *17-segi aejŏng chŏn'gi*. Seoul: Wŏlin, 1999.

Yi, Sŭnggyu, ed. *Inhyang chŏn*. Kyŏngsŏng [Seoul]: Chunghŭng sŏgwan, 1937.

Yi, Sŭngil. *Chosŏn ch'ongdokpu pŏpche chŏngch'aek*. Seoul: yŏksa pip'yŏngsa, 2012.

Yi, Tonggŭn. *Suijŏn ilmun* (Lost work from *Eccentric Tales*). Seoul: Chimanji, 2008.

Yi, Tuhŏn. *Han'guk kajok chedo yŏn'gu*. Seoul: Sŏul Taehakkyo ch'ulp'anbu, 1969.

Yi, Yumi. "Kŭndae kyemonggi tanp'yŏn sosŏl ŭi wisang: 'taehan minbo' sosŏl nan ŭl chungsim ŭro." *Hyŏndae munhak ŭi yŏn'gu* (2004): 130–66.

Yŏm, Sangsŏp. "Yŏja tanbal munje wa kŭe kwanhayŏ." *Sinsaenghwal* 8 (August 1922).

Yu, Sŭnghŭi. "19 segi yŏsŏng pŏmchoe e nat'anan kaltŭng: ch'ujo kyŏlok rok ŭl chungsim ŭro." *Taedong munhwa yŏn'gu* 73 (2011): 159.

Yun Hŭigu [Udang, pseudo.]. "*Sinsosŏl*." *Maeil Sinbo*. April 5 and 8, 1916.

Yun, Sasun ed. *Kidang Hyŏn Sangyun*. Seoul: Hanul, 2009.

Zeitlin, Judith. "Xiaoshuo." In *The Novel*, edited by Franco Moretti, 249–61. Princeton, NJ: Princeton University Press, 2006.

Index

Harvard East Asian Monographs
(most recent titles)

Harvard East Asian Monographs

243. Kyung Moon Hwang, *Beyond Birth: Social Status in the Emergence of Modern Korea*
244. Brian R. Dott, *Identity Reflections: Pilgrimages to Mount Tai in Late Imperial China*
245. Mark McNally, *Proving the Way: Conflict and Practice in the History of Japanese Nativism*
246. Yongping Wu, *A Political Explanation of Economic Growth: State Survival, Bureaucratic Politics, and Private Enterprises in the Making of Taiwan's Economy, 1950–1985*
247. Kyu Hyun Kim, *The Age of Visions and Arguments: Parliamentarianism and the National Public Sphere in Early Meiji Japan*
248. Zvi Ben-Dor Benite, *The Dao of Muhammad: A Cultural History of Muslims in Late Imperial China*
249. David Der-wei Wang and Shang Wei, eds., *Dynastic Crisis and Cultural Innovation: From the Late Ming to the Late Qing and Beyond*
250. Wilt L. Idema, Wai-yee Li, and Ellen Widmer, eds., *Trauma and Transcendence in Early Qing Literature*
251. Barbara Molony and Kathleen Uno, eds., *Gendering Modern Japanese History*
252. Hiroshi Aoyagi, *Islands of Eight Million Smiles: Idol Performance and Symbolic Production in Contemporary Japan*
253. Wai-yee Li, *The Readability of the Past in Early Chinese Historiography*
254. William C. Kirby, Robert S. Ross, and Gong Li, eds., *Normalization of U.S.-China Relations: An International History*
255. Ellen Gardner Nakamura, *Practical Pursuits: Takano Chōei, Takahashi Keisaku, and Western Medicine in Nineteenth-Century Japan*
256. Jonathan W. Best, *A History of the Early Korean Kingdom of Paekche, together with an annotated translation of* The Paekche Annals *of the* Samguk sagi
257. Liang Pan, *The United Nations in Japan's Foreign and Security Policymaking, 1945–1992: National Security, Party Politics, and International Status*
258. Richard Belsky, *Localities at the Center: Native Place, Space, and Power in Late Imperial Beijing*
259. Zwia Lipkin, *"Useless to the State": "Social Problems" and Social Engineering in Nationalist Nanjing, 1927–1937*
260. William O. Gardner, *Advertising Tower: Japanese Modernism and Modernity in the 1920s*
261. Stephen Owen, *The Making of Early Chinese Classical Poetry*
262. Martin J. Powers, *Pattern and Person: Ornament, Society, and Self in Classical China*
263. Anna M. Shields, *Crafting a Collection: The Cultural Contexts and Poetic Practice of the* Huajian ji 花間集 *(Collection from among the Flowers)*
264. Stephen Owen, *The Late Tang: Chinese Poetry of the Mid-Ninth Century (827–860)*
265. Sara L. Friedman, *Intimate Politics: Marriage, the Market, and State Power in Southeastern China*
266. Patricia Buckley Ebrey and Maggie Bickford, *Emperor Huizong and Late Northern Song China: The Politics of Culture and the Culture of Politics*
267. Sophie Volpp, *Worldly Stage: Theatricality in Seventeenth-Century China*
268. Ellen Widmer, *The Beauty and the Book: Women and Fiction in Nineteenth- Century China*
269. Steven B. Miles, *The Sea of Learning: Mobility and Identity in Nineteenth- Century Guangzhou*
270. Man-hung Lin, *China Upside Down: Currency, Society, and Ideologies, 1808–1856*

Harvard East Asian Monographs

Harvard East Asian Monographs

Harvard East Asian Monographs

Harvard East Asian Monographs